Praise for
Preaching Methodist Theology and Biblical Truth:
Classic Sermons of C. K. Barrett

"At a time when a great gulf exists between serious biblical scholarship and most preaching, the sermons of C. K. Barrett—arguably the most significant New Testament scholar of the twentieth century—offer an instructive and rewarding corrective. Barrett had a gift for drawing out the theological significance of passages so as to stimulate the intellect of the most sophisticated thinkers and at the same time make the biblical truths interesting, understandable, and relevant to ordinary Christians. These sermons are pure gold."

— **David Bauer**, Ralph Waldo Beeson Professor of
Inductive Bible Study, Asbury Theological Seminary

"Like many others, I first encountered C. K. Barrett as a great New Testament scholar. But the sermons published here reveal another Barrett—Barrett the preacher. He was a preacher who knew how to unravel a biblical text and put it back together again, a preacher whose sermons sounded like a summons from the God of eternity. It is wonderful to have this treasury of Barrett's pulpit work to inspire a new generation of Christ's heralds today."

— **Timothy George** is the founding dean of
Beeson Divinity School of Samford University
and general editor of the *Reformation
Commentary on Scripture*

PREACHING
METHODIST THEOLOGY
& BIBLICAL TRUTH

CLASSIC SERMONS OF
C. K. BARRETT

EDITED BY
BEN WITHERINGTON III

Preaching Methodist Theology and Biblical Truth: Classic Sermons of C. K. Barrett

The General Board of Higher Education and Ministry leads and serves The United Methodist Church in the recruitment, preparation, nurture, education, and support of Christian leaders—lay and clergy—for the work of making disciples of Jesus Christ for the transformation of the world. The General Board of Higher Education and Ministry of The United Methodist Church serves as an advocate for the intellectual life of the church. The Board's mission embodies the Wesleyan tradition of commitment to the education of laypersons and ordained persons by providing access to higher education for all persons.

Wesley's Foundery Books is named for the abandoned foundery that early followers of John Wesley transformed into a church, which became the cradle of London's Methodist movement.

Preaching Methodist Theology and Biblical Truth: Classic Sermons of C. K. Barrett

Copyright 2017 by Wesley's Foundery Books

Sermon text copyright Ben Witherington III

Wesley's Foundery Books is an imprint of the General Board of Higher Education and Ministry, The United Methodist Church. All rights reserved.

C. K. Barrett's sermons in their original form were donated by Penelope Barrett Hyslop to B. L. Fisher Library, Asbury Seminary, through the efforts of the rights holder, Ben Witherington III.

The sermons are in their original form with minor editorial updates.

Biblical translations are C. K. Barrett's own, primarily based on his translation of the Greek New Testament.

All web addresses were correct and operational at the time of publication.

ISBN: 978-0-938162-32-2

17 18 19 20 21 22 23 24 25 26—10 9 8 7 6 5 4 3 2 1

Manufactured in the United States of America

HIGHER EDUCATION & MINISTRY
General Board of Higher Education and Ministry
THE UNITED METHODIST CHURCH

*For Penelope, without whom none of these
sermon volumes would have seen the light of day.*

CONTENTS

The Epistles and Revelation

INTRODUCTION

In a sermon on St. Paul's conversion, Charles Kingsley Barrett, better known as C. K. Barrett, shows us how he views preaching. He says:

> There is a difference between a sermon, on the one hand, and a lecture or essay on the other. A sermon is not simply a public address on a religious subject; it is not simply an exposition of a passage of Scripture. It is these things, yet if it really is a sermon and not a lecture, it is something else too. *It is a means by which God himself speaks to us.*[1] This is not an event the preacher can command or arrange. It is independent of his learning, his eloquence, his enthusiasm. But it does happen, and it is the only *raison d'etre* of preaching.

Preaching, for C. K. Barrett, is not merely the conveying of information or even an exercise in transformation, but an encounter with the living voice of God speaking quite directly to the individual listener through the proclaimed Word. That is, God uses proper preaching to speak to us, sometimes with the help of the preacher, and sometimes even in spite of the inadequacies of the preacher.

According to James Dunn's memoir, C. K. Barrett (1917–2011) will be long remembered as the "finest English language commentator on the New Testament in the twentieth century." Dunn goes on to say, "As the commentator who mastered the central section of the New Testament—the Gospel of John, the Acts of the Apostles, Paul's letter to Rome and his letters to Corinth, all of them served with weighty commentaries—Kingsley Barrett surpassed his contemporaries." (*Biographical Memoirs of Fellows of the British Academy*, XII, 3–21. © The British Academy 2013.)

Son of Fred Barrett, a well-known British United Methodist evangelist and preacher, C. K. Barrett was a remarkable student, and later an even more

---

1   Editor's Note: emphasis added.

remarkable scholar and preacher. After excelling in the study of theology, he was called to teach at the University of Durham. During his career, he not only lectured widely and published numerous works but also sustained an active pastoral ministry, preaching nearly until his passing.

In C. K. Barrett, we meet a masterful biblical scholar and gifted preacher who never lost touch with his Wesleyan heritage and who can still instruct us today. In addition, C. K. Barrett, and later his daughter, Penny, carefully kept his sermons, most of them together. As Penny says, "There are very few strays." In the wake of examining a myriad of his sermon notebooks, all written out word for word in longhand, it became immediately apparent that these hundreds of sermons were of immense value for both students of modern Methodism and its homiletics as well as theologians who want to see how the interweaving of insightful biblical exposition and Wesleyan theology could be done skillfully and with clarity at almost any level of discourse.[2]

These sermons reflect a masterful biblical scholar with considerable homiletical skill and are an interesting window into twentieth-century Methodist preaching of a sort that is very much in touch with the original sermons of John Wesley, the hymns of Charles Wesley, and the biblical witness of St. Paul and thinkers like Martin Luther, but at the same time conversant with modern theology and biblical scholarship. It is rare to find this level of skill with all three of these factors—the Bible, the Wesleyan heritage, and the art of preaching—and well worth a close reading. Elsewhere in these sermons, C. K. Barrett makes clear that in his view, preaching must always be based on a biblical text, not a poem, not some extraneous passage, however uplifting or meaningful. He says repeatedly in his sermons that the preacher must preach Scripture, or it is not proper preaching. He appeals to Wesley's famous remarks about being *homo unius libri,* a "man of one book," when it comes to the text for preaching, and above all when it comes to the matter of salvation. Here is another revealing quotation from these sermons:

> Years ago, I read an article by Karl Barth with the title *The Basic Focus of Theological Thought.* Those, he said, are these. First is exposition, by which the Christian goes to Scripture and works at it so as to bring

---

2 I came to have this material through discussions with Penelope Barrett about her father's library. I was hoping to acquire it for Asbury Theological Seminary, and as it turned out, I did, but with it came a bonus—all the sermon notebooks of C. K. Barrett and his father. I immediately realized the value of this material and determined to see it into print. C. K. Barrett without question was the foremost British Methodist NT scholar of his age, but these sermons reveal another side of him, the preacher, and even evangelist, like his father.

out and make available the truth that it contains. The second is criticism, a word Barth used in its sense of passing judgment. You put the truths you have learned from the Bible alongside of what you see in the world about you and in your own heart; and what you see in the world and in your heart is judged by the Word of God. And the third focus is proclamation. The truth you have discovered you must tell the world. There is no proper Christian theology that does not come to voice in preaching; not necessarily what is done in pulpits on Sunday, also what is done on street corners and what is done when man talks to man and woman to woman.

It is clear enough as well from these sermons that he sees preaching as the main task of the ordained minister, and even says at one point that the preacher ideally should be in his study (when there are no crises to deal with), every morning studying the Word, praying, preparing sermons. True enough, he also emphasizes visitation in the homes of the parishioners and various other duties, but preaching is the prime task, that which mainly distinguishes the minister from other servants of the Church.

In a sermon on 1 Corinthians 11, C. K. Barrett adds: "A preacher has only one task; to expound, to explain, to compare Holy Scripture, and consequently if he is not continually speaking of the death of Christ for sinners, he is not true to his own appointment." For C. K. Barrett, the heart of not only the Gospel but of the whole New Testament, indeed the theme by which the whole Bible is tied together, is Christ and him crucified. This explains in part why even various of his Old Testament sermons lead to a discussion of Christ and him crucified. For C. K. Barrett, if the essence of sin and human fallenness is self-centeredness, the heart turned in upon itself (C. K. Barrett even suggests self-centeredness is the real meaning of the Pauline term "flesh.") then the essence of grace is unmerited self-sacrificing, self-giving love. A revealing anecdote from the same sermon makes clear his views about this matter, and about the fact that a sermon should be text based, not audience based.

On one of his visits to Oxford, Dr. Johnson[3] heard the official sermon preached for the benefit of those criminals who had been condemned

---

3   Dr. Samuel Johnson was the foremost British literary figure of the eighteenth century and well known to many including the Wesleys. He made lasting contributions to English literature as a poet, essayist, moralist, literary critic, biographer, editor, and creator of English dictionaries.

to die at the assizes. A week or two later, the same learned preacher preached the university sermon before the University of Oxford. He did a thing which is evidently not restricted to Methodists. He preached the same sermon. Dr. Johnson commented on this and received the usual reply. It was a good sermon and therefore worth preaching more than once. "Yes sir," said Johnson, "but the university was not to be hanged the next morning." Do you preach a different sermon to those who are not to be hanged the next morning? No doubt circumstances can and do give extra point to a sermon, but as the old preacher said, "All sermons should be preached as by a dying person to dying persons, and we may add they should be about the dying God."

In all this, C. K. Barrett stands in the line stretching forward from John and Charles Wesley, but he makes their emphases contemporary. If one analyzes C. K. Barrett's three hundred–plus sermons as a whole, you see that the typical recipe is the same: (1) a biblical exposition; (2) a drawing on the theology not only of the Bible but of the Wesleys, chiefly as expressed in Charles's hymn texts, which are quoted again and again in these sermons, and (3) an insistence on plain, practical application of the source material. Sometimes one could wish for more exposition and a bit less application, but in all of this C. K. Barrett is following in the footsteps of his Methodist predecessors, who were noted not only for "preaching for a verdict" but also "speaking a strong word into the practical affairs of life." It is plain speech for plain folk.

One should not however be deceived that the plainness and directness of the address suggests something superficial or lacking in profundity. To the contrary, C. K. Barrett had that gift of great scholarly preachers of distilling the profoundest things of the faith to any level of discourse, even, and very often, to the coal miners of the small pit villages in the northeast that surrounded Durham and Newcastle.

It is perhaps a propitious moment for these sermons to appear as Methodism continues to face the crises of "the law of diminishing returns" as it wrangles over major issues such as the disagreements about Christian views of human sexuality. Wesley's warning, that should we lose biblical preaching and a zeal for evangelism we stand in danger of becoming a dead sect, is one that should be heard and heeded today. We need to return to the original recipe of what made Methodist sermons powerful to convict, convince, and convert.

And that recipe can be seen at work in these sermons of C. K. Barrett. He ably offers us a nourishing treatment of God's Word, of our Methodist theology and musical heritage, and of practical applications that are both helpful and necessary often punctuated by powerful and personal illustrations. These sermons show the humility of the man and his deep insight into human character, human need, and the things of God.

Many of these sermons were preached at Elvet Methodist Church in Durham, which I and my wife attended for three years in the late 1970s. Indeed, we were the caretakers of that church during that period and had occasion to hear some of these sermons along the way. It is interesting to see just how many of them composed after 1945 (the year C. K. Barrett left Bondgate Church in Darlington to become a professor at Durham University) were first preached in Elvet. Elvet was not, and is not, simply a colliery village church. It was a church in the center of Durham City full of university folk, both faculty and students, as well as many successful business persons. And yet if one looks at the listing of the places C. K. Barrett preached a sermon first composed for Elvet (e.g., the sermon on Phil. 3:7 and Paul's conversion) clearly he did not think the sermon too high brow for any of his audiences.

Again, clarity, perspicuity, and plain speaking should not be confused with simplicity of thought or a lack of profundity. Apparently, C. K. Barrett had not only taken the advice of his one-time Cambridge professor, C. H. Dodd, who spoke of "teasing the mind into active thought," but he believed that all Methodist listeners should be challenged with the whole Gospel, even the complex and puzzling bits. This is all the more interesting because C. K. Barrett's *modus operandi* was to preach on major themes or topics in a given scriptural text. He does not tend to do old school expository preaching where one walks through the text explaining one verse after another. No, he picks out some of the big and interesting ideas or themes that the text suggests and milks them for all they are worth. In part, this means that these sermons are unapologetically theological and ethical in substance, just as the biblical text is. In addition, he does not reduce the biblical text to mere sociology or political discourse.

C. K. Barrett does not spend a great deal of time on explaining historical background, grammatical curiosities, political context, *unless* it is directly relevant to the illumination and proclamation of the major themes on which he is dwelling. A sermon then is not like a commentary on a biblical book; rather, a sermon is based on careful exegesis of the text. There is a difference between preaching one's exegesis and preaching *on the basis of* one's deep engagement with the text, and the latter is what we get in the sermons of C. K. Barrett. What of course distinguishes his sermons from many other

Methodist sermons of that era is that C. K. Barrett was an expert in theology and the exegesis of the biblical text especially the Gospels and Epistles, and he could bring that expertise to bear on his sermon preparation (including his expertise in the biblical languages) in ways that ordinary preachers could not and perhaps cannot.

I remember well the reaction of the Elvet church members when they heard that Professor Barrett was coming to preach. That Sunday would be marked on the calendar "must attend church without fail." They knew that a powerful sermon, with value added that only someone like C. K. Barrett could bring, was forthcoming, and this very volume is a testimony to that fact.

The seventy-five sermons in this volume, many of which go back to the period of 1943–1945 when C. K. Barrett was the full-time minister at Bondgate in Darlington, were preached some 828 times over the period of 1934–2009, or on average eleven times each. This is all the more amazing when one notes that many of these sermons were preached only once, for example the wedding and funeral messages or the special occasion sermons. But some, however, were preached thirty, forty, even fifty times over seven decades. Overall, C. K. Barrett preached about five thousand times using the three hundred sermons he wrote during this period.

It is also intriguing to probe the question: What was the relationship between C. K. Barrett the scholar and C. K. Barrett the preacher and minister? In a revealing quote in his sermon on 1 Thessalonians 1 and turning from idols, he says:

> For me the idol commonly takes the form of pure and scientific scholarship. Most folk may find it hard to understand but I do take real delight in setting the precise meaning of a Greek particle or a Hebrew root or in determining just what Alexander the Great did in 350 B.C. Now undoubtedly when I have found out things of this sort, I have found something true, which therefore has its own proper value, but if it be left to itself it is something that is not living; what is more it is something that dries up the source of life and breeds dry rot.

Scholarship for its own sake is not a living thing. Scholarship in service of the preaching and ministering of the Gospel is something else, both living and life-giving. One can also see the humility and frankness of the man in this quote.

What counts as a *classic* Methodist sermon, one might ask? By *classic* I do not mean that these sermons are perfect or always hit the center of the target necessarily, or even always offer the best possible interpretation of a biblical text. What I mean is that these sermons, time after time, provide us with an excellent model of how good preaching in the Wesleyan and Biblical mold should look. They set the bar high in terms of study, preparation, organization (usually three points), and delivery of the biblical and Wesleyan goods, involving a deep engagement with matters crucial to the faith.

Frankly, I have grown weary of sermons that have illustrations that do not illustrate the point of the appointed biblical text—story sermons only loosely connected to the Bible—and sermons based on the perceived wants and needs of the congregation, rather than on the substance of the subject matter of the Bible, in short, sermons with little biblical or Wesleyan content, because they amount to little more than words of general encouragement or some sort of ethical harangue. As Mr. Wesley was wont to say to his preachers—you are not called upon to preach your experience, however profound, your opinions however lofty, your tradition however noble, or your own logic, however reasonable. No, you are called to preach the Bible in season and out of season, when it is well received and when it is poorly received. And as C. K. Barrett was apt to emphasize, it was not about the preacher and his eloquence anyway. If Jonah could put his hand over his mouth and weakly utter "repent" and "all Nineveh responded to God's call," then surely it is mostly about the message, the living Word of God, powerful and active, and not so much about the messenger.

A good Methodist has only one thing to preach—the biblical text—and if one wants to narrow the field of focus even more, C. K. Barrett would say in Pauline terms, "Know nothing among them but Christ and him crucified."[4] Above all it is Christ that one is called to preach, whether it pleases the ears of the listeners or it does not, whether it is fashionable or unfashionable. Christ is not only the heart of the good news but the center of the Scripture, and one can see how very much C. K. Barrett affirms this fact in his Old Testament preaching, which almost always comes around to Christ at some juncture or in some way.[5]

---

4   Referring to 1 Cor. 2:2.

5   Editor's Note: What we do not hear much about in these three hundred sermons is the Parousia, or Second Coming of Christ. In part this is not surprising, since like many NT scholars CKB was influenced by both the strong emphasis on realized eschatology of his teacher C. H. Dodd when it came to the Gospels, and the equally strong emphasis of Schweitzer on the perils of emphasizing the possible imminence of Christ's return, whether one focuses on Jesus' or Paul's eschatology. Nevertheless, the subject does come up once in a while, usually in association with talking about the Creed, and Barrett says repeatedly he is not budging from Christian orthodoxy on those matters of doctrine.

Most of these sermons were quite literally battle-tested, by which I mean they were first preached during the stresses of World War II, forged during the Blitz and bombings England endured. That the messages hit home to good effect is clear enough from how many times C. K. Barrett was invited back to preach at Bondgate and many other Methodist chapels and churches he first visited during the war. This continued long after he had left the full-time pastoral ministry and had become a professor at Durham. In fact, this pattern continued to the end of his preaching ministry. The listing of the chapels he preached in tolls like bells performing a Grandsire triple peal, mostly ringing the same notes. In some cases, he had preached eighty or more times in a chapel between 1934 and 2009. By my count, there must be several dozen such chapels, and he was preaching to two or three different generations of church members in those places. This involved a good deal of travel, whether through buses or being driven to a preaching appointment, for C. K. Barrett did not drive (though Margaret, his wife, did).

It is good to hear once more the voice of my doctoral supervisor as he breaks the bread of life for his Christian audiences all over England, and especially in the northeast. I not merely suspect, rather, I know that these sermons will repay repeated readings and pondering. It is my hope that these sermons will intrigue and edify you as much as they have done for me over the course of the months I have been transcribing these little gems.

Easter 2017

Old Testament Sermons

"Covenant"—Exodus 24:7; Jeremiah 31:31-34; Mark 14:24f.

[Preached once at St. John's College, Durham University 1/10/06][1]

Covenant: You have heard something of the way early Methodism took up the word and used it as they developed a new service of their own; a new service or a new appreciation of an existing service. The covenant service is not a third (still less an eighth) sacrament, but a special use of the familiar sacrament of the Lord's Supper, held usually at a time, especially at the beginning of the year that gives it extra weight and a special application.

Covenant: The word of course is not specifically religious, and the world is full of covenants explicit and implicit. When you come to a university there is an implicit covenant, an agreement between you and the institution. You will pay some money and accept some academic disciplines; the university will put on a teaching program for you. Marriage is a covenant. Husband and wife promise most usually love, care, loyalty, faithfulness. Covenant is a great biblical theme, and that is the main theme before us now; but there are all kinds of minor covenants that help us to understand the major one. Isaac made a covenant with Abimelech, king of the Philistines, a non-aggression pact. More personal was the covenant between David and Jonathan, a covenant of friendship. "If anyone injures you, he injures me too. We defend and support each other." But these only illustrate the great covenant theme that runs through both testaments. For that we need at least three texts (not three sermons, and there ought to be four).

For the first text we go to Exod. 24:7. "Then he took the book of the covenant and read it in the hearing of the people and they said, 'All that

---

1   Editor's Note: This is one of the two last sermons CKB seems to have written, this one in 2006 and "The Scandal of the Cross" on Galatians 5 in 2007.

the Lord has spoken we will do, and we will be obedient.'" That of course is not the beginning of the story. For that we should have to go back to Abraham, who has perhaps more right than Moses to a text of his own. But this marks the acceptance of the people as a whole, the covenant God has already made with the chosen family. The two sides of the covenant are clear and we shall have to keep them in mind throughout. The initiative is God's, and the initiative was one of sheer grace. They had done nothing to deserve it, yet God in love for their fathers and mothers chose them out of all the nations of human beings that they might be his representatives in the world, a people whose very existence, the fewest of all peoples, was a testimony to the grace and power of God. As a further gift, and as a means of sustaining their distinctness, he gave them the Law. It was a good law. Parts of it can be quietly dropped in a new civilization, who keeps the law of wearing no kind of mixed cloth or never eating pork,[2] but it was a good law. Here first, centuries before Jesus, was to quote them, one of the two primary commands: "Thou shalt love the Lord thy God with all thy heart, soul, mind and strength; and thy neighbor as thyself." So keep the Law, and the covenant lasts. Break it, and God is released from his commitment.

And that should be the end of the story, but it moves on. The covenant begins in grace and deliverance. He rescues the people from their slavery in Egypt. Ungrateful, they turn in disobedience against their deliverer. "Right," says God, you may read it again and again in the Old Testament— "I've finished with you." But his love is too great for that and he can always provide a way of repentance, and then of forgiveness and renewal. But this cannot go on. The schoolmaster curses the disobedient schoolboy and threatens to expel him, relents, cautions him again, and so on. Eventually, then if the boy isn't worn out, the cane is. You need a new device.

The person who saw this most clearly was a prophet, Jeremiah, and this brings us to our second text—Jer. 31:31-34: "I will make a new covenant with the house of Israel . . . not like the covenant which I made with their fathers when I took them by the hand to bring them out of the land of Egypt, my covenant which they broke . . . this is the covenant which I will make with the house of Israel after these days. . . . I will put my law within them, and I will write it upon their hearts, and I will be their God, and they shall be my people. And no more shall each person teach his neighbor and his brother

---

2 Editor's Note: There are in fact many orthodox Jews who avoid such things, at least in North America and Israel.

saying 'Know the Lord' for they shall all know me . . . for I will forgive their iniquity, and I will remember their sin no more."

That prophecy represents the triumph of hope and disillusionment. There is a story attached to it. The good king Josiah found that workers in the Jerusalem Temple were not being properly paid. This had to be put right and he sent Hilkiah the priest and Shaphan the secretary to look into the Temple papers and accounts. They were honest men and they did so. In doing so they found something they were not looking for. They found a Book of the Law. What was it? No one knows. Perhaps it was the Book of Deuteronomy. They read it with some dismay. "We must take it to the king." They took it to him and the king rent his clothes in horror. "We have broken the covenant. We have not kept the commandments that the Law contains." Not only Deuteronomy but all the five books of Law are pretty explicit about what will happen to people who do not obey the laws they contain. The covenant is ended; God will cut us off; we are unprotected in a hostile world because for decades no one in Jerusalem had cared two pence about the Law and its demands.

"We must reform our ways," said the king, the priest, and the secretary—among the few who needed little or no reform. Jeremiah was full of hope; this was a key turning point, all would be well. But it wasn't. A few years later, and Jerusalem was back where it had been. No one bothered about the Law and we can't take the trouble to learn all those stupid commandments. We can do what we like, God won't bother. And what can he do anyway? We are free, we can please ourselves. And in the end God will forgive, "*c'est son métier.*"[3]

A second blow, and you might think a knock out for Jeremiah—reform had not worked. Surely this was the end. The king couldn't do it, the priest couldn't do it, the people wouldn't do it, would not come back to the old ways of an obedient people living under the authority and protection of the Almighty. "We prefer to go our own way, and we are quite capable of looking after and protecting ourselves"—a proposition which was demonstrated false in generation after generation.

So, the position was hopeless? No, for Jeremiah was capable of seeing the one thing that prophets exist in order to perceive. He saw the situation

---

3   Editor's Note: This phrase, which means basically "it is his job" is quoted a good deal by CKB. It is sometimes attributed to Heinrich Heine, a German poet, supposedly as a death-bed quip, but it has also been attributed to one or another of the French free thinkers, like for instance Rousseau.

coram Deo in its relationship to God, the one actor in the story which a minute ago was left out. King, priest, and people foiled, but what about God? He had always been in the business; in it with Abraham, in it with Moses, and it was his Law anyway, covenants began with God; that was grace, mercy, love, began with his creative action, as he gave hundred-year-old Abraham and Sarah, as he gave Moses a mouth and wisdom and signs to perform. Perhaps he would act now and make a new covenant.

What would he have to do? You can picture Jeremiah working it out. What was wrong with the old covenant, a daring question that, for God himself had made it, but Jeremiah had to ask the question for without it we could never get things right. And how could we make a new beginning? Well the Law was a good law; it must be for it was God's own Word. It had been written with his own hand on the stone tablets that were given to Moses on Mt. Sinai—most impressive. But (you catch Jeremiah thinking) wasn't that just the trouble? Tablets of stone are cold and they are external. Who is going to take the trouble to read them? And if he reads them who will bother to keep them? The fault is not in the commandments but in the way they are perceived and received—or not received. We need something warmer, more immediate, more acceptable, so that loving your neighbor as yourself becomes not a grievous burden wearisome to bear, but something you want to do. God will write his will not on bits of stone, but on human hearts, so that it becomes their very nature, and they will want to do it. Love will be part of their makeup as it is God's. "On their hearts will I write it."

But so far this is impersonal. It needs personal contact to bring it to life and that was lacking. It was alright of course for Jeremiah, he was a prophet. It was alright for Hilkiah, he was a priest. Priests and prophets might be expected to know God. But what about the person in the street? He could only listen to what Jeremiah and Hilkiah told him. "Maybe they are right and there is a God. And maybe they are saying the sort of things he wants. But I don't know. It takes me all my time and strength to plow my land, to lay the stones for their precious Temple." "It's not good enough," said Jeremiah as God himself prodded him. "They must all know God for themselves. Priests and prophets may help them, but they mustn't be dependent on priests and prophets, they must know in their own hearts."

"Yes it will be fine," said Jeremiah to himself, "but how do we get there with such a crowd of rogues and ruffians, sinners and unbelievers, as I see about me?" There is an answer. God is the same God who gave a child to Abraham, and freedom to slaves in Egypt. And he is creative forgiving love.

That will do it. But it didn't, not for 500-odd years. And there is a third name to add to Moses and Jeremiah.

Jesus

And I will give you a third text, one which will suggest the whole context of which it is a part. Mark 14:24f. "He took a cup, and when he had given thanks, he gave it to them, and they all drank of it. And he said unto them, 'this is my blood of the covenant, which is shed for many.'" The old covenant with Moses had been sealed with sacrifice. The new covenant which existed in Jeremiah's mind, and on the parchment in his book lacked sacrifice, but it received it now and at the very hand of God, the pierced hand of the Son of God himself.

There is nothing special in a covenant service except its context. Every time we receive the bread and wine at Christ's table, and at other times too, we enter into and renew the covenant which he set up, taking as always the initiative of grace. And Jeremiah at least can tell us the basics of the covenant we enter. There is a renewing power of divine goodness which creates an answering love within us. Loving God with all our heart, and mind, and soul and strength becomes natural and right. Of course, we can resist it and most of us sometimes do, but when we give it freedom to create a love for our neighbors, including the most objectionable of them, as great as any love we have for ourselves. And this as it joins us together, in a covenant people which we call church is the hope of the world.

And this is knowing God, for God is love, and he or she who dwells in love dwells in God. Of course, prophets and priests (under other labels) can help us to understand what God means, but essentially we know him, even if we do not understand him ourselves. And we are free, free as only forgiving love and justifying grace can make us free, free to serve him who at the cost of a broken body and shed blood set us free, free to serve our covenant keeping God, who will never let us go.

"The Great Inheritance"— Joshua 17:14-18[1]

A sentence or two will suffice to remind you of the historical situation out of which these words come to us. The twelve tribes are out of Egypt. They have traversed the desert and crossed the Jordan. They have reached the promised land, the land flowing with milk and honey. The next question, being who they are, is naturally—Who is to have the best share of the milk and honey? For answer to that question I shall not go into the details of the settlement described in Joshua. Out of that I pick this one very human scene. The leaders of the great tribe of Joseph, and they were a great tribe, really a double tribe, approach the national leader: "Look, don't you think there is a misprint in this list somewhere? I see that we are only down for an ordinary share like everyone else, and of course you couldn't have forgotten who we are, I mean to say, not quite the ordinary tribe, don't you know." Joshua's answer is stiff and full of all the natural dignity and hardness of the man—"You want a bigger portion, do you? Well no one's stopping you. You see that forest country, thick and threatening where the enemy are? Then show your greatness, and make that yours."

That is the piece of history and that the divine word we shall have in the back of our minds this morning. I will however admit I have been driven to that word as an answer to a question which I hope rings in the ears of every Methodist Church. It is the prime question among many that which Conference has sent us to consider. It is very simple—to ask "What is this Church for?" I don't know if you are ever struck as often I am by the apparent absurdity of everything the Church does. If not, I hope you will be now.

---

1 Editor's Note: Unfortunately, the cover and first page of this notebook are lost, and so we don't know where and how many times this sermon was preached, nor do we have the title page with the title of this sermon, so I have titled it on the basis of the content. If, however, this sermon was used to a like degree as the others in this notebook from the late 1940s, it was preached more than a dozen times over the many years.

We come here and sing. That is understandable for some of us, but not for all. And we talk. We talk to and about things that cannot be seen. We are no richer and no more comfortable for being here. On the contrary, yet we urge others to join us. In fact, the Church often looks like an automatic gun; the recoil from one shot provides the energy for shooting the next. We keep the Church going in order to keep it going. What is this Church for? All the energy and work we put into it; to what are they directed? To a point inside, or outside the mechanism? That means, are we going somewhere or going round in circles? These are big questions. Let us look back to the text, and let us start with something we certainly can understand. It gives us firstly a definition of—

True Greatness

What Joshua said to a tribe, a national unit has often been so said, and truly. I have just re-read the great story of Herodotus, the father of history. It is the story of the rise and fall of the Persian Empire. At the end, he brings in the story of the great Emperor, Cyrus, to pronounce a sort of epilogue. He bids his fellow Persians to take their choice either to live in a hard, bad land and be conquerors, or live in luxury and be slaves. I know at least enough history to be very cautious about generalizations. But it is pretty safe to say that that choice is always presenting itself. The nation placed in the lap of nature's luxury goes soft—witness in India, Bengal, and compare with that the hardy heroic hill tribes, the Afghans for example. Can you remember how Wordsworth says

> When I have borne in memory what has tamed
> Great Nations, how ennobling thoughts depart
> When men change swords for ledgers, and desert
> The student's bower for gold, some fears unnamed
> I had, my Country!—am I to be blamed?

Greatness is not developed by luxury and privilege, but by hardness and struggle. This is true in personal life as in national life. Recently I saw an advertisement put in a paper by a young man who wanted a job. He listed his qualifications, named the salary and conditions he would require, and concluded "Don't miss this splendid opportunity." I don't know whether experienced employers were impressed by that, but I wasn't. I shall not rush at the splendid opportunity of employing a man who evidently thought that his splendid talents qualified him for a post with a magnificent salary and little work. True greatness is not produced that way. Human greatness is only evolved in struggle. How often have you compared two men: It has all been made easy for A, but B has had to struggle every inch of the way. B is the man you respect.

But my real point is that this is true of Churches too. We show greatness not by asking to have a double share without the labor of getting it; a preacher is developed, not in ease but in hardness. This is a great time for the Churches. I say that deliberately and I say it because it is a hard time for the Churches. It is a great time because Jesus said "blessed are you when people revile you and persecute you and say all manner of evil against you; and woe unto you when all shall speak well of you." It is a great age, because it is like the apostolic age. The Church is a small remnant, fighting for its life. The Church has once more the opportunity of developing heroic stature.

Of course, you will all agree with me there. You may not do so if I speak, as I intend to do, with the utmost plainness. I know some Churches, and in varying degrees I think this is true of all Churches, which in fact work on a very different scale of values. They are great because they are wealthy, they are great because they are influential, they are great because they have a magnificent history, they are great because the right people go there, they are great (all too few of them) because they have large congregations. But that is no true scale of values. A Church is great insofar as it is faithful to its Lord, and fighting the good fight. And it follows that there are back street missions which are greater Churches than some of Methodism's most splendid edifices.

I believe this is a great Church. You will not show it by sitting still and waiting for sinners to be given you as your lawful due; you will show it only by getting your coats off and down to work; by buckling your armor on and going out to fight. There is another side to this. I want to show it briefly but firmly.

The Church's Inheritance Is Prepared

I don't want you to think that you have to wring success, or any good thing, out of the hands of an unwilling God. What I have said does not mean you have to create your own achievements while God looks on critically. Look back to the story. The land which Joshua challenged the tribe of Joseph to win was land that God had promised. It was land God meant them to have.

It was land which in the last resort and for all their own conflict, was God's gift to them. It is so here.

There is no more complete perversion of the Christian faith possible than the notion that it all depends upon what we do. The great truth is that all rests upon what God has done through Christ. The tragedy of the present situation is that so few of us believe or even understand that. As a result, we waste time and energy, as well as grieving the heart of God. We are like a person frantically rushing around with half a dozen burst pipes in his house, never thinking of the shutoff valve that would keep his house dry. We are like an army of men busy sharpening our arrows and stringing our bows while someone holds out to us the secret of the atom bomb.

I am telling no one there is no work to do. I am not taking back a word of what I have said of the grim struggle which will develop our muscles and prove our worth. But I am saying that every task worth accomplishing is a task God means us to accomplish. And above all I am saying this: that for every task Christ summons his people to perform he had supplied abundant forces and resources. In effect, what he summons us to do is to possess what is already ours.

For the rest, I can only illustrate that. The inheritance which Christ has made ours, which he summons us to possess, and which the truly great Church is possessing, is twofold. You might say that it was inward and outward. First then,

The Church's Inward Inheritance

I mean by that the qualities of personal life, and opportunities of personal service and devotion; which God in Christ has made available to us, and which for the most part we do not possess. I want to say quite simply they are your inheritance; don't stand grumbling because they aren't put into your hand, go and win them. I can only make a selection of things that might be said here. But I will speak first and speak plainly about the means of grace. You know what they are—public worship and the preaching of the Word, the sacraments, prayer common and private, fellowship, reading the Bible. No doubt there are others, but these will serve; they are the most important. Now all of these things are already available to all of us. They are beyond dispute the things by which Christians live.

How seriously do we take them? Some of us, I know, very seriously; and for those who do so the relevant questions are—How can we make our services more effective and helpful? How can we learn to pray better? How can we obtain a deeper understanding of the Bible? But there are all too many of us just now, who have hardly reached that stage. Take our ordinary weekly services for example. What means of loyalty do we show there? The sacrament of our Lord's Supper; what is the matter there? Why can so few of our people find time for that? No one for a half an hour more on a Sunday evening will lose his life, lose his wife, his money or his business. There is something here I cannot understand.

I don't want anyone to rush off into an orgy of pietism, no one could hate that more than I. I am really asking throughout this sermon for nothing more than a little quite straight and sincere thinking. If you think (or if you don't) that prayer is bunk, say so and I shall not be shocked. But don't, for God's sake, come to Church and sing "Prayer is the Christian's vital breath" and then spend two drowsy minutes a day at it. Say if you like (people have said it to me) the Bible is a pack of lies, but don't pay a subscription to the BFBS[2] and then let the pages of the book stick together with disuse. Say if you like that religion is the opium of the masses, and Churches are tedious irrelevant monstrosities, but don't call yourself a Methodist and abuse, I will not say the discipline of your Church, but the dying love of your Lord who summons you to the feast of his love.

One other item of our inheritance—holiness. Holiness is perhaps a special Methodist emphasis, but it is a universal Christian privilege. Universal—I stress that. This is no optional subject for the top class. It is for everyone. I know what holiness means. It is consecration. It means a life that belongs not to humanity but to God. But that has consequences. And the consequences depend on who the God is. If the god is Astarte, the women will be prostitutes. If the God is Christ, the men and women will be what—people like you and me? God forbid. The plain fact is that Christians are not good enough. I am not good enough. And we are not good enough because we are not possessing our inheritance. "Answer that great end in me, for which thy precious life was given."

Again, let us have no mistakes. I want prigs no more than I want pietists. The Lord saves some people from being drunkards; he has saved me from being a prig—and for many things I prefer a drunkard to a prig. I believe that if we would have it, Christ would make us so good that people would

---

notice it. As it is, they don't. They ask us in every factory, what difference does being a Christian make? I know there are invisible differences, differences the questioner can't guess. But I cannot answer his question. The only answer to his question will be when the Church is living differently. How much do you love one another? I am not talking about loving other classes, or the Germans, or the Indians. Are you really a family of brothers and sisters (and that doesn't mean you always agree) in this Church? That is where we begin, if we cannot even begin then God help the world. I must turn to—

The Church's Outward Inheritance

The Church must grow inwardly; it must also grow outwardly. That too is part of our inheritance, it is the essence of the Church's life. I remember a friend of mine describing the road that winds up the dale from Ilkley to Granington, a greedy road he said because it doesn't run straight, it winds backwards and forwards, crossing and recrossing the stream in order to take in every farm on the dale; it would leave none out. The Church's way is like that; it must leave none out. "The arms of love that compass me, would all mankind embrace." If you cannot sing that, you are no Christian.

We know it. The tragedy of the situation is that so often like Joseph we expect to sit down and have our inheritance added unto us. But no! That way will never be yours. Up to the hill country and the forest and fight. Every day it becomes clearer that the Church that will sit still will sit by itself, and sit so until it dies of its own longevity. I am saying little of this, because I have spoken of it here before, and today many my chief aim was to stress our inner heritage; but I cannot leave this unsaid. All Christians share in this inheritance that is to be fought for, but none more than we.

I have said strong things today; so strong, I am afraid. Not afraid of you; I don't mind what you say. I am afraid that because I have had to say these things to myself, and to blurt out my own wretched failures. I have no right to say what I have said but one—my authority as a minister of God's Holy Word. It is in his name, not mine that I speak. And in his name, there is one more thing to add. You are to go nowhere he has not already gone. These things are not his demand but his gift. Prayer, holiness, witness are not your effort but his benefaction. They are your duty, but they are also your privilege. It was to this end that Christ died and rose; that you might live with him. What is the Church for? For this.

"Choose This Day Whom You Will Serve"—Joshua 24:13-25

[Preached thirty-seven times from 7/5/42 at Vicar St. to 8/20/95 at Bishop Auckland]

It is a scene well worth painting. By whatever standard you measure him, Joshua was a great man and he had done a great day's work. Moses had died at the critical moment, just before the big offensive. It had been a time when the people could easily have gone to pieces, lost their nerve, and given up everything they had worked so hard to win since the day they left Egypt. Only a strong person would have assumed command and fired up his folk for a supreme effort, for one last mighty assault. And Joshua had done it. He had led the tribes across the Jordan and they had subdued the promised land. They were at last able to enjoy the milk and honey of it. But Joshua's turn was over. He had played his part and he could do no more. He gathered his people together for a last address to them, and the sum of his words is our text.

It was a great appeal to them to serve the Lord, the God of their fathers who had delivered them from Egypt and brought them into their promised land. The scene had the drama of the enactment of a covenant between the people and their God. There is no need to stay to point out the value of a like decision now. There is no need to make general observations, however true and useful about the folly of indecision. This is the word of God which is addressed to us and that is all that needs to be said. God still addresses us: "Choose, make up your mind whether you will follow and obey me or whether you will do something else." We shall consider this command of God under four heads.

The Basis of God's Claim

The first part of this chapter is an account of the things God has done. Joshua begins before the time of Abraham, he recounts the history of his people, their wanderings, their sufferings, their experiences of God's grace and power. Above all, there is the story of Egypt, and of the mighty deliverance that God had wrought for his people there. There are the battles in the wilderness, there is the tale of Balaam, an account of the pleasantness of the land into which they had been brought. All this Joshua records and concludes, "Now therefore, fear the Lord, and serve him in sincerity and in truth, and put away the gods which your fathers served beyond the River and in Egypt, and serve the Lord." The basis of God's claim is the things he has done in the past. It is no idle promise, though indeed there is promise in it—promise authenticated and warranted by the performance in the past. It is not the imagination of the fanciful mind, it is the concrete event of history. Joshua, putting all his cards on the table, says "That is what God has done; that is the sort of thing God can be relied upon to do. Now, what are you going to do about it?"

Now it is undoubtedly true that history in general has that meaning, that force. It demands appropriation. If it is to be a real thing, it must be realized in the present. That can be illustrated. Take a great event in English history, the signing of the Magna Carta by John at Runnymede in 1215. Now what was that event? In the boldest possible description, it was that a man wrote his name at the bottom of a sheet of parchment in the presence of other men on a small island in the Thames. There was nothing very striking or revolutionary in what King John agreed to. Life in England changed very little immediately afterwards. But the power of the Magna Carta lay not in the things that happened immediately after it. What is important is not what it meant to King John in 1215 but what it meant to Hampden and Pym in 1625, when, fired by its possibilities and their interpretation of it, they stood up to a tyrannical king and brought him down. Their reading of the Magna Carta forced them to a decision to act in a particular way, a way that brought them trouble and hardship, danger and loss, but a way that meant new life to this country. Of course, the same thing is still true. The Magna Carta requires a decision from us. We may, if we will, regard it as a scrap of paper. Or we may honor it by remembering the price of liberty is eternal vigilance, by hazarding everything that we have in defense of our free and democratic institutions. But choose we must, decisions are wagers forced upon us by the heritage of the past.

I have taken as an example a monument of our political liberty because that is a thing we are all thinking of. It is even better to consider our heritage of religious liberty, and the Protestant tradition in which we are born. To take one example only, people have died in agony in order that we, their children, might be free to read the Bible. Again, that very fact forces a decision upon us, and I want to make it a clearly conscious decision for every one of you. You are of course quite free to decide that these men shed their blood for nothing and that the Bible that was life and breath to them you can dispense with. Or, on the other hand, you can accept their gift. I truly want you to see quite plainly what you are doing. Either you are turning your back on the death of men like Tyndale, or you accept their dying gift. What you can't do is to pretend that something which did happen didn't happen.

But there is more to say than this. Joshua reminded his people of the thing God had done for them—which they could waste if they would by turning their backs on him. I will do precisely the same thing. Christ died for you. He died that you might be forgiven, he died to make you good. Again, you can waste that (humanly speaking) by turning your back upon him. You cannot undo what has happened in the past. The Cross will still tower over the wrecks of time when your insignificant little points against it are clean forgotten. But the Cross, the thing which God did, forces a decision upon you, and again I will make that decision a conscious one for you. You are not to be allowed to drift on, ignoring what he has done for you. If you want to say I shall not respond to it, I cannot stop you. But I want you to see that unless you do definitely accept Christ, that is the alternative to which you are forced.

The Alternatives

One alternative was the gods which your fathers served which were beyond the River, or the gods of the Amorites in whose land you dwelt. Joshua, you see, takes for granted that these people will have to serve something, someone. That is a penetrating and true piece of observation. There are some folk who reject Christianity because they want to be free, independent. Why should they be bound to God, to Christ? They don't want to be bound to anything. They want to keep an open mind.

Unfortunately, that is a thing that simply can't be done. If you find people with really open minds anywhere it is in a lunatic asylum, and you don't find many, even there. Whether you will or will not, you must serve something. If you won't volunteer, you will be conscripted. Jesus told a story of a man who had had an evil spirit thrown out of his mind. You can imagine the man left panting, as it were, after the struggle. The spirit comes back and finds the mind still vacant; a no-good spirit has come in to take control in the absence of the evil spirit. So back he comes himself bringing seven even worse spirits with him. There must be alternatives, if you do not serve Christ you will serve someone else. Joshua lists two alternatives, which you may call, if you will, the gods of the past, and the gods of the future. They are mighty idols still.

We all know people who live in and on the past. There is nothing like the good ole days. All change is change for the worse. There is a great deal of attraction in the sayings about old friends, old times, old wine and so forth. So said these people. "Let me go back behind the days of this God of Moses, this God of startling changes. Let us go back to the old soft gods who never troubled anyone. You know that attitude too. This Christian God is too vigorous for our liking, let us stick to the old conventions, like the people of Luther's day, of Wesley's, of General Booth's.

There are also people who live for the future. The present, let alone the past, has no attraction for them. Life is all ambition, all change, all restless striving. "Still striving after knowledge infinite." Joshua's people said, "Times have changed, we must adapt ourselves to the new environment change our methods, outlook, ideas." People are saying it still, even Church people. We must adapt our message to the modern mind, give folk what they want. Any gods but Christ, Christ who stands in the midst of time, who is never out of date, but belongs exactly to our world.

The Difficulty of Serving the Lord

"You cannot serve the Lord." This is not what you expect Joshua, or any preacher to say, but it is honest. Joshua gives two reasons: (1) He is a holy God. That means life has to be taken very seriously. The holy God requires that his servants be holy too. He is not to be fobbed off by a sentimentalism about the past or a ready enthusiasm for the future. He demands simple straightforward obedience and he demands it here and now. There is no putting off, there is no concealment possible. God is holy and he expects holy people. So, you may well think twice before you make up your mind to follow him. It is not that you have to produce a certain standard of goodness before you can become a disciple of Christ, and it is his job and his delight to start with you where you are and to make you holy whatever you have been. But if you are to follow him it does mean taking goodness and taking him seriously; (2) He is a jealous God. That means that he will brook no divided allegiance. You cannot serve God and mammon. It is all or nothing. It is a hard saying; Joshua knew that and I know it. But it is quite certainly true. Half and half just doesn't work. It gets nobody anywhere. No commander in a battle would dream of leading soldiers who said "We'll follow, if and when we feel like it; if we don't, we won't." But many people seem to think that Christ can put up with Christians like that. We'll go to Church, but not if So and So is preaching. We'll communicate, if it doesn't rain. We'd take a Sunday School class, if only we could get home in time for *The Brains Trust*.[1] If your mind works like that, Joshua's saying is true—"You cannot serve the Lord," it is the gift of God.

Therefore, Choose

"How long do you hesitate between two opinions. If the Lord is God, serve him." If God really did do everything for you in Jesus Christ, then serve him. Serve him in order to see that history coming true in your life. Serve him rather than the gods of the past or the future. Serve him in holiness and with all your heart.

Gilbert Murray says that the old writers of the ancient world are like these ghosts which can only become real by sucking blood—vampires. If we do not give our heart's blood to Plato, to Virgil, to Augustine, they are lifeless empty ghosts. They live as we give them life. The parallel I am making is not exact. Christ is no ghost, he and what he did are real whatever we do. But by the gift of our blood, our very life, what he did can become real for us. Therefore, choose now whether you will serve him; whether you will allow him to give you the forgiveness, the life, the joy which he died to win for you.

---

1   Editor's note: *The Brains Trust* was a popular BBC radio, then TV show in the UK.

"Faith"—2 Kings 6:16-17

[Preached twenty-seven times from 7/19/42 at SHMABC to 9/1/85 at Trimdon Station]

What are we to say about this strange story? Who can understand it? What has it to do with us? I have told you many times that the Bible is a book that deals with real life and with real people. I have said that if you read it with your eyes open, you can always see yourself in it. You will find your life, your problems, your temptations, your doubts, your hopes and fears, successes and defeats in it; because the Bible never wanders from the way of stark reality. Well, have I been caught out at last? Have we now found a passage which has nothing to do with us, which we can safely leave aside, or in which we can interest ourselves solely for literary and historical reasons?

Certainly, we can admit that the framework of this story is foreign to our experience. Hitler has not found any of us so personally dangerous that he has sent out a special Panzer division to surround Wednesbury. And since that presupposition is absent we may well expect that we are not likely to catch visions of tanks and guns and fire circulating around the parish Church. No this is one of the Bible's picture lessons. Again and again the great themes of biblical theology, and of the Gospel, are illustrated not by specific discussions but by stories. That is why the concordance is not an infallible guide to what the Bible has to say on any given subject. For example, if you wanted to learn about faith you could find out a good deal by looking the word up in a concordance. But the concordance would not send you to this passage, because the word faith is not here, but the idea is. Faith is the theme, and the theme is worked out, as it were, in five movements, so that there are four things for us to say about it. First—

Faith Is the Gift of God

It is not a natural possession, it is not innate. It has to be given. The young man in the story could not see until God opened his eyes. No one can. A blind man, when Jesus healed him said—"Since the beginning of the world it was never heard that anyone opened the eyes of a man born blind" (John 9:32). That is true. Only God can open the eyes of people that are born blind. And we are born blind, all of us. That is the meaning of the doctrine of original sin. We cannot naturally see and know God; of ourselves we cannot understand his world. We are born blind and only God can give us sight. It is in vain that we grope about by ourselves, in vain that we try any quack medicine that is offered to us with the promise that it will set us right. We apply to guides as blind as ourselves, but they do not bring us to the light, but only make us fall into a ditch.

We have no natural knowledge of God and we do not learn about him by looking at sunsets, or contemplating the immensity of the sea or any other of the wonders of the world. We do not really see him until he has opened our eyes, as he opened the eyes of Elisha's servant. We are then like the blind man whom Jesus healed. We do not know as much as we ought to do about the healer and we cannot explain what he has done to us we can only say "one thing I know, I was blind, now I see." A new thing has happened, God himself has made us to see—to see himself and see his world.

There is only one sort of human activity in this story and it is prayer. Elisha prayed for his young servant. "Lord I pray thee, open his eyes that he may see." That is a right and proper thing for us to do. We cannot give people sight, that is we cannot give them faith, but we can and we should pray to God that he will do so, and in his infinite mercy he hears our prayers. This is not the time to go into the wonders of prayer. But it is the time to urge you to pray. Maybe there is someone you are trying to win for Christ, and you're not getting very far. Pray for him, specifically by name. Take your friends one by one and pray. I will tell you what to say: "Lord there is so and so; open his eyes that he may see." That is the first thing. Faith is God's gift and we are to pray for it, for ourselves and for others. Second—

Faith Is the Reversal of Human Judgments

When the blind man, the man without faith, looked out upon the scene, it was obviously a good thing for the Syrians. There they were their amassed troops all around the little town, the prophet a fast prisoner. The powers of evil are on top. It is a good thing to be a Syrian and a bad thing to be a prophet of the Lord. Humans are on the point of putting God to flight. It was a different scene for the man whom Elisha had prayed to have his eyes opened. The roles were reversed. It was humans after all that were running away, and God was the master of the powers of evil.

Now this is characteristic of the reversals that faith is always making in our judgments. Faith finds its center in Christ crucified. There above all other places, we see the reversal of our judgments. We look at the Cross and we see weakness and foolishness. And in that judgment there is no intellectual mistake. I have not very much patience with those (especially pacifists) who assert that the way of the Cross was the wisest way, that submission can wield a stronger "however" than compulsion. The Cross then becomes a method of getting one's own way. And it wasn't. When the intelligent man sneers at the Cross as foolishness and weakness, he is dead right—on his own level. And what makes us see it as the power of God and the wisdom of God is not mere intelligence, but the faith that God gives.

Faith reverses our ideas about humanity and God. Everywhere, and this has never been truer than today, we see humankind planting his lordship firm on earth and sea, land and air. Everywhere we see God being pushed into the background. It is only by faith that we see that the God who is content to use as his messenger to the nations the herdsman of Tekoa, who is willing to entrust his Son to a manger in Bethlehem, is quite capable of ruling his own world, and needs neither our sympathy nor our assistance.

Faith means the reversal of our opinion about ourselves. The person without faith sees himself as the center of his own stage. His own personal safety and welfare is what matters, and the question that rises to his lips is "Alas, my master! How and what shall we do?" The person of faith learns that he is not after all the middle of the picture. God is in control and God is able to look after his own interests and in particular is able to look after his own servants. That is the characteristic difference that faith makes. Lack of faith always asks "How and what shall we do?" Faith is able to see and rely upon what God has already done. It looks back to the foolishness and weakness of the Cross, and beholds the wisdom and power which are fighting on our behalf.

Faith Is the Way of Understanding

That is to say that it is the means by which we are able to take a true and balanced view of life. Without faith, we see only the King of Syria's army, and it is a sight as should drive any one to despair. It is only by faith that we get a balanced view that can take in both sides of the situation. And make no mistake, faith does see both sides. Just because it can see the horses and chariots of fire, it does not fail to see the horses of flesh and blood and the chariots of war. Faith does not mean shutting our eyes to facts, it is rather like opening our eyes to more facts. It is this, and I think only this, which can keep us sane and hopeful among the changes and chances of life. But for this double vison of faith, we should despair.

I came across recently a bill copied from an account book. It ran like this: Bill of charges for burning Ridley and Latimer:[1]

> For three loads of wood faggots to burn Ridley and Latimer—12.0
> Item, one load of fringe faggots—3.4
> Item, for the carriage of these four loads—2.0
> Item, a post—1.4
> Item, two chairs—3.4
> Item, two staples—0.6
> Item, four laborers—2.8
> Total 25.2

Total one pound five and two. That's one way to looking at the event. And there is tragedy enough in it. The price of the lives of Latimer and Ridley 25 and 2. But there is another way of looking at it, the way of faith. Here is Latimer's own words: "Be of good comfort Master Ridley and play the man. We shall this day light such a candle, by God's grace in England as I trust shall never be put out." It is by faith that we can see the meaning of events, even events like that. And who can say that Latimer's faith was a mere pious hope?

Faith Is the Way of Victory

This is the victory, says 1 John 5:4, that has overcome the world, even our faith. This follows, of course, from what we have already said. Faith is the

---

1 Editor's Note: This is a reference to these martyred English saints, not the later buildings named after them. Both Ridley and Latimer were burned at the stake in Oxford, England, October 16, 1555, for their views against Roman Catholicism.

reversal of human judgments. When humans in this world, and evil humans at that, seem to be top dog, we can be sure that in spite of all appearances God is conqueror, God rules, God is the Lord. Faith is the way of understanding. It is by faith that we perceive the resources are ours in the battle with evil. It is by faith we see that they that be with us is more than the they that be with them.

Of course, it is not our victory, it is not a triumph achieved by our cleverness, our determination. It is God's victory. But for that very reason it is all the more secure. Above all it is by faith that we are brought into contact with the victory of the Cross. Because of this, the Gospel is the power of God unto salvation for all who believe. Let me finish by quoting a hard saying that will take thinking over, but which is true. We know all too well the shabby inadequacy of our lives, their grim ugly failures, the sin that so closely clings to us. We know that. And we know too what God has prepared in glory for those who love him. We have ideas at least of what this life of glory is—life with him. Now here is the hard saying: By faith we are, what we shall be.

"Light in Darkness"—Isaiah 9:2

[Preached twenty-four times from 12/18/38 at Bloxwich Wesley to 12/6/98 at Kelloe]

I cannot read these words, or the whole passage, to you easily or lightly. They are *either* the greatest truth in the world, a truth which revolutionizes and transfigures every other truth, a truth of God, beside which the truths of human beings are a lie, because it speaks of the light of God, compared with which the light of humankind is darkness, *or* they are a bitter and cruel mockery. We do not think often of the terrible knife edge on which the words of the Bible hang. We do not see, as Luther did, that apart from faith God's word is full of impossibilities and foolishness. We take it for granted, we do not press beneath the surface to find out whether or not what appears to be is the truth.

Impossibilities and foolishness! Do you think the language is too strong? The prophet speaks of a great light shining on humanity living in a dark, a painfully dark world. He says that one is born who shall be Wonderful Counselor, Mighty God, Everlasting Father, Prince of Peace. Very well. Now go to Spain and stand in the blasted streets of Madrid, and proclaim the Prince of Peace. Go down the air raid shelters and cry "Arise, shine, for the light has come!" Or go to China and tell those who dwell in that land of the shadow of death that upon them the light has shined. Do you think that you would be believed? Is light credible in such darkness? Is not the Bible, are not we, talking nonsense when we proclaim such things?

We ought to notice that the prophet was writing at a time almost if not quite as dark as our own. He was no blind optimist. The two Jewish kingdoms of Israel and Judah were threatened by Assyria. Judah was for submission but Israel was trying to compel its neighbors to mount a resistance. It was a nice choice between the frying pan and the fire. In these very verses, Isaiah speaks of the hardship, the hunger, the darkness, that was to befall his people. He was not one of those who think that things will of themselves get better and better. It was not to progress and improvement that he looked, it was to deliverance by God. And just there where the darkness was blackest, he proclaimed the day, before ever the streaks of dawn had begun to tinge the sky. The true prophet always sees the dawn at midnight, when it seems least likely.

And this has a bearing on a question that occurs to everyone at some time or another. Does religion, does Christianity break down in the darkness? It is question raised by the fact that religion of a great many people does indeed break down in the dark. As long as things go well, they are happy and trusting. When trouble comes, when darkness falls, they give everything up. Their religion does break down. It gives no light. It is useless. But there are others in the same circumstances who cling yet more clearly to their religion. "The Lord," they say, "is my light; in him will I trust." Paul and Barnabas in prison, in the stocks, in the innermost dungeon at midnight sang hymns and praise to God. Who is right? Are the prophet and Paul and Barnabas fools? Or have they got something, have they found some truth which those who so loudly proclaim the obscurity and uselessness of faith, have not suspected? Is there light in darkness? In fact, it is always, not just on one special occasion—

God's Will to Be the Light of the World

If I were an artist in words, as some are, I would paint three pictures. The first is one that demands the vivid imagination of H.G. Wells and more. It is a picture of a world formless and void before land was separated from water, before all hills and valleys, seas and lakes, before there were trees and plants, before the beasts and the birds lived. "I beheld the earth, and behold it was waste and void; and the heavens, they had no light. I beheld the mountains, and behold they trembled, and all the hills moved to and fro. I looked and behold there was no human being, and all the birds of heaven were fled. I beheld lo the fruitful field was a wilderness" (Jer. 4:23-26). And then see a point of light breaking out upon the surface of the deep, spreading and expanding, touching the wave crests with silver, and glinting along the troughs, the light glowing, because God said—"let there be light, and there was light." We do well to remember that God is the author of old light and we see and appreciate all the beauty of the world because of his act. He is the author, giver of all good things.

The second picture would require an even larger canvas. It too is a picture of the world, but this time of the inhabited world. It is full of busy men and women noisily occupied in the everyday commerce of life. Here and there is a student thinking great thoughts of God and the world. Here and there wise, sober, diligent statesmen are governing their people considerately and well, but we cannot help seeing that a dark shadow hangs over the whole world. We see at least as many slaves as free persons, slaves who have not even the rights of a dog. We see cruel and bloody wars. We see immorality such as I cannot describe to you in public, carried on not secretly but openly and uncondemned. In God's own people we see a hard, superficial legalism and hypocrisy. A world benighted indeed! And again, there is a point of light and it is centered in a stable in Bethlehem, and it issues in a life of perfect purity and love, a teaching of joy and peace and righteousness and death and a new life whose power has in some degree permeated the shadowed world.

The third picture is a miniature in comparison—the soul of a single individual. And there is much here that is good. There is sincerity, honesty, strength of purpose, a brilliant and restless mind. But there is also profound dissatisfaction. There is mental temptation which is all too easy to succumb to. The very command of God provokes evil passions and desires; there is a bitter hatred of one, and of his followers. This is a persecutor, this is Saul. "And as I made my journey and drew nigh unto Damascus, about noon, suddenly there shone from heaven, a great light round about me" (Acts 22:6). And there shone a light in his heart too. Faith and love were kindled. Jesus was Lord and Christ and he had brought with him peace and light to Paul.

And it was left to Paul to discover the great truth that God is the source of all light, whether the physical light that floods the earth, whether Jesus the light of the world, or the light which through Jesus shines in the sinner's heart. "It is God that said light shall shine out of darkness, who shined into our hearts, to give the light of the knowledge of the glory of God in the face of Jesus Christ" (1 Cor. 4:6).

And in that verse you have it. Can religion keep going in the dark? Can we believe the prophet is right when in the eighth century B.C. or the twentieth century A.D. he sees the dawn at hand? If God is like that certainly we can. If when our human hope fails and facile optimism fades "yet God the Son abideth" there is light, and the light is our faith, and it will not let us down. It has pleased God that this light should be seen in the face of Jesus Christ.

He Is the Light of the World

He is the light of the world because he came from God and went to God, who is the source of all light. The light of Jesus has nothing to do with the optimistic view of the world, which is so provoking today. I have just been reading it in a sermon. I looked at the date of the volume—1910. You could write that sort of thing then, but since 1914–18 it is not so easy. Abyssinia, Spain, China, Czechoslovakia—it is not so easy. Jesus gives light because he speaks not of some transient world order, but of God. We are apt to be impatient about that. We want Jesus to proclaim pacifism or the reverse; socialism or the reverse; he does neither. He gives Good News of God. He is firmly fixed on the one unchanging factor in history, namely that which is outside history, God. And because of him, we too may find an anchor which cannot be moved, we too can be rooted and grounded. We can find a resting place, a security, and the world of eternal reality, from which we shall derive power, not to go out of but to live in this world.

For he alone is the light of life. There is little enough of commandment in his teaching, but there is enough. "Thou shalt love"—God and neighbor. Do not think that there is anything sentimental (in a bad sense) here. Truly, to love one another will at times need all the strength and at times all the severity that we have. There is a love that takes and a love that gives, and the love of Jesus is the latter. He gives to us, and we must give to him and to each other. We must give from the heart because we love from the heart.

Jesus is light to those who are in the shades of death, literally understood. Here is the test. Again, we ask, does religion break down in the dark? Perhaps we can live as he taught us when all is well. When good spirits reinforce the peace of God we may indeed know what joy is. But when life is dark; when all the human lights of life have gone out—what then?

One of the greatest of modern preachers whose sermons I have read is Dr. [Arthur John] Gossip. It is a moving experience to read "the first sermon preached after my wife's bewilderingly sudden and undreamed of death." He uses an illustration to express his discovery: "What I have to say is this: when Claverhouse suddenly shot Brown of Priesthill, he turned to the wife and asked, the callous brute 'what think ye now of your brain guidman?'[1] And she, gathering the scattered brain, made answer. 'I aye thought much of him, but I think more of him now.'" "I aye thought much of the Christian

---

1   Editor's Note: a "guidman" or "goodman" was an owner or tenant.

faith, but I think more of it now, far more." That is the word of one who passed through as black and staggering a darkness as most of us are likely to know, and the light shone. Does religion break down in the darkness? Ask the prophets, ask the apostles and saints; ask millions of humble men and women who have put their hand in God's and walked with him, and they will tell you, with no uncertain voice. But this fact, that light has come into the world is one of which—

No One Can Be Independent

Not even if one wishes. Many think it to be a sign of freedom to have nothing to do with religion. I was glancing a little while ago at a book by a descendant of Francis Asbury, the Methodist pioneer in America.[2] It was called *Up from Methodism* and the author was extremely proud of having escaped from the bondage of religion. And it was quite apparent on the most superficial examination that the man was writing as complete nonsense as I have seen. Free! All the time he was bound by his monumental pride and self-assertion. And was he even free from the religion he despised? Perhaps he would have nothing to do with Jesus, but has Jesus nothing to do with him? The fact that light has come into the world means that all the world is under the judgment of God. Light reveals, it enforces a choice; do you choose darkness because your deeds are evil, or do you come to the light?

The judgment is there and you cannot escape it; the only thing to do is to face it. I wish I could get as excited and urgent about this as the New Testament. The writers of the New Testament look back to Isaiah crying heroically in the darkness, believing in the light, and they say—"it is here, it has come." That which the prophets desired to see, you are seeing. Read again the first two chapters of Luke's Gospel. Feel the thrill of the new life bursting into the world. I am often very much afraid that we may sentimentalize Christmas. By that babe in the manger, the Incarnation, the life and death of Christ, the light of God shining in the darkness, we are judged and we are saved. And all depends on our attitude to Him.

There were three men to be beheaded in China. The third, a lieutenant asks for time to pray, is spared and spends his life in service of God. The

2   Editor's Note: Francis Asbury never married, nor had he any children, so presumably C. K. Barrett means a relative or cousin rather than a descendant.

center of the Chapel was filled with soldiers brought there by him. And they salute Jesus. The wise men worshipped him. These Chinese soldiers salute him. Cannot we come to him, and give ourselves to him, God's gift to us all? We give our obedience and loyalty, knowing that we could never come to the light at all except God had drawn us and given us his unspeakable gifts.

"Mighty God, Prince of Peace"— Isaiah 9:6

[Preached fifteen times from 12/15/40 at Pinfold St. to 12/23/90 at Trimdon Station]

There is no need to linger over the difficult political background of this prophecy. Politics certainly do lie behind it, but it is more than politics that lies ahead of it. I do not know how we should explain such anticipations of the Gospel and of the Gospels but here they stand rooted in the Old Testament, and this is a Gospel text, and a very great one. The Bible is not the only book that talks about God. Human beings have always had the name of God on their lips. Unlike other books, the Bible in its speech about God has a Gospel, good news, because it is not merely meditating on God, is not content to describe what it has pleased theologians to call his attributes, to put each one in its proper place, and to suppose that that is another problem dealt with—God like so many other awkward things securely tied up with red tape. Not so much the attributes as the activity is the theme of the Bible. The Bible does not bother to tell us who God is but rather what he has done, what he is doing, and what he will do. It does not look down its research microscope at God, and describe him, with careful diagrams. Its witness can be summed up in the line of the hymn—"to God be the glory, great things he has done."

So, in this text, God's activity is both direct and indirect. He will work directly in the gift of the child, and he will work indirectly through the child whom he has given. And he will do things for his people, he will be a counselor, a leader, a father to them. He will give them peace. I have said this is a great text. It is too great a text for me to deal with the whole of it. I shall pick out only two things—Mighty God, and Prince of Peace. I pick them out because they offer such a contrast.

Some people want to translate Mighty God as Hero God. That is, at least,

30

not far wrong, for the word used here with God is one that is often applied to the mighty men of the Old Testament, the heroes of Israel's history. David, for example was a "mighty man" and the leader of mighty men. Once he was a fugitive from the Philistines, penned up with a few followers in the cave of Adullam. And he was homesick, as great men can be, and thinking of his own ancestral home, he said "I wish someone would give me a drink from the well by the gate in Bethlehem." It was not a command, but three men left their hiding place and stormed through the enemies ranks and back again just to fetch a cup of water. Because they were heroes, men of great personal courage they would not only do this, but also turn to flight great armies of aliens. And the picture of the Mighty God is frankly borrowed from the picture of the mighty men of valor. The hero God is the champion of his people, the Lord of hosts, mighty in battle. "Who is this that comes from Edom, from Bograb with blood-stained clothes, glorious in his apparel, marching in the greatness of his strength? I that speak in righteousness, mighty to save." (Isa. 63).

And at the same time Prince of Peace. A governor not only in time of war, but one who orders the life of his people in prosperity and well-being. He administers justice, liberty and happiness abound. If the mighty God could be symbolized by David, the prince of peace can be represented by an idealized Solomon, a Solomon without his oppression and injustice. The Mighty God and the Prince of Peace, this text finds room for both.

Fulfillment

In only one other place is there room for both the mighty God and the Prince of peace, that is in the character of Jesus Christ. But there they are found in such an increase and quality that can hardly even be hinted at from any parallel one could quote. Partly, this is because there is so much more than personal heroism and inward peace in Him. Indeed, it is not unusual to find these two combined in great human beings, and even in those who were not so great! Capt. Scott set out for the South Pole and he and his five friends reached it—a few days too late. Another had anticipated their discovery. They set out for home but were engulfed in a blizzard. Their daily march decreased day by day. One after another fell to rise no more. Dying in a tiny tent, isolated by miles of snow, Scott could yet write in his diary, quietly rejoicing that Englishmen could still be found who would face adventure and accept death with as great a fortitude as ever.

Heroic daring and quiet simple peace are there, and we may see the same thing in Jesus, see his resolute forward tread as he goes up to Jerusalem, the place of death, the city of battle, the city of sacrifice. It may be a comparatively easy thing to charge into the valley of death and the charge of the Light Brigade with the cheer of companions, the courage of the heroes, the flash of the guns. It cannot have been an easy thing to weigh up the possibilities and costs and calmly set out for a Cross, with no one to understand, no one to share the burden. Yet that is what Jesus did, facing death with courage and serenity.

Yet that is a side of the picture that the prophets seem singularly disinclined to show us. You will not find much of the human touch there. Jesus is true enough a man going to his death but he is also the Son of God going to his victory. He is a hero but not a hero giving his life in a forlorn hope. It is true indeed that the way of his victory was through his death, but because of the victory there is no tragic waste in his death. Someone has described the tragedies of J. Galsworthy as tragedies of waste. The horrifying and pitiful action of them, the ruin of men and families, in many respects noble and good, were not necessary but that some defect, some flaw was there. So great a good is wasted and great evil happens—waste. It is impossible to speak that way of Jesus. He is not the mighty man for whom the end of his ways is dust and dishonor. He is the Mighty God who redeems his people and leads them up to the hills of God.

And in the same way, he not only has peace in himself, he has the power of creating peace. He brings peace where there was strife, he gives courage to the faint-hearted. So, with him the contrast is all the more striking. He is supremely the warrior of God and he is supremely the peacemaker. He is ever of war, he is always making wars to cease. All of this illustrates the universality of the character and of the appeal of Jesus. He is himself both the Hero of God and the Prince of Peace. His sovereignty extends over every aspect of human life. Paul asks in one of his arguments "Is God the God of Jews only?" Obviously not. But we have misunderstood Paul if we think that Jews stand only for a human division of blood and soil. You could paraphrase "is God the God of religious people only?" Is he concerned only with the pieties of life? Does he restrict his interest to Sunday? Does he stay inside the Church? Does he never go into the streets, the slums, the factories, the shops, the army camps? God does not belong to the religious people. They belong to him, and so do the folk outside the Church, the folk who are working day and night, the men who guard and fight, the people who are struggling to make this a better, safer world of liberty and justice. They belong to God and God claims them.

And the people who cannot speak with full assurance of faith, those who are worried and anxious, who do not know what peace of mind is; does God neglect them in favor of the strong men and women of faith and serenity? And the bad people; the man who ruins his home because of his lust for pleasure, the man who steals and kills, be he dictator or starving and out of work; the man who gives way to his temper and bitterness and makes life a hell for his friends? Do these not belong to God? Is he not their God? He is, and he claims them, claims a share in all their lives. Bishop Westcott once said in conversation with C. F. Andrews "the one denial of Christ is to leave him out of *any* sphere of human life, as if he were not, in very truth, the Son of Man." Christ the warrior and Christ the peacemaker. He calls us to himself, making his claim upon every sphere of human activity.

His Call to Heroic Service

In the first place the hero God calls us to service in the spirit in which he leads. One of the greatest of the Spaniards died during their civil war, Michael Unamuno. He had had a checkered life, doing for the most part an unpopular work. He was for many years a professor of Greek in Salamanca, but his real work was to spread the knowledge of the Bible in a land in which it has almost been expelled. He found the key to life in Don Quixote's exclamation "Religion is knight-errantry, is the soul on the march uniting in its ranks the brave and gallant seekers of the truth from all lands and all ages."

In the early Church, there was no more popular symbol of the church than the army. The Roman Army was known to all. It was the model of courage, discipline, organization, efficiency; and the Church was the army of Christ. It was pledged to follow the Lamb wherever he might go. It marched with the Cross as its standard. The Church is still God's army, and Christ is still at work in the world. He is still the foe of all evil. He has won the victory of his Cross, but it must be dispensed through all the world. Satan was conquered on Calvary, but he still has a large army and there is moral mopping up to do.

A few weeks ago, a missionary (Dick Robertson) told me this story. A young Indian couple were married and went to work as teachers in an untouched south Indian village. They were only 20 and full of hope and enthusiasm. They had a tiny home in the village, and their first job was to set about the making of a Christian home. That was not easy. It can never be easy, but in an atmosphere of unchecked cruelty and immorality it must have been infinitely worse. But the village decided it would not have them. Persecution began. They were insulted in the streets. Their house was filled with refuse from the village dung heap so that it could not be used. They slept in the open. They had to walk eight miles for every drop of water because the village well was closed to them. At the end of a month they went to the district prayer meeting and asked what they should do—"Go back, we shall be praying for you." They stuck it a little longer and then came cholera. They nursed or buried everyone. Now the village has sent an official letter to the Methodist Church that in no event should they be taken away.

God calls us into a sinful world, maybe into beastly surroundings, to take our share of hardship. Not for our afflictions, but so that we might serve and redeem. God has given us in these dark times a glorious opportunity for hard thinking and hard working. We see the break-up of great civilizations, we see universal systems of thought and life falling from dominance. We see morale and integrity smashed from within and without. And into this chaos Christ leads his army like a rescue squad. For there is rescue work to be done. There is demolition to be done. Above all there is the restructuring of a world to be carried through.

His Offer of Peace

This leads to the third point. There can be no reconstruction of our cities until peace comes. There can be no reconstruction of character until peace comes. You cannot build up a well-constructed character on a divided life. If you are not yourself at peace, you will not bring peace and well-being to anyone else. Now Christ is the prince of peace and he brings peace to those who need it. But not by any means the peace of complacency or self-indulgence. That is a very different thing. The peace, for example, of Paul was in that sense, a very uneasy, uncertain thing. It is peace with God, the peace that can only come to a person who is relying entirely on Christ and not on anything he can do for himself and which sets a person free from self-centeredness and enables him to serve others.

Two American missionaries were captured in 1934 by the Red Armies in Kivei Chow. After grim privations over 13 months one was ransomed and the other not for another six months. Christmas Day 1934, judging from outward appearances could not have been a more dismal day. The weather was cold, there was no fire, and their sole pastime was sitting on the floor. The only thing to relief the monotony was the three meals of rice and vegetables which were brought to them and which were eaten in silence. Truly, as seen by the outward eye the day was dreary, gloomy, cheerless. But the Lord sent them a message in one word which made a world of difference—"Immanuel, God with us." "I longed to pass it on to Mr. Hayman. The idea came to me to form the letters with pieces of straw. And so, unbeknownst to the guard, it became a message of cheer to my companion also. The whole scene was changed into one of joy. 'If God is for us, who can be against us?' And so, knowing that we should be imprisoned no longer than he would allow, we rejoiced in tribulation." That is his offer of peace, which lies in the love of God, from which nothing, life, death, sin can separate us.

These Are Not Two But One

Wordsworth paints the picture of the happy warrior. A man who in war is possessed of inward peace, is "happy as a lover. And the Christian warrior is inevitably a happy one, grim and determined no doubt, perplexed and defeated at times. Yet always governed by an invincible joy which springs from the peace of God. "In war, my peace" said Charles Wesley. Christ's call to service and his offer of peace are not two but one. He makes no demand on us, for we are too weak to respond without his own help. But while we were yet sinners, he brought us within the orbit of his dying love. The Cross is his army's banner, and his resurrection promises the peace of his eternal presence.

There are not two but one. It is mutilating the Christian message to divide it as is sometimes done as if Christ called young people to difficult service and offers old ones a little peace before they step into the grave. Very humbly one might suggest that there are old people who have forgotten to fight. And it is undeniably true that there are young folk who are seeking peace in their own lives. Anyone can see adventure nowadays; it is peace and serenity that are hard to find. Christ offers us his peace, the peace of confident trust in God, the peace that opens a way into a world of service, in which we may serve the Mighty God who reigns for us as Prince of Peace.[1]

---

1   Editor's Note: Stuck in the pages of this sermon is the outline of another one on this same text, Isaiah 9:6, a sermon more apropos for Christmas. The outline begins with a recalling of the jubilant cheer of these words in Handel's *Messiah*, "Mighty God, the everlasting Father, the Prince of Peace," and then Barrett adds: "But we know it only because it brought disappointment and disillusionment—the King in Isaiah's day didn't bring it off. This means that the hopes, real hopes, that God evokes are fulfilled only in God. And Christmas means that in God they are fulfilled. God doesn't let us down, and he comes and speaks to us in our disappointment and disillusionment of which there is plenty today. Consider first the hope of the fulfillment. This is too rich for detail. Consider 2 Sam. 15:12 etc.—the King's court, Mighty God, and David and his mighty men (25:23), longing for a father figure, the role of the kings. Second point—Solomon the Prince of Peace, but note the disappointment in all these human illustrations. Best take up the four points again in Jesus—wisdom, victory, Abba, peace. This leads to the third point—the diversity of his offer and call. Wisdom, involves understanding life, Conflict, against evil of all kinds, Abba, reproduced in us. Peace, that passes understanding. On the strength of this we return to the jubilee of Handel's *Messiah*."

"Sold for Nothing"—Isaiah 52:3

[Preached thirty-three times from 10/19/47 at Bishop St. to 6/25/00 at Wheatley Hill]

Short as the time may be, I must claim a few minutes for the historical setting of these words. They were uttered in the cause of God by a prophet who was in a position to look back, to review as a whole the first long chapter of Israel's history, a history of petty political intrigue, myopic in the conception and appalling in its consequences. Centuries before, an older prophet had declared "Israel is like a silly pigeon, fluttering this way and that." Now she thinks she will be safe with Assyria, now she flaps away to Egypt. And in the end Babylon had sacked Jerusalem and carried away the people captive. That was the final dividend their policy had paid. So many brilliant schemes, so many well laid plans, and this was the end.

But there was more in it than that. This was more than the tragic failure of human plans. At stage after stage the will of God had been presented to this people, clearly, unmistakably, and at stage after stage they had rejected the plan of God for their own scheme. They had sold their destiny, they had sold themselves. There were two brothers the old story said, Esau and Jacob, the ancestors of Edom and Israel. Esau in his hunger sold his birthright for a mess of pottage, the whole thing for one meal. Jacob was too prudent for that, and his descendants were too foolish. Instead of exchanging their inheritance for a belly full of food, they frittered it away for nothing. Here they were homeless exiles, with no rights and no homes, no inheritance and no hope.

Now what is unique about Biblical history is not that similar things have never happened elsewhere, but that there was someone on hand, a prophet or an apostle, who would see through the event to its meaning. The event, this event, was not unique. I wish it were. But in fact, it will be easy to see it elsewhere—

The Bargain That Never Pays

It is never safe to bargain with your divine destiny. It is never profitable to sell yourself. There is no truer saying, no more immediately true saying in all the teaching of Jesus than this—"What shall it profit a person if he gains the whole world and loses his own soul?" There was a time perhaps when evangelists made too lurid a use of these words; perhaps we have dropped them a bit. They don't need to be exaggerated. They are simply true, and they only need to be stated.

The classic story of this is of course Faust, told in English by Christopher Marlowe and in German by Goethe. Faust knew everything, had everything, supreme in every science—philosophy, medicine, law, theology. He was the greatest person of his time. But he wanted one thing more. He wanted to be more than merely human, he wanted to be lifted above the ordinary run of the mill humanity. So, he sold his soul to the Devil for 24 years of unlimited power. Everything was his, even the beauty of Helen of Troy, "the face that launched a thousand ships, and burnt the topless towers of Ilium." And at the end of 24 years the Devil came to claim his purchase, then all the price, all the glittering gaudy price turned to ashes and Faust knew he had sold himself for nothing. He had gained knowledge, power, the world and he had lost his own soul. Faust is a legend. It never happened. I don't know that human beings can sell their souls to the Devil.

But the truth of the legend has been written on every page of human history. And there is perhaps no page of it on which the writing is larger and clearer than today. We are living on the stage of what may well prove to be the master tragedy of all civilization. I do not say that to grab attention. I say it because I am persuaded it is true. We live in a society which is based on the attempt of gaining the whole world. What? Faust had knowledge and power. He had less of both than a secondary schoolboy. There was a real Faust about whom the legend was spun. He died in 1538. What did he know?

Copernicus was his contemporary, but his book on the sun and the planets was not published until 1543. Galileo was not born until 1564. There was neither modern science nor even modern literature. But we have everything in our hands, even atomic energy. It would be tedious to attempt a list. We have more than Faust dreamed of and we are losing our souls. Not indeed to the thunder and lightning of the last act of Marlowe's play, but in a dreadful still quietness as when you sit by a bedside in a great hospital, equipped with every modern scientific resource, and yet must sit and watch life slowly and gently slipping away. Is that not true of our world? Is it not losing its soul in a wave of blind materialism? Is it not losing its conscience in a dull drugged apathy to right and wrong? If I say nothing else tonight, let me say this. It is increasingly the duty of the Church to confront the world, to confront civilizations and governments and cry "What shall it profit a person if he gains the whole world and loses his soul?"

But not worlds, societies, nations only. People too. This is far more than political economy. Esau sold his birthright for a mess of pottage, and which among us are not in danger of ranking our daily bread, our physical necessities, and a great many things that are by no means necessary, above the glorious liberty of the children of God? I will show you how we do this.

We do this in our lust for power, our desire for financial security. Let my head be well above the wave under which the other devils drown. We want to get on; when we have succeeded there will be time for the spiritual values of life. But there isn't. We get on and we find that we have gotten out, out of the real world. It was not a minister, it was a business man I heard the other day say "Unhappy? Of course, he's unhappy. Everyone is unhappy who lives for money."

We do it by stifling our consciences. Not so much perhaps by doing what we know to be wrong, but by hardening ourselves into looking upon what is wrong without feeling, the searing pain in our conscience which makes us spend ourselves in succoring the oppressed and risk ourselves in fighting evil. And it is a poor bargain; we gain a few paltry pence, we keep our soft skins on the soft cushions for a few moments longer. . . . And then?

I will show you how we do this in Church, we the people of God in 1947. We smooth out the offense from our Gospel. We offer people what they want, not what they need. We are so anxious to be friendly we forget to be faithful. And it doesn't pay. If the precentor keeps dropping his pitch so as to bring in everyone, he finds himself in the end ruining the chorus, the music won't sing. All the petty intrigues, all the disregard for God's word, and in the end you have sold yourself for naught. But if this is the bargain that never pays, there is also—

The Bargain That Has Never Been Made

It's a very odd one, for there is no money in it. Our prophet is looking back but also forward. You have sold yourself into slavery, but God will buy you out—without money. Have you ever looked in a pawnbroker's window? I always do when I pass by, and never without a poignant feeling. It is not just the thought of poverty, it is the wastefulness of it. There are articles in the window that ought to be in use; if you've any imagination you can see them being used. The clothes on someone's back, the kitchen utensils on someone's stove, even the other little palliative ornaments looking quite at home, even if not very artistic, on someone's mantelpiece. But now they are all pressed up together in one shop window. How can they be released? How can they be returned to their proper places? The answer is simple—pay over the money and the goods in the pawn shop will be returned.

But suppose they are not saucepans and china dogs in the pawn shop but people? People who have pawned themselves, people who have sold themselves for naught and are free no longer. Will money release them? Indeed, it will not. Nor will many another thing. Our prophet does not tell us how it will be done. He knows that God will do it and in his next chapter he captures a marvelous glimpse of how it will be done—in the suffering of the innocent for the guilty. But he does not really tell us how people are released from the bondage into which they have sold themselves.

But we know. There are two things to do. There is a restraining power to break; and there is the soul of a human being to free from his prison home. And both these things were done on Calvary. You remember the words with which Rousseau began the Central Social which did so much to provoke the French Revolution? "Humanity is born free, and everywhere he is in chains." A fine saying, and truer than that anti-clerical deist knew; a saying which might provoke a revolution but which couldn't really change the world. Why? Because fine phrases cannot alter the framework of life in which people are imprisoned. Even revolutions can't. Paul and Silas were thrown into the dungeon in Philippi. Fine phrases would not release them, nor could they batter down the walls by hitting their heads against them. It took an earthquake, something from outside that shook the whole framework of things, to set them free. And so people can only truly be set free when God stoops to shake the world. Matthew tells us there was an earthquake when Christ died on the Cross. He was right. There was. That was an act of liberation, of victory over the forces of evil, that help people in their grasp, the victory of the free love of God.

But there is a deeper reason why—there were and there are people who do not want to be free. They are comfortable where they are. It has always been so. From the Jews who found that life in Babylon could even be preferable even prosperous there to ourselves who are very well as we are and need no religious excitements to disturb the even course of our lives. But look! Here is the dying Son of God who shed his blood to free you. Is it nothing to you? Must he die and die and die for nothing? "He sees the souls for whom he dies, / still clinging to their sins." Must he do so? Must he open the prison door only to watch you toil in your chains? What does he offer you? The freedom of the children of God.[1]

---

1   Editor's Note: This is a very rare sermon indeed that simply breaks off at this point, with a note to mention that freedom is given for a particular use and to mention the pawnbroker illustration again. Almost all the other sermons are written out completely in longhand.

"A New Covenant"—Jeremiah 50:5

[Preached twenty times from 1/2/44 at Bondgate, Darlington, to 1/13/85 at Howden-le-Wear][1]

This text describes God's people as they find themselves facing a new opportunity. For years, they had been exiles in Babylon; now as the prophet hailing the first light of dawn, announces to them they are to be free. God is setting them free. And this is what they will do. Hence we may find help here in our great task of discovering what we Christian people are, and what we must do. Already, it seems to most of us, politically, militarily we see the flags of dawn appear. What is God's word for us now? What does God want of a Church in days like these? We may first of all learn—

Two Things about the Church

The first of these is that the Church is a redeemed Church. Christian people are saved people. That means you. I don't know why it should; I don't know why it should mean me. But it does, and for a moment I want you to think of the grandeur of it. "Who is like unto thee?" says Deuteronomy, "a people saved by the Lord." Think of it from God's side. That is the place to begin. You and I are pretty poor stuff, but poor as we are God loves us. He didn't love us because we were good, or even because we were potentially good. He just loved us. For our sake, Jesus Christ, the Son of God was content to live a human life and die a human death. God the Creator and Redeemed is among human beings in yet a third activity. As the Holy Spirit, he works in our hearts, creating in us faith and righteousness. I don't know why God does all this. I don't know why he loves us. It can only be because it is his nature to do it, because he is the mighty lover of humankind, and it is true

---

1   Editor's Note: This sermon also appeared in some form in 1991 in the *Methodist Recorder*.

"all the attributes divine, are now at work for me." Sovereign might and sovereign love are ours.

Think of it from the human side. We are redeemed, saved people. We are saved from our sins, there is no disputing about it. It is there in the New Testament. "Thou shalt call his name Jesus, for he shall save his people from their sins." Sin shall no more have dominion over you. We are saved from our cares, for we are to cast all our cares on Him, since he cares for us. There is no doubt at all about this Christian claim to deal decisively with sin and sorrow. There is no mistaking the triumph with which the primitive Church confronted the ancient world.

Have you ever read the Greek and Latin apologists of the second century? If you haven't take my advice and don't. They aren't worth it, except for those of us whose trade is scholarship. They are tedious old men. Many of their arguments are very poor. But again and again they come down to this. "You may slander us," they say, "with tales of profligate banquets and more; but have the patience to really look at us. Where will you find good life—humility, patience, honesty, endurance, love—like that? "You may torture and kill us," they say, "but look at our martyrs, look at their sheer happiness, their complete victory over suffering and death. Where among all your philosophies will you find the like?" And they were right, and in the end the pagan world had to admit it. The Christians were holier and happier people than they were.

Of course, this holiness and happiness was not now in a state of complete attainment. That leads to the latter of the two things to say about the Church. The Church is not only a redeemed people, it is also a Church on the march. These folk, 500 years or so B.C. were released from exile in Babylon, but they had several hundreds of miles of desert pilgrimage to cover before they got home. God set them on their way, he guided and guarded them, but they had to use their legs. You probably know the story of the lugubrious man to whom someone said, "You know So and So is not the man he used to be." "No," replied the man, "and he never was." A Christian will go further than that and add, "and he never will be, not in this world." If there was time, I could put this in many ways.

You are not yet the persons you ought to be, the persons you were meant to be. Is there one of you who will deny that? Is there one of you who thinks himself so much better than Paul that "I have already attained. I am made perfect"? Of course, there is not. No one will blame you that you are not. One must be very young to expect people to be perfect. But the vital question is this—Are you on the march? Are you going? Are you seeking this holiness, this happiness of which I speak? There may be some of us who have never set out with God at all, who have never paused in quietness to let God take hold of us, and set our feet on the road. There may be others who once set out, but turned back, or turned aside, or just stopped in our tracks. Maybe tired, maybe lonely, maybe afraid, maybe just idle. Well then, to you—up again! Set your feet toward the highway. Forward march. Christ frees you in his power, set out and aim for the prize of the high calling he sets before you. Leave the past behind. To it again.

This is not yet the Church it ought to be. I know it is a great place, and we love it very much, but it is not yet the pure bride of Christ, without spot or wrinkle or any such thing. Darlington is not yet staggered by the quality of Christian life that we show. We are not yet filled with a burning zeal for the work of the Lord, with a passion for souls. People do not yet think of Bondgate as a place where men and women are brought to God, a place where Christian faith burns bright, a place where the glory of the Lord is revealed. I know why. We don't pray enough, we don't work enough, we don't care enough. And not because I am in any way more virtuous than you, but because I stand here as the minister of God's holy Word and sacraments it is my duty to beg you "abound more and more" in the work of the Lord. But how? That is the second point. These ancients wanted to get to Zion. How did they inquire?

With Their Faces Thitherwards

That is, they faced in the right direction first. They did as much as they knew before they asked. This was no casual dilettante inquiry; they meant business. That is the only kind of inquiry I have time to deal with now. I am not very interested in the person who merely takes a polite interest in religious questions, except to feel sorry for him. The only people you can really answer are the people who really want to know. It is remarkable how often we fail here in regard to the Christian faith when we would not do so in any other department of human life. If you wanted to learn about biochemistry you wouldn't go to the library for books on Baroque art. If you wanted to hitchhike to Durham, you would go and stand hopefully on Crosscliffe Road. It is like the story of two of Wesley's preachers, one of whom heard the other praying, "Oh Lord send me a good wife, and Lord let it be Betsy." When it comes to religion, we all think we know. God is told his business a good deal more commonly than the average fireman. We will serve him, provided he can do it in our way. He can give us what he will, provided it meets our approval. He can tell us what he likes, provided that the message can pass the censor we have ourselves appointed. Really, it would be comical if it weren't so serious.

And it is serious, in some respect this is the most serious, the most dangerous thing there can be in Church life. Nothing can more easily vitiate the whole of our work. We want to dictate to God about time. You know the famous prayer of Augustine: "God give me chastity, but not now." A little longer to enjoy myself, to do as I please, and then and only then—chastity. Or we say, there can be no forward movement, no real advance in the Church during war time. Why not? You may not be able to see in the blackout, but do you suppose God can't? It is high time that we remembered that our times are in his hands and not vice versa.

Or we want to restrict God with regard to methods. There are some who will hear of nothing but the old ways; others are never happy unless they are doing something no one has done before. Or we are finicky about the people we are prepared to work with. If So and So is in the committee then we won't serve. And so it goes on. Consistency is not a strong point with some of us. We blame the age for its laxity and indifference, but we show a pretty poor example when active support of the Church is concerned. We expect our children to go to Sunday School and be good. But we don't go to Church or set up the framework of a Christian home. To ask your way to Zion with your face thitherwards means consistency.

It also means purpose, genuine purpose, hard-grained intent. Nothing else will do. A stranger once asked a farm boy "Where does this road go to?" The boy replied "It goes nowhere, it stops where it is." The man tried again "I mean where does it take you?" "It takes you nowhere, if you want to go, you'll have to walk." Wise answers where life is concerned. If you want to get anywhere, you'll have to walk. There is no other way to go. There is another question to the country lad, the answer to which doesn't apply. "How do I get to So and So?" "I don't know, if I were going there, I wouldn't start from here." That is wrong. In this matter, you do start from here. There is nowhere else to start from.

That is why I say to you all; from now on in the work of this Church, let us be at it together, we need one another. We are all alike in that we all need God. There is a great word before us in what, God willing, will be a great year. Let us start now, with no looking back. There are no shortcuts. The way may be hard, it may be long. Nearly four years ago, this country faced a hard job with the consistency, the purpose, the determination of which I have spoken. Will you show less now in this job, in this fight? Or are you persuaded that your battles are worth more than God's? Therefore comes the third thing. Let us join ourselves to God in a—

Covenant

A covenant that shall not be forgotten. Some of them are. Some of ours have been. But not this one, not this time, by God's grace. The Scots are the great people of covenants. Here is the first of them—They promised, "Before the majesty of God and before this congregation, that we by his grace shall with all diligence continually apply our whole power, substance and our very lives to maintain, set forward, and establish the blessed Word of God and his congregation."

But Methodists too are people of the covenant. Covenant services are one of our special contributions to the life of the whole Church. For we shall be joining in that service. Let us make it the pledge that in covenant with almighty God and one another we are going into battle this year; to find ourselves in the true life of the Church, to set about the powers of darkness, and to bear witness to the mighty love of God in Christ Jesus our Lord.

New Testament Sermons

"Come unto Me"—Matthew 11:28

[Preached once at Bondgate, Darlington, 12/19/43]

We have taken these texts beginning with the words *I came*, quite deliberately for this last sermon I have turned the word around. Here it is not indicative, a statement; it is imperative, a command, or rather an invitation. "Come unto me all ye who labor and are heavy laden." I want you to notice—

Who Are Invited

We have been singing that glorious carol "Angels from the Realms of Glory." I have loved it, and especially the tune, for years, but a few years ago it struck me that there was something wrong with the words, only I couldn't think what it was. I know now. The trouble with that hymn is that it leaves me out. It keeps on saying Come and worship Christ, but to whom is it speaking? Listen "Angels from the realms of glory." You would probably laugh if I said "I'm no angel" but it's true for all that. Then "shepherds in the field abiding." A lovely romantic picture, how we admire it. But it is a far cry from the lonely hillside in Palestine with all that pastoral beauty and simplicity to industrial war-time England. We don't fit there. "Sages leave your contemplations. But we are not sages and we have no contemplations to leave. We're ordinary prosaic men and women. And last "saints before his altar bending" that's the hardest of all for we know we are not saints.

Do we then not come in at all? Not into the hymn. But that is just where the hymn is wrong and incidentally where the Wesley hymns are always right. Wesley says "Come sinners," and that does mean me, and you too, I suspect. The call, the invitation of Jesus himself is not addressed merely to the picturesque, the romantic, the learned, the holy. What does he say? "Come unto me all you who labor and are heavy laden." The only people not invited are those who are quite sure they don't need him and are perfectly happy

49

by themselves. It is of course no use asking them. "There are tears in things" wrote Virgil long ago and he was right. You have felt, have you not, that dull and distant ache in your heart, hard to locate, hard to define, but which nevertheless means that all is not quite well, that life is after all not quite complete and satisfying as you had hoped. You have felt tired. I don't mean tired in body for at least when you are young and healthy that is a fine comforting feeling, full of contentment. How often have I walked off the rugger field bruised and weary but infinitely happy! No I mean tired inside. Weary with the feeling that life is getting you down, that you are loaded above the limit. To you, Jesus says "Come unto me. . . . My invitation is for you."

What Does He Offer?

"Come unto me and I will give you *rest.*" That is a very great promise and a true one. Christ does give rest to the burdened and tired. But it is only a small part of the meaning of this text, a meaning that the ordinary reader does not suspect and is only found out by a good deal of philological burrowing (I must justify my trade!). It is not only that the Greek word here means not so much to give a passive sort of rest, but rather to quicken, refresh, restore, what the seconds do to a boxer in the intervals between the rounds of a boxing match. When you get back to the word which Jesus probably spoke you find that he was not simply referring to rest in general but to a very particular rest. In his time people often spoke of the age to come, God's new age as like a perpetual Sabbath, a period in which there should be no toilsome servile work but all should be gladness and praise in the service of God. A name sometimes given to the Messiah was based on the root in question. Now Jesus picks up this picture, this metaphor and says "It has come true! All you weary, burdened people who are looking and striving so hard for the promised Kingdom. It is here. Come to me and you shall find what you need and what you seek."

And that, very briefly, is the word I pass on to you for Christmas. All you folks who are so busy seeking rest for yourselves and a new world to live in, the new age has come. It came in Bethlehem, it came at Christmas, the mighty inbreaking of God's redeeming power. And Jesus who is it bearer and messenger says "Come unto me, all ye that labor and are heavy laden, and I will give you rest."

"God Is Not Business-like"— Matthew 20:1-16

[Preached thirty-one times from 2/22/59 at Elvet to 9/26/04 at Brandon]

Many of the parables of Jesus, and this is one of them, are a very curious mixture. On the one hand, they have the unforgettable quality of a photographically exact observation and drawing of real life. They are perfectly real and true to life. On the other hand, they contain somewhere the oddest of tricks. Something happens which simply doesn't happen in real life. This is true here, and Mr. Short has summed it up in his epigram (I can take no credit for it), "God is not business-like." Most of this story shows us just exactly what did go on in a Palestinian vineyard. There were certain times in the year when an almost unlimited amount of extra laborers was needed too, and the owner or manager would hire workers anywhere and at any time. And there was and is a scorching heat; or better, with the marginal reading, a hot wind, the sirocco which swept in from the eastern deserts and made midday work almost intolerable. All this is given us with complete realism. It is also true that one denarius per day was a normal wage for laborers. But at the end of the story we find an employer behaving with the most hare-brained lack of concern for economics and good business. Instead of scaling down the pay to the amount of work done, he hands the same reward to everyone. But this is the end of the story, not the beginning, and we have other things to do before we reach it. Here is the first thing to observe—

God Is Always Seeking People for His Service

The owner of the vineyard is out at daybreak, 6 a.m., calling men to come and work for him. He gets what workmen he can find, but he is not satisfied

51

and by 9 he is out at the market place again and cleans it out, sweeping out everyone off to work in his vineyard. He is out again at noon, and at 3. And now it is 5 p.m. There is only an hour left, and anyone left by this time can't be much of a worker. The bottom of the barrel will be scraped by now. But no, out he goes again, and rakes up the last sweepings—"come and do what you can in the few minutes that remain." There is work for all.

Now this is God, and God is always looking for workers. And we for our part, I am speaking of the majority, the general run of us, are equally thinking of perfectly good excuses for not heeding his call. But a good many of them are out from under our feet in this parable. One thing we say—"it is too early to start, God can't really expect us to begin yet. We are too young." This is not a new excuse. Jeremiah tried it. God called him to the work of prophecy, and Jeremiah replied "Ah, Lord, I cannot speak; I am only a lad." It is true that not all of us in our youth are obsessed with our sense of inadequacy. Quite the contrary. We sometimes think we are a good deal too good to waste our time in God's service. I well remember overhearing a conversation among some spectators at the University Rugby ground at Cambridge, "Look at him!" said one, "A triple blue, and throwing himself on the Church." No! Let us first use all our powers to get blues, and to make money, and to enjoy life, and then when other interests fail, then let us think about the service of God. This may seem very well, but it is not God's idea. He is out at daybreak looking for workers. Fix yourself up elsewhere, the odds are you will never be free to take up God's service. If you are afraid of your inadequacy, he will find work you can do. If you have a high opinion of your powers, he will find work that will stretch that to the utmost.

Others of us say: it's too late now. If we had had the chance when we were young, we could have done something; but now we are past it. We are not much use to people, and we cannot be much use to God. Don't believe it. The owner of the vineyard comes out at the eleventh hour to see who is still available and he is glad to use all he finds. One of the most depressing feelings in life is the thought that we are no longer useful to anyone. "Too old at forty"—no longer wanted. But you are not too old for God.

We are all prone to say "the conditions are too hard. There is a scorching wind. The work is too hard. The day is too long. We should never stand it." That is something you need not consider, for the conditions are God's affair. What he calls you to do, you can do. He will see to that. Often when we talk about the Church we speak of the ministry and the laity. Often it is useful to do so. But in fact, the whole Church is in ministry, for ministry means service, and there is not a single person God does not call into his service. He does not call us all to the same kind of service, but he does call us all to service of some kind and there is no valid excuse. One of the chief dangers of the Church at the present time, is simply the unavailability of its members. They like the Church and they wish it to continue its work; but they are not willing themselves to take responsibility for any part of that work. Perhaps this is the besetting sin of our age; we want everything to be "laid on" for us. But the Church is not, and never will be "laid on."[1] It depends absolutely on the power of God, but the power of God operates through the actual responsible service of each member of the community. "Christ doth call, one and all, Ye who follow shall not fall" (J. Neander). There is a second thing to note in the story—

God's Servants Should Not Judge One Another

Recall the parable. The owner of the vineyard agreed to pay the men when he called at the beginning of the day, the standard rate for the job, one denarius for the day. It was a fair bargain. At the end of the day those who worked for only one hour received—one denarius each. Those who worked all day expected their pay to go up, *pro rata* and it didn't. There was no breaking of the agreement, they simply grudged the generosity he had shown to others. It is not a pleasing attitude.

I have the suspicion that something might be said on this basis in a number of industrial disputes, including one I have read of in the last week. But I must avoid the temptation to preach to people who are not here. There is plenty to say along this line as to what goes on in God's own vineyard. Indeed, I am going to leave out a number of things that could be said on this score. Let me be as practical and as personal as I can be. Is it not true, shockingly true, that we can find it in our hearts to grudge and envy the ability and the success of some of our fellow workers in the Church?

Even the early church was riddled with this sin. John comes to Jesus "Teacher we saw someone actually seeking to cast out demons in your name, though he doesn't belong to our set. But we soon put a stop to him." "Oh no," says Jesus, "if he can cast of devils in my name then you'd better let him get on with it. It is not for you to judge him." As we look back we can see that there was no greater man in the apostolic age than Paul. Yet there

---

1   Editor's Note: The British phrase "laid on" means "done for you" by someone else.

certainly was no man who suffered more distraction of such an unpleasant kind. They even stooped to say that when he made a collection for the poor, he embezzled the funds.

Paul himself met with a situation in Rome where two groups of Christians were sharply divided against one another. One group was saying "Look at those old stick-in-the-muds. They have no idea what Christian freedom means. They are as bad as those Jews with their prohibitions and taboos." Then others said: "Look at those unprincipled creatures! They don't keep Sunday as they ought and they are not as careful as they should be about what they drink!" To them both, Paul says, "What business is it of yours to judge someone else's servant? It is to his own Master that he stands or falls." Yes, and since the Master is on both sides Christ, Christ will make him stand.

It would not be hard to modernize all this. How sticky we can all be when someone poaches, as we think, on our own preserves; gets on with a job we supposed was ours, even though we were not doing very much about it. How easy it is to criticize, let's say the Billy Grahams, who don't do the job quite the way we should do it, and with courage and sincerity and (let us be honest) a humiliating measure of success. How easy it is to complain of the ways and habits of our fellow-Christians without really trying to understand their point of view! Surely it ought to be possible for all the servants of Christ, if not to love one another, though God knows why they shouldn't be able to manage that, at least to understand and sympathize with one another.

It is indeed a measure of the wonderful grace of Christ, that he should be willing to accept into his service the persnickety old curmudgeon in the next pew whom you find it so difficult to get along with, but he does accept him. And if Christ accepts him, can't you? And if we can start there can't we begin to build up the kind of fellowship, the kind of love, that will be visibly a miracle within the world? It is time to come to the last and vital point.

God Is Not Business-like

Here is the sting in the tale of the parable. I can think of no better way of bringing it out than telling you another parable told by the rabbis and coming therefore from the same background as Matthew's parable. "To what can we compare the case of R. Buni the son of R. Hiyya? To a king who engaged many workmen for his service. One of them was more active in his work than the rest. When the king saw this, what did he do? He took the man off, and walked with him up and down. In the evening, the workmen came to get their pay and he paid the whole amount equally to the man with whom he had been walking up and down. Seeing this, his companions complained: 'We have wearied ourselves with work through the whole day, and is this man who has only exercised himself for two hours to receive as much as us?' 'That' says the King, 'is because in two hours he has done more than you have done in the whole day.' In the same way when R. Buni had studied the Law up to the age of 28, he knew it better than a scholar or a saint who had studied it up to the age of 100."

What more do I need to say? God is not business-like, God is love. It is true that he calls persons constantly into his service. It is true that he should be served in the right way. But when all is said and done, it is not our service, neither the quality of it nor the quantity of it, that matters; it is his goodness. This parable does not teach that God has no rewards for those who love and serve him, it teaches that the rewards do not hang upon the thin and fraying string of our desert, but simply upon God's indestructible love.

It is only here that we can turn to and make sure of the first two points. God calls you into his service. Well, why should you take any notice? Why not take it easy instead? Because he is not a business-like employer, because he is the God who loves and gives without reference to our deserts; because he is the God who made himself known in Jesus Christ, who never calls people to carry crosses, except—after him. A taskmaster who drags you to work, you can say no to with a good heart; but a lover who means to give us our full reward, even though we cheat him out of his due, it is a different thing to rebel against him.

And then you get beyond the romanticism of Christian service, and you learn how dull it can be, and how very unpleasant and provocative your fellow workers can be, and of course you lose patience with the whole lot of them. "I wouldn't be seen dead in a Church full of people like that," we say. And then you remember. There is one always to be seen dead in a Church full of people like that. He died for them as well as for me, and every single one of them is my brother or sister for whom Christ died. He came not to be served but to serve and give his life for us. That is precisely why we give ourselves to his service.

"Watchnight Service"— Matthew 25:14-30

[Preached three times from 12/31/54 at Elvet to 12/31/70 at Franwellgate Moor][1]

Why do we have Watchnight Services on the 31st of December? We are all quite intelligent enough to know that there is no real difference between December 31 and January 1, so we might as well draw the dividing line of time anywhere else. If the calendar were to be reformed in our time, we should make no fuss about losing eleven days of our lives. The point of course is that the dividing line is here, and that passing it makes us aware that we are moving on through time. The train is always going; the milestones remind you how swiftly you are speeding on your journey. And the fact that tomorrow you will write 1955 on your letters reminds you that we are moving on into an unknown future and leaving behind us a past which we can now experience only through memory. The whole process can be summed up (you may think flippantly) in the words, the further off from England the near it is to France. As one leaves the remote days of childhood, old age and the end draw near.

What is to be done with this diminishing period that remains? One of my Christmas presents was a detective story by Anthony Barkley, *Trial and Error.* I have only skimmed enough to see the opening theme. A man is told by his doctor that he only has one or two months to live, he invites a number of friends to dinner and asks the question how a person could most profitably occupy himself in these circumstances. To his surprise, all those

---

1 Editor's Note: One of the more distinctive practices of Methodism instituted by John Wesley himself was the Watchnight Service on the last evening of the year. It was a form of a covenanting service, the Methodist equivalent to serious religious New Year's resolutions, but resolutions and carrying them out make persons answerable to God at final judgment, so the service involves hard questions being asked as the New Year dawns.

present (except one not very bright person) agree that the greatest benefit such a person could convey on society would be to remove some source of evil in society—in a word, to commit murder.

How would you answer? That is not a literary puzzle, it is the most important question any of us could face tonight. How best should we occupy our time and use our talents with the time remaining to us? The word *talents* of course brings me back to the text. The New Testament is always reminding us that we are people left on earth with a trust from the Lord, and we must ever be ready to make up our accounts with him. What sort of life does this mean?

It is our first task to make sure we are right with our Maker. The little symposium I spoke of had no difficulty in agreeing that what the dying man should do should be for the good of humankind. They never considered the man himself. In a way, that was right and healthy. There are few things worse than spiritual narcissism. It is far better to do good for others than to always be bothering about your own salvation. That sort of thing leads quickly enough to a mental asylum. It nearly led John Bunyan there for example. But a moment's thought suggests that no one is likely to put the world right who is wrong himself. As persons who sooner or later will stand before the judgment seat of God, our first business is to make our peace with Him.

I suggest that our first thought before we enter upon the activity of the New Year should be to examine our own relation with God. On his side, he has done everything to make it right. He came in Christ to reconcile us to himself, to give us peace. It remains for us to put our trust in Him, to accept his grace. It is as if you had quarreled with a friend, and found him after this service with his hand outstretched waiting for yours. Bunyan got it right in the end, he knew that Pilgrim had to find the Cross before he could begin his journey.

What we do with our time should be governed by the character of the judge we shall meet. You know me, says the master in the parable, you knew I was a hard, grasping man. Why didn't you act accordingly? Why didn't you at least put my money in the bank? We know the character of our Master, who has committed our talents to us. How would he use them? He may say one day—You know me, why didn't you act accordingly?

May I therefore suggest a second thought for the New Year? We should take more seriously the Christian obligation of measuring our life by Christ himself. It is so easy to let convention be the standard by which we judge ourselves. We do the usual thing, the ordinary thing, the thing everyone does. We do so for what on the surface is not a bad reason. In a sense, the people around us are our judges, the judges whose verdict we heed. What do they do? What do they say? Could we be a little less concerned with what they do and say, and more concerned with what Christ did and said, and what he will do and say? He is our judge, and in the long run it is what he says and does that matters.

If you knew you were not going to live through 1955; if like Mr. Todhunter in my story you knew that in two or three months your heart would go, all these questions would be far more pressing than they seem to be even in a Watchnight Service. When you see the steward coming with the plate you begin to feel in your pocket or your handbag. Some of us, I suspect, know what this means. "No life lives forever." "I see that all things come to an end." God uses time to bring pressure to bear on us. But that is not the whole truth, and it is well that others should remember the other side of it too.

God presses upon us through his Spirit, who works upon our consciences, who tells us of the things to come so urgently and so personally that the judgment is always upon us. That is why the Christian life is, in the strictest sense a responsible life, an answerable life. We are answerable to God. There will be a day when this life is over, when we cannot escape his questions, but he is asking them now. And God, is "answerable" to us all.

"Suffering and God"—Mark 2:1-5

[Preached once at Harrowgate 4/29/84]

What a disappointment! You will easily see what I mean. Suppose that, in the next few minutes, I collapsed here in the pulpit, suddenly struck down by some grim disease, surrounded as I am by the leading members of the nursing profession; and suppose further that you could find nothing better to do than say "Never mind old fellow, we forgive you." Well, my opinion of the Royal College would go down a number of points.

I am being serious, for this is a serious matter. It was serious from the beginning, for I suppose that paralysis, whatever be the case with the scientific description of it, is a serious illness. At all events, it was serious enough to send the stretcher bearers and their patient up to the roof, and to lead to the invention of the first hospital lift. So much anxiety, so much ingenuity, and we know what they were hoping for. They didn't get it, not at this stage anyway. The man thought he was being lowered into the surgical theater and he found himself in the hospital chapel!

When you are confronted with physical suffering, does it make sense to talk about God? About God, for the scribes are quick to see that when you are talking about sin and forgiveness, you are talking about God. Let me make clear what I am not talking about and what I am talking about. Many an expositor has taken this and other stories from the Gospels, and said, yes these miracles are credible, in fact they are not really miracles in the sense of something that constitutes an exception to the uniformity of nature. Disease can be caused by psychological conditions such as a sense of guilt, and the first step, perhaps the only necessary step, towards a cure is treatment of the psychological condition, a sorting out of the stops, checks, inhibitions that exist within the mind. Perhaps, they say, that Jesus perceived that this man's trouble was psychological, that he needed, more than anything else, healing of the mind; that given this, the rest would follow. I can only say, I do not know; it may be so, but the Gospel doesn't say so, and I don't know.

And I am not going to talk about the psychological treatment of psycho-somatic diseases, not because I think the subject unprofitable, or that I don't believe in the cooperation of the medical with the classical professions. It is the sort of thing that should be encouraged. I am not speaking on this theme for the excellent reason that I have no qualification for doing so. My theme, and Mark gives it to me at once is—Does it make sense to talk about God in the presence of suffering? Or is this the place where we must leave him out.

No one will understand my question better than you; many of you have had to face it. To the rest of us it may come less frequently, but come it does. Last Sunday I preached at Easter morning service. We sang the great triumphant Easter hymns, and I think had a good time. I found myself speaking on the church porch to a lady I knew. She had a hip replacement a few years ago and can barely walk, and must go to hospital to see about a second one. And now there seems to be thyroid trouble, and she must have a blood test to see what can be done about that. And in the background a second cataract operation is waiting to be done. She said to me in the Easter sunshine, "I'm afraid." Do you strike up the Easter hymns again? Can you go on talking about God's victory over suffering and death?

Does it make sense in the presence of the world's battles, its physical suffering and all its other agony, to talk about God? Can we do it? Is it not an insult to suffering humanity? Well it depends on what you mean by God. There are some kinds of gods that are out of place here. There is, for example, what I call the Father Christmas kind of god, the god whose whole business is to give us nice gifts and make us happy. Life is not like that, and God is not like that.

Here is the seed out of which this sermon began to germinate in my mind. Student nurses are pushed in at the deep end. They come, some of them at least, out of a Christian background, but you can hardly expect them to have more than an adolescent faith, idealistic and somewhat sentimental, confessing that God is love and religion is following Jesus, and pursuing a wonderful vocation. Then comes realism to drown out idealism. The sights and smells; the people who really are in pain. There is death, probably never glimpsed before. But now you see people die, you deal with the physical remains, you meet the relations, this dead man's widow, this dead child's parents. There is no need for me to go on in this vein. One of two things is bound to happen. You can't simply go on with the image of God as someone who likes being nice to nice people. That immature kind of faith must either go or be deepened. There is no third way.

Let us suppose it is going to be deepened. How? What is the alternative to an immature adolescent idea of God? A philosophical one? Is it tolerable in the context of suffering and death to talk about a philosophical God? There are two things to say here. One is intellectual. Suffering is the rock on which all kinds of philosophies have foundered. Suppose we set out to prove the existence of God by the argument from design, the famous old picture of the watch. This complicated piece of machinery with minute parts that actually work. Surely, the watch implies the watchmaker—God. Fine, if the universe ran like an accurate unfailing watch. For some of the time, for some of the people, it does and we shall have no problems about God. But this is just the time and here are just the people we are not talking about. What of all the things that contradict the idea of design? A human being in good working condition; perhaps we can believe God made him. But what of the paralyzed man for whom the body doesn't work any more? Can you say to him—"Look at yourself, your motionless limbs, you are incontinent again, your atrophied brain, and think how wonderful the God is who made you!" It doesn't work.

The second thing is personal. The widow, the parents of the dead child have no use for philosophical abstraction, even if it can be made to work and robbed of its logical contradictions. They want a person they can talk to, and some to talk to them. They want not the coolness of abstract thought but the warmth of personal affection, and assurance of a love that is wide enough and big enough to encompass both them and their dead. When the crunch comes, I do not want to be put off with either the children's image of the heavenly grandfather nor the philosophical concept of pure being. What then?

To answer, I go back to Mark and the story he has left us. "Son, your sins are forgiven" and the theologians are quick to pounce. They are good theologians and they are quite right. No one can forgive sins but God. True; for sins though we express them in the various wrongs we do to one another, are all of them sins against God. If you have injured someone, I do not know and cannot say that I forgive you. If you have injured God, then only God can forgive you.

Very well, Jesus replies, you think it is easy to talk about forgiveness because there is no way to see whether the sins really are forgiven or not. Let me show you something; "Get up you; pick up your mat and go home." What I am concerned about here is the logical connection. No one can forgive sins but God and Jesus forgives sins. I doubt whether Mark was a sufficiently sophisticated theologian to draw the explicit conclusion "then Jesus is God." But he means not less than this. The only God that matters, the God we can deal with in fair weather or foul, the God whom we share both joy and sorrow, both life and death is the God whom somehow or other we encounter in the person of Jesus of Nazareth. This is the God you can take with you into the world, into the theater, into intensive care, to the death bed.

For this God is one who understands what suffering and death means. He has passed through the whole process himself, seeing it from without, seeing it from within, both spectator and participant in the whole game. Agony of the body, dying, dried up in the withering heat; agony of the mind, deserted, lonely, unfriended, uncomforted. There is nothing he doesn't know about our human condition. I can think of some environments in which I believe Jesus would have felt uncomfortable and not at ease—some of our more elaborate and stately services at church, some of our more venomous debates, when self-seeking and self-importance prevails. But he would have been at home when you get back to the hospitals, back to the people like the paralytic, the leper, the blind man, Jairus and his dead little 12-year-old girl. There is someone who will know what to do.

He will know (here is a second reason), for he, the God we see in Jesus, is love. His love is not a soft thing, it did not spare hatred or lust or hypocrisy. It is not acquisitive love, it is giving love, in the end self-giving love, and such love is better than philosophical explanations. They are fine, when and if you can get them, but love is better because love is creative. A God who understands, a God whom you can bring into a context of suffering, distress, and despair. Indeed, you don't need to bring him, he will come of his own accord. But there is one thing more and it is there in large letters in Mark's story. Here is a God who offers forgiveness. Forgiveness is not the curing of the guilt complex, which may lead to the curing of a physical condition. Forgiveness puts right the relationship between human beings and God and that, and that only, puts us in a position in which (and I don't say this lightly) it doesn't matter whether the issue is life or death. We can cope with both. "The sting of death," said Paul with acute insight, "is sin." He could have said with equal truth, the sting of life is sin. For sin is the breaking off of relations, with God and with our fellow human beings. When it is dealt with, real life begins. Does it make sense in the context of suffering to talk about God? If the God is the one we see in Jesus, nothing else does make sense.

"Follow Me"—Mark 2:14

[Preached eleven times from 1/4/42 at Toll End to 9/21/75 at Brandon]

I am not going to waste any time in introducing what I have to say in this sermon. I shall not give an account of the incident from which the words are taken in its setting in the life of Jesus. I shall not even make any attempt to show that Jesus, who once called people to follow him in Palestine, still calls us to himself today, though that is certainly not an obvious thing. I shall assume that, and simply try to find out what following Jesus today means. I shall do it by asking and trying to answer three questions: (1) Who is it that we are to follow? (2) Where will he lead us, by what way? (3) Why should we follow him?

Follow Whom?

That question is not by any means as easy and as superficial as it sounds. Whom are we to follow? Why Jesus; we know him well, we have heard about him since we were children—the founder of the Christian religion. But I can answer the question differently. An obscure Jew of peasant or artisan class, of little education who lived nearly two millennia ago. He was a member of a subject race generally, and not without some justice, despised for its lack of interest in and knowledge of the humane arts and the civilizing power of philosophy. In the course of time, he became one of a fairly numerous group of persons, the Galilean prophets or preachers. Like the others he gathered and taught a few disciples about him. After some time, he went up to Jerusalem and was crucified by the Roman authorities, but this, of course, was no uncommon occurrence, it was merely part of the revolutionary disorders which just under 40 years thereafter resulted in the great Jewish rebellion and war of 66-70. And now in the words of this hymn—"Who is this Jesus?" Why should we follow him?

First because he is one who has gone our way and knows our road. He did live in this world. He is not a philosopher who withdrew himself from human affairs or an ascetic who knew nothing of life's joys and their attendant problems. Still less was he an angel or a spirit entirely foreign to our world or just a myth—someone who never lived at all. In one of his books Turgenev, the Russian novelist, tells of a vision that he had. He was in one of those low-roofed country churches in Russia. He could see it all. The little dabs of red that were the candles in front of the holy pictures, the dim light, the mysterious priests, and a big crowd of worshippers in front of him, ordinary peasant folk they were, their fair-haired heads looking like a field of corn. As he stood there he became conscious that another man had moved up from behind, and stood beside him, and inwardly, without looking he knew that this man was Christ. He felt the desire to turn and see him, but he dared not. He overcame his fear and looked. Immediately there swept over him a surge of disappointment—this could not be the Christ! So ordinary a man! And then he knew better. That was just what Christ was, an ordinary man, in some ways at least belonging more truly to that peasant congregation than to the priests who were leading their worship.

He is one of us, one of us in the sense that a great leader is one with his people. He does not share our weakness, but our strength, and for that very reason he is more truly ours—he is what we ought to be. This is the one who calls us to follow him, the one in whom men and women of old recognized their master, one of themselves, yet always above them, always to be followed and obeyed.

And second, because though he was like us, one of us, he was more than we are. He has gone our way, that is true, but it is not the whole truth. He is one who has come from somewhere else to fetch us. He belongs to this world and somewhere else too. He is no mere human leader, no colossus of a man who stands head and shoulders above his fellows. For though there were those who recognized his imperial splendor and the undeniable imperative of his call, those very men, at the hour of his need, left him friendless and alone to go to his end, to defeat, to dust and dishonor.

Why then was that not the end? We shall not go into a difficult piece of history. Let it be enough to say that if he had been merely a human being, though a great one, his death would have been the end. Julius Caesar was a great soldier, but people did not follow his corpse nor even his ghost into battle. His death was the end. But the death of Jesus was the beginning, and his followers fought for him ever since. Jesus was like us, and he was infinitely more. He sprang from our midst, yet he came from without. You could put this more precisely, but let this suffice. This is he who calls us to follow.

Follow Where?

That was a very significant question to people like Peter and Andrew, fishermen; to Levi the customs officer. They were engaged in ordinary decent jobs, perhaps not very lucrative but fairly comfortable and secure. Peter at least was married and had a home of his own. Then appears the new teacher and says "leave it all, do the rash thing, the thing people will call stupid—follow me." To say where, was indeed a fair question. What right had Jesus to break up the plans and schemes of a life time? What had he got to offer in exchange for the things they would have to leave behind?

They do not understand at first. It was enough for them to follow him. They did not really understand at all until after he had died, and he had repeated his call from the other side of death. He had told them before hand, but they had not taken it in. He had told them where the way he was treading would lead him. Again and again he said it—"the Son of Man must suffer many things." Perhaps even less had they understood what he meant when he said "if anyone would come after me, let him deny himself, and take up his cross and follow me." That was not easy to comprehend, for a cross was a real thing. It didn't mean in those days a vicious attack or a difficult mother in law, it meant something you got crucified on.

But that was not the only thing Jesus offered them, though he was careful to put it in the foreground. They continued with him in his tribulations and they were afterwards to share in his glory. "There is no one," he said, "who has left home, or brothers or sisters or mothers or fathers or children or lands for my sake, and for the Gospel's sake, but he shall receive a hundredfold now in this time, homes and brothers and sisters and mothers and children and lands with persecutions; and in the world to come, everlasting life." That was his offer to them, a way that began with leaving things and people behind, which led through persecutions, and at the same time brought with it the recompense of a new family, the family of God; and after all everlasting life.

Now what about us who are not going to follow an earthly Christ? Who will not leave our homes, who, maybe will not be persecuted? If you can just change the background from a Palestinian mountain path to an English road, the same conditions hold good. This is how perhaps the greatest book on Jesus that has been written in this century finishes "He comes to us as one unknown, without a name, as of old, by the lake-side. He came to those men who knew him not. He speaks to us the same word—'Follow me!' and he sets us to the tasks which he has to fulfill for our time. He commands, and to those who obey him, whether they be wise or simple, he will reveal himself in the toils, the conflicts, the sufferings, they shall pass through in his fellowship and, as an ineffable mystery, they shall learn in their own experience who He is."

Do you know who wrote that? Albert Schweitzer, the man who had Europe at his feet. Still at this moment one of the greatest theologians and philosophers in the world; one of the greatest and most famous of organists; who gave up all prospects of European fame, or rather the fame itself, for at the age of 30 he had fame, to go to a miserable African village in a wretched climate and heal the bodies of filthy Africans.

That seems to me to indicate the very thing I mean. The cross taken up, and the consolations of Christ and his Church, for if you read Schweitzer's books you will not find a picture of a miserable man. You will find his sense of humor going strong and more than that a sense of complete rightness with life. So the way in which he leads us is not necessarily an easy one, it has the odor of the cross about it, but it also has the joy of the Lord in it too.

Follow—Why?

In the first place because of the things that have already been said. Because he is who he is. Because he is a person like ourselves who knows our life and how to live it. Yet more, because he is not like us, because he lived and spoke as no other person lived and spoke, because he came into our world from outside, because he came from God and went to God, came bringing God's love and God's power, into our dying world and has gone to prepare a place for us, to take us into the glory of God.

And we must follow because of the way that he offers us. You don't really want an easy life—do you? No affront, no hardship, no struggle, no blood sweat and tears? You don't want to go through the world so smoothly that you leave no mark on its surface, do you? A cutting tool, pressed into the stone may wear out quickly, but it is better to leave your mark and wear out than to be idle. "I want to live, live out, not wobble through this life somehow" (Studdert-Kennedy). And Christ offers a way of concentrated, dedicated, self-forgetting service.

Nor again do you want to live, do you, a solitary, glum life, left to yourself to stew in your own juice, to wallow in your own failure and despair? On the way of Jesus is travelling God's family, those who hear the Word of God and keep it. You can say a lot against the Church—I can, but I must say too that I have found in it the best people I know, the people in whose company I want to make life's journey.

Follow him then because of who he is, and the way he leads, and lastly this. The very fact of his presence in the world precipitates a crisis. He himself was always pointing that out in his parables which again and again lead up to the question—What are you going to do now? You couldn't miss the choice then. Either you were one of the followers of Jesus or you were not. Why should there be any difference now? No one will take any notice if you simply pass him by, but you can take your place on his side quite as definitely as Peter or Levi, when he said "follow me."

Of course, it won't mean leaving your home or being a martyr. It may perhaps mean nothing more exciting than doing your work rather better and more conscientiously than you did before, and confessing your faith. And you say, "that's only a matter of belief then. It doesn't matter what a man believes."[1]

Last winter my friend was in a blitz in London. He was in a shelter with a crowd of people, listening to the things that were coming down pretty close. A man in the shelter sitting near my friend began talking to say, among other things, that it didn't matter what a person believed. My friend almost lost his temper. "Doesn't matter?" he said, "Do you mean to say that it doesn't matter that those men up there in the airplanes have a certain faith? A crazy damnable faith it is, but it is a faith that makes them leave their homes and drop bombs on London."

Of course, it matters what a person believes. You can see it when you think of the difference it makes to a person's life whether he believes in Christ or Hitler. You don't believe in Hitler. It may be that you don't believe in anything very much, or in something fairly good—such as yourself. Why not believe in the best of all, and find out the way that faith leads?

1　Editor's Note: As the last paragraph of the sermon shows, he is being ironic here.

"Following Jesus in the Gospels"— Mark 2:17

[Preached four times from 12/23/84 at Houghton-le-Spring to 11/28/04 at Crook][1]

You have been pursuing an intensive course this Advent, as Sunday after Sunday you have considered what following Christ means in daily life, in prayer, and so forth. This is the very stuff of what being a Christian means. I wonder if you have noticed what a dangerous course it has been. I should not like you to misunderstand what I mean when I say that. I do not mean that those who have preached here the last three Sundays have led you along dangerous paths you ought not to go; that they have persuaded you to do things you ought not to do. I know them all too well to think that.

What I mean is this. We talk about following Christ and doing so in the only setting in which we can follow him—in our own lives, lived today in the modern world. But he is someone we cannot see with our eyes or hear with our ears; and it is very easy to create a Christ in our own image, a Christ who will be sure to lead us where we have already decided we want to go. In Shaw's *Saint Joan,* Joan says "I hear voices telling me what to do. They come from God." Robert replies "They come from your imaginations." And Joan answers, "Of course, that is how the messages of God come to us."

That is true, and it is the danger I am speaking of. How do I know that the Christ I am trying to follow in my daily life, the Christ to whom I say my prayers, the Christ I makes theologies about, is not just a figment of my imagination? Do not all of us imagine Christ for ourselves and make him who we want him to be? People have always been doing it. Look at all the pictures people have painted. One person paints a soft loving face bordering on the effeminate, another paints the frowning judge, evidently on the

---

1   Editor's Note: This sermon is a replacement for an earlier sermon on the same text.

point of condemning all of those of whom he does not approve. People in our day have made Christ a pacifist, others a violent revolutionary. I don't say that there is no truth in any of these pictures of Christ, there may in fact be a measure of truth in all of them. I am saying we need a check, an objective check, external to ourselves and our imaginations.

Hence to the text. When I have to prepare sermons for Advent and Christmas, I often turn to these texts, there are a number of them, in which Jesus says "I come" to do this or that. Thinking about them this year, I have noticed especially how many of them are in two parts, negative and positive; he says "I came not to do this but to do that" and this form of the saying, before we get to the content of the saying, is interesting and important and shows that back in the time of the Gospels, people were making up their own minds about Jesus and getting him wrong. Let us find time for a few examples.

They said, "Here is one who has the gift of getting on well with everyone; he will be able to find the right religious formulas on which we shall all be able to unite, there will be no more controversies between Pharisees and Sadducees; we shall bury the hatchet and all be good friends." And Jesus said "No! You have misunderstood. I did not come to bring peace but a sword. My work, my message will split society in two, not only society on the large scale but families, a family of five will be split three against two, father against son, mother against daughter. You will have to take sides. Not peace but a sword!"

They said, "this man does not care for God's Law; we have been brought up to keep the Sabbath, with the greatest strictness—no work is to be done. But he does not mind how many sick people he looks after and cures on the Sabbath. We have been taught to carefully distinguish between clean and unclean foods, beef we may eat, pork we may not and so on. But he says this doesn't matter, he says that it is not what goes into a person that defiles, but what comes out of his heart and mouth." The man defies God and his Word. And Jesus said, "No, you have misunderstood. I did not come to destroy the Law or the Prophets, but to fulfill them. I am bringing out the real meaning of the old commandments, showing you that violence of thought is just as wrong as violence of action, lustfulness of thought is as wrong as lustfulness of action."

What all this means is (though I may not be putting it well) you need tonight's sermon as well as the others. Following Christ in daily life, in prayer, in faith means following Christ in the Gospels because this is the one check we have, by means of which we can know we are following the real Christ and not an imaginary one. This is not a matter of listening to a Sunday evening sermon for a few minutes. It means living in the Gospels, and getting through them to know the living person they put forth. You cannot do this in a quarter of an hour. At the end of a lifetime you are more aware of how little you have achieved. I am not under the illusion that I can do it all for you in the last few minutes of this sermon. But let us go back to the text with which we started. I picked it out of all the various possibilities, not only because it tells us so much about Jesus, but also because it goes so well with Christmas. Perhaps in the end these two things are the same.

Again, it is "not this but that." People said, "here is a good moral teacher. We know what he will do, he will seek out all the best people, the most religious, the most intelligent, the most virtuous. You will have to pass a short test before you become one of his disciples. He will not mix with ordinary people like us. Only the best will do." And Jesus said "No! You have misunderstood. I have not come to invite righteous people, I come to invite sinners. Think of a doctor. He does not pick out all the hardiest specimens he can find, he looks for the sick. So with me." There is nothing, I think, that gets us more deeply into the story of Jesus than this, nothing that shows us more directly what following Jesus means. We can see these things in this saying.

First there is a stinging rebuke for the Pharisees. But I put it that way with some limitation, because the Pharisees were nothing like as bad as they are often painted. And we need to understand the term in the light of the tale of the Sunday school leader who told her class the parable of the Pharisee and the Publican and concluded it by saying, "And now children let us thank God we are not like the Pharisee." Or better perhaps we can recall the title of a volume of sermons by Edwyn Hoskins *We Are the Pharisees*. True, for it is spiritual pride that Jesus condemns, and it is to be found on both sides of most moral and ecclesiastical fences. There are the strict moral disciplinarians who look down on their more liberal-minded fellows who don't much mind what they do; or the free who look down on the fusty stick-in-the muds. There are those who love an elaborately order liturgy and those who practice a Quaker spontaneity in their worship, each one despising the other. There are those who at Christmas dismiss the shepherds and wise men as so much pious legend which we ought to have grown out of, and those who say "these people are destroying not only the romance but the fact of the Incarnation." I am not saying there are no rights and wrongs here, but there is nothing so wrong as the spiritual pride that is so sure it is right that it alone is the object of God's affection. "No," says Jesus, "I did not come for your benefit, if you are so sure you are right, you can look after yourself."

That leads to the second thing. There is something here for the sinner's comfort. At bottom, when we get past our spiritual pride and self-righteousness, we know that we all belong here. And he has not come to condemn, he has not come to pass by on the other side of the road with lofty superiority. This is the point we note the saying "I came to invite sinners." The saying is set in the context of a meal in which Jesus sits down to eat with some outcasts. "These," he says, "are the very people I have come to invite."

> Come, sinners, to the gospel feast;
> let every soul be Jesus' guest.
> Ye need not one be left behind,
> for God hath bid all humankind. (Charles Wesley)

He lived this out through the whole course of his life, and in the end, it led him to the Cross, but it is clearly to be seen in the first chapter of the story, the Christmas story. Born, not in a palace but in a stable, worshipped not by the great ones of the earth but by ordinary men doing an ordinary job. And if you say what about those kings, I say they are kings only in the later tradition they are not kings in the New Testament, and in any case the significant thing about them is that rich or poor, they were outsiders. They came from outside the closed religious circle of the people of God.

That leads to the third thing. In this verse, as in the story of Jesus taken as a whole, there is for the Church a commission. Perhaps it is at this point that we need to be sent back again and again to the Jesus of the Gospels. We all find it so easy to settle down in our church groups, where we get on well with one another, understand one another's language, and try hard not to hurt one another's feelings. We don't want this harmony destroyed by the profane secular world outside. This is why we want a Christ for ourselves, a Christ who will be flattered and gratified by our piety, who will join us in condemning the wickedness of the world outside, and at the same time turn a blind eye to the sins of spiritual pride, vainglory, and the bypassing that we practice.

The Christ of the Gospels will give us no peace as we settle down in these comfortable, well-padded seats. "Lord, Lord" we say, "did we not prophesy in thy name and by thy name cast out devils and do many righteous works?" And he will say "I never knew you." Those are his words, I think he could add "And you never knew me, you never took the trouble to see me, you never took the trouble to understand my love for the outcast, the sinners. So, you can go, you are no people of mine."

We come here to this Church service to learn the truth, the Gospel truth about Jesus of Nazareth, and this you must do because it is where everything begins. But it is not where it ends. From this point, you can go out to follow Christ in daily life, in your prayers, in your thinking about faith. But we have not begun to understand the Jesus of the Gospels, the only Jesus there really is, if we have not learned to find and serve him as we care for the needy, and take the Good News to the poor.

"The Seed Growing Secretly"— Mark 4:26-29

[Preached twenty-five times from 7/16/44 at Bondgate, Darlington, to 9/28/03 at Lanchester]

A large number of the parables in the Gospel have a rural background. There is seedtime and harvest and vineyard and vintage, trees and fishing. In particular, there are several which conclude in different ways, involving the simple fact of sowing seed and reaping a harvest. There is the parable of the sower which brings to light the different yields of different kinds of soil, some 30, some 60, some 100-fold. There is the parable of the wheat and tares which shows that the field which is white unto harvest is not pure grain; there are weeds in it. There is the parable of the mustard seed, which stresses the contrast between the tiny seed, and the huge shrub which comes from it.

Today's parable is the simplest of them all. It states simply that a man sows a seed and the stuff comes up. The man does nothing; he sleeps at night and gets up in the daytime and the crop comes. He does nothing to make it come. It simply appears. I have unfortunately no time to indicate the Old Testament background which lies behind this apparently artless selection of material. It all points to the fact that the Kingdom of God is (to use Otto's phrase) "God's seed not humanity's deed." The man in our parable is asleep. He doesn't know how the seed grows. The sprouting of the new plant is a miracle, a sheer miracle. Our ideas of growth have changed recently and that is why this parable is sometimes misunderstood. You good gardeners think of growth as a natural and inevitable process. You need to be a bad gardener like me to understand this parable. If I put a seed in the ground and it comes up, it's a miracle, a joyful surprise. And that is what is in mind here.

The Kingdom of God is the miraculous working of God's power. It means God exercising kingly power. It is that notion I want to expound. First—

The Kingdom of God Is Power

So it manifestly is in the seed parables. It is the uprush of life which forces the oak tree out of the acorn. So it is in the related parable of the yeast and dough, and in many another place in the Gospels. So it is in more straight-forward sayings such as for example this: "If I by the finger of God cast out demons, then the Kingdom of God has come upon you." The divine power which drives out the forces of evil, is the indicator that the Kingdom thunders at the world's gate. So Paul sets the Kingdom of Christ over against the power of darkness, and says that it means righteousness, peace and joy in the Holy Spirit.

The Kingdom of God is power, simply because it means God exercising power. It is not a domain, an area governed, but the Rule, the Reign. It signifies God in his activity as King. When the Old Testament was translated into the language Jesus spoke, such a phrase as "the Lord is king forever" was translated as "the Kingdom of the Lord endures forever." The Kingdom of God means God as King, hence it connotes unbreakable power.

The Bible is always talking about the power of God in many different ways. It speaks of God's power in nature. The old Hebrew saw God's work in the storm that swept in a mighty wind over the eastern desert and burst upon Palestine with unquestionable fury. God thundered with his voice. God made the cedars of Lebanon to skip like calves with his voice. He could send a storm of hail to beat down his enemies. The lightning and the thunderbolt were at his command. Naïve and primitive is this? Perhaps, but not more so than those people who talk about the miracle of Dunkirk.

But the Bible speaks especially of the power of God in the lives of human beings. Hear for example this—"Truly I am full of power from the spirit of the Lord, of judgment and of might to declare unto Jacob his transgression and unto Israel its sin." Don't just pass over that as a Biblical quotation, a cliché. Think what it meant to Micah the prophet. He stood alone in the midst of a people who were sinning. The easy and obvious thing was to do what everyone else was doing. The next thing was to stand out in silent protest, to refrain from joining in. Micah did neither. He stood out and he spoke out when other prophets of his day, false prophets, would say whatever they were paid to say. Not so Micah. He would stand up to the world and denounce crime and oppression and national apostasy. How did he find the strength to do it? "I am full of power by the spirit of God." God's power was his, and by that power alone he lived.

It is not hard to find a similar instance in the New Testament—in St. Paul. His was a different lot. He was summoned to a job of almost incredible difficulty, a life of pain, anguish and loneliness. How did he endure it? You remember the words of Christ to him, "My grace is sufficient for you, my power is made perfect in your weakness." I should have no great difficulty in citing such instances of God's power from every Christian generation since the days of the New Testament. Of course, I must be content to pick out one or two. I will give you one off the beaten track and one on it.

We often think of Anselm, Archbishop of Canterbury, simply as a theologian, or as the stiff-necked ecclesiastic who stood up to the English king. Hear this story. On one of his journeys to Rome, the Duke of Burgundy, tempted by the rich prey offered in the form of an Archbishop of Canterbury, tried to carry him off. Galloping up to the pilgrims, "Which of you," he asked "is the Archbishop of Canterbury?" Anselm quietly stepped out from his retinue and gave him the kiss of peace. "I have seen the face of an angel" said the robber, as he slunk off with his troops. There again is divine power for the rebuking of transgression and sin.

And now the illustration on the beaten track which you expect me to use.

Our conquering Lord Hath prospered his word,
Hath made it prevail,
And mightily shaken the kingdom of hell.
His arm he hath bared,
And a people prepared His glory to show,
And witness the power of his passion below. (Charles Wesley)

You know who wrote that, Charles Wesley. As you know, I think, how true were the words he used. There has rarely been a mightier and more manifest outpouring of the power of God than the Evangelical revival of two hundred years ago. No wonder John Wesley stepped back with awed astonishment to say "What hath God wrought!" I opened my copy of his Journal at random and the first page I opened will do. "So general an outpouring of God's Spirit we have seldom known as we had at Epworth in the afternoon, 'like mighty winds or torrents fierce, it did oppressors all o'er run.'" And on the same page a passage I cannot forbear to quote especially in view of the Commando Campaign, and my own hopes for this Church. Wesley is speaking of some other men and implies by contrast what the Methodists had done. "They have neither sense, courage nor grace to go and beat up the Devil's quarters in any place where Christ has not been named. That is the way to see the power of God. The two famous sentences of William Carey belong together, 'expect great things from God, attempt great things for God.'" If you and I attempt nothing more than the tame and the feeble, if we pitch our standard low, if we have no higher aim than to be an entertainment center, then we need not be surprised if we do not see the power of God. Go and beat up the Devil's quarters and we shall find that the Gospel is the power of God unto salvation. I have stressed this point, that the Kingdom of God signifies his power, at length, but there are two shorter points to be added.

The Kingdom of God Is Hidden Power

The life is in the seed but it is small. It is pressed down and hidden in the ground. The power of the Kingdom is not immediately manifest. This is not merely parabolic, but historically true. Jesus went to his death. That grain of wheat was hidden in the earth and died. There was no noise of trumpets or thundering from heaven. He died in agony, alone. There was no universal proof of his resurrection, only his friends saw him.[1]

You will recollect the words of 2 Corinthians which I quoted just now. The word of the Lord to St. Paul "my strength is made perfect in weakness." Paul did not travel the Empire dazzling the minds of people by strange and staggering deeds.[2] He was a little mission preacher whose followers were neither wise, nor mighty, nor noble who changed the course of European history. The Church has often worked in obscurity and with lack of success.

On the same page of the Journal which I quoted just now, John Wesley went into Crowle Church looking for a tomb. He found it. "Here lieth the body of Mr. Solomon Ashbourn. He died in 1711 and solemnly bequeathed the following verses to his parishoners: 'Ye stiff-necked and uncircumcised

---

1 Editor's note: This is not quite true. Saul of Tarsus was no friend of Jesus, and there was at least one other non-disciple who saw Jesus after he rose, his own brother James, of whom it is said in John 7:5 that he did not believe in Jesus (nor did the other brothers). The proof of this fact is shown by the fact that none of Jesus' brothers fulfilled the prime Jewish filial duty of seeing a deceased brother got a decent burial. They were missing in action.

2 Editor's Note: But see Rom. 15:18-19. Nevertheless, signs and wonders does not seem to have been Paul's main way of doing ministry.

in heart and ear, ye do always resist the Holy Spirit. As your fathers did, so do ye.' 'I have labored in vain. I have spent my strength for naught and in vain. Yet surely my judgment is with the Lord, and my work with my God.'" God's power is often hidden power. Not every district today is a Mass Movement Area. We work and work, and nothing happens. The war goes on with all its train of suffering and loss. We ask why God does not do something great and striking to draw all people's wonder and obedience. Why does he not?

That is too big a question to answer in a minute or two, but I think it is in order that God's salvation may be of faith, that we may not be compelled to Him by the force of evidence but may trust him. 'Though he slay me, yet will I trust him. In hope against all human hope . . . desperate I believe.' In this way, we are led to put our trust only in God's mercy, and rest upon the God we have not seen. One thing more.

The Veiled Presence of the Kingdom Demands a Decision

A decision of faith. God will not hustle you into the Kingdom. God will not force his power upon you. In his mercy, he opens your eyes that you may see the truth of the seed, that you may trust in his harvest. The question is whether you will receive the Kingdom of his, whether you will let him rule you. The old Jews had a striking phrase in which they said that Abraham made God King. Of course, God was always King. But when a man was found who would obey the royal command, who would dare all in the King's service, then the King of heaven had become a King on earth as well. In that sense, some of you too can make God a King. Not that his sovereign power depends on you and me; thank God it does not. But you can accept his sovereignty. "Crown him with many crowns!"

"Faith"—Mark 5:25-34

[Preached twenty-eight times from 11/9/58 at Elvet to 11/21/04 at Spennymoor]

In a sermon preached just 433 years ago in 1525, Luther said that you can see depicted in this woman what the Gospel is. He was right. In particular, you can see what faith is, and that is what we must try to see this evening. I can't see any need in using words and minutes in introducing a story that is so well-known. We can jump straight into it. If this woman is a picture of faith, what is the outline of this picture? The first thing to say about her is that she was—

In No Doubt of Her Need

She had been ill for twelve years. That is long enough for anyone to recognize that he or she is dealing with no passing disorder. After so long you have stopped saying "Well it will probably be alright tomorrow." You know it won't. It wasn't that she hadn't tried. "She had suffered many things of many physicians and had spent all that she had (before the health service that is), and was nothing bettered, but rather was worse." No human advice helped; rather it hindered. If you look at Luke's account of this story you will find that he has left out the statement that all her expenditure on the medical professionals had made the poor woman worse. Some people say that was because Luke was a doctor himself. And indeed, the medical profession does not come out of the story very creditably. They only succeeded in demonstrating to the woman that her case is completely hopeless. That is why she turns to Jesus.

That is where faith, real faith, begins. It cannot begin earlier. Religion can; we can be interested in religion, amateurs of theology, friends of the Church, certainly we can be deeply moral and highly respectable people

78

without any sense of our absolute need. But these things are not faith, and we do not have faith in God until we have scraped the bottom of the barrel of human resources and know that there is no more to be had from that quarter. I believe that it is true in our day that there is a real danger in the development of sedative and narcotic drugs; there is the possibility of merely cloaking disease by treatment of its symptoms. But everybody knows that you don't get rid of toothache simply by taking aspirin.

This is certainly true of our age in matters other than physical disease. We have learned how to condition ourselves so that the real ultimate need in which we live is concealed. We have, even the poorest of us, so many comforts and pleasures, that we are well cushioned from the sharp, raw edges of life. That is why this is in no sense an age of faith, why it is easy for the most earnest and sincere Christian to grow feeble and lethargic in his faith. Why should we bother?

But it would be a great mistake to suppose that because we do not so often or so easily feel it, that the need does not exist, or that it can easily be met with the help of spirits and drugs and television. I have only once been down a mine, and one of my most vivid recollections is of a miner squatting on the ground eating his lunch out of a tin. The official who was conducting us around told him to move, and not unnaturally the man was angry. Why shouldn't he sit there and eat in peace? Without a word the official pointed upward to a wooden prop in the roof. It was cracked right through and there was reason enough for us all to move.

Well we sit under a cracked roof, eating our comfortable meals, but the roof is cracked whether we know it or not. We are not secure. I am not thinking of the fact, though it is a fact, that the material universe itself is insecure, that if the wicked, or even the merely stupid had their way, the great globe and all that is in it might "dissolve." I suspect we make too much of that. I am thinking of the structure and the destiny of our lives, which we have from God, and therefore cannot come apart from him. There is a sickness in every human life, an unhealthiness, which we cannot cure by our own efforts.

What we need is the forgiveness of our sins, for what is wrong with life is that it is separated from God, and it is sin that does the separating. And there is no human source of forgiveness for the sin that stands between us and God, for in the nature of things only God can forgive our sins against him. From others, we can get wisdom, learning, inspiration and good examples but we cannot get the one thing that we need. She [the woman who had been ill for twelve years] knew her need then, and she made—

Contact with Jesus

It was not a very formal, respectable, orthodox kind of contact. It would have been more usual to listen in the crowd to his preaching, or to seek a private interview. Instead, she sneaked up in the crowd, and put out her hand to touch his clothes. One has read, not without distaste, of the same sort of treatment of film stars. Not respectable or orthodox, but it was contact. And that is faith. Conscious of its need, it gets, somehow, anyhow, to Jesus. There is no other way. When I watched the other day the televising of the coronation of Pope John XXIII I heard with interest that the plenary indulgence he had issued would apply not only to the throng in St. Peter's Square in Rome, but to all those who looked and listened to the broadcast, in fact to me. But the true way is both easier and harder than that—you only put out your hand to Jesus.

Of course, I should like you all to do that in a decent, orthodox, regular way. I should like everyone to attend Sunday School and Church from childhood, to go to the preparation class for Church membership, to learn there about Christ, to enter into his Church and to have communion with him in Word and Sacrament. I should like you all to hold the faith of the Nicene Creed. But let me say quite plainly that that is often the end of faith, not its beginning. And for a beginning, the best kind of contact you can manage will do. You may start with complete ignorance to orthodox formulas, ecclesiastical ceremonies, Church fellowship. All right, so long as you start. It wasn't long before Jesus had brought this woman into conversation. That is what he does, and once that starts, he can be trusted to look after himself.

The trouble with many of us is that we simply cannot believe that it is as easy as that; we think we must go all around the world first. We must solve all the problems of philosophy and theology; we must achieve a really satisfactory moral life; we must conform with all the practices of religion; we must work ourselves up to having the right kind of feelings and experience. God's way is too easy for us—as it was for Naaman. "If the prophet had asked you to do some great thing, would you not have done it? How much more when he says 'Wash and be healed?'"

Of course, there is theology and there is morality in Christianity. But to try to begin with them is bad for theology, bad for morality, and bad for you. You begin by trusting Jesus to do the job you cannot do for yourself, to meet the need you cannot meet for yourself. That is the very essence of faith. But we have not done yet. The next thing we have to say about our woman is that—

She Confessed Her Faith

Jesus was well aware of what had happened. The woman could not stay concealed. She came through to the front of the crowd and acknowledged what she had done. Here is another element of faith. It begins inwardly with the secret soliloquy "If I can just touch his clothes, I shall be alright." But the inward connection leads to action, and the action leads to confession. Faith and confession always belong together. They stand together in one of the earliest descriptions of Christian faith—"if you confess with your mouth Jesus is Lord, and believe in your heart that God raised him from the dead, you shall be saved." It was a perfectly clear matter in the earliest days of the Church. To become a Christian did indeed mean, as it always does, an inward, personal, essentially private turning to Christ, a matter that was between a person and their God alone. But it also meant a life marked out from the rest of the world by no outward sign but simply by an acted and vocal acknowledgement of Jesus as Lord.

I am inclined to believe that it is when circumstances have led to clear confession of faith that the Church, and Christians have been strongest and healthiest. Times arise when the Church over against the world has to make a confession of its faith; times like the Reformation, times like the '30s in Nazi Germany, when the Confessing Church took its name from the duty it performed. And similar occasions arise in our private lives, when the only honest and the only safe course is the way of clear and open confession of faith. If faith is real there will be no question about it. If we are aware of a need that can be satisfied nowhere else and fling ourselves upon Christ, trusting him only, how can we keep the fact a secret?

But we do, and the fact we do is bound to throw doubt upon the reality of our faith. Hardly anything could make so much difference to the religious situation in this country as a decision on the part of every Christian to take his faith seriously, without any attempt at self-assertion, and make quite clear to all his associates where he is and where he serves. Nothing makes me so ashamed of my own cowardice as the thought of what some of our fellow Christians have gone through. Think, for example, that some of you, if you had lived in East Germany would never have reached a University, would never have taken an advanced level certificate unless you had prepared to renew your Church membership. And from the thought of what the faith costs some of our brothers and sisters, it is only a step to think what it cost Christ to be the object of our faith. Remembering all this shall we hesitate to confess our faith before others? There is one further point to learn from this woman, that—

Faith Works

I use these words reluctantly because I do not want to give the impression that faith is a sort of patent medicine and can be recommended like a patent medicine. It is not so. Yet this is also true; the woman was cured and she knew that she was cured. She felt in her body that she was cured of her plague. And Jesus himself summed it up in his words "your faith has put you right, go in peace." The root of the matter is that faith and faith alone puts us into a right relation with God, and out of that relation all other good things flow. I believe that sometimes, not always, not often, one of those good things is physical health, but the root of the matter is what Jesus calls peace, the perfect relationship with God in which for example it becomes a matter of indifference whether you are sick or well, in the sense that you know, like the woman, you know in yourself, whether in sickness or in health, in life or in death, you are in God's hands, and completely and absolutely safe. Faith doesn't necessarily make a sick man perfectly well. It doesn't even make you perfectly good, but it does give the release, the freedom that comes from knowing that nothing stands between you and God, and that there is nothing in heaven or on earth or in hell that you need fear anymore.

There is the story and there is the picture of faith. How does it conform to what passes for faith in so many of us? We are not conscious of our need; consequently, we do not reach out at all costs to Christ crucified; we trust too much in ourselves for that. Again, it follows that we do not confess our faith. There is so much of ourselves in it that we inevitably become far too self-conscious to speak of it; self-conscious when we ought to be Christ-conscious, and of course it follows too that our faith doesn't work—how should it? Of course, I am caricaturing—it is not as bad as that. But here and now you should examine your faith, and if as you look you become much more conscious of need than of peace, stretch out your hand to Jesus.

"One Thing You Lack"—Mark 10:21

[Preached twenty times from 9/10/44 at Bondgate, Darlington, to 6/3/73 at Skinningrove]

One thing you lack—only one? Then surely it cannot matter very much; one thing cannot make so much difference. If a person is alright but for one thing, there can be nothing much for him to worry about. While I was away in August I was reading a piece of Greek. I came across a word I didn't know. I don't think I was much to blame, it was a queer word. But on holiday, one cannot carry many books about and I had no dictionary. So the word remained unknown and I couldn't translate the sentence. Only one word, but the sentence remained nonsense without it.

About a dozen years ago, before I began to try to be a theologian, I was taking an examination in London in chemistry, among other subjects. It was a practical examination. Some of you know better than I do now that in inorganic analysis, certain kinds of group tests have to be carried out in a definite logical sequence. In this examination, it became obvious that something had gone wrong, and I began to feel hot and cold. I went back over all I had done, and then I got it. I had missed out one reagent early in the process, and it had upset the whole experiment. Only one thing—but I nearly failed the examination because of it.

That is all interesting enough but we are going to dig a bit deeper. Think about the great classical tragedies. True tragedy is not the story of a bad person; it is the story of a good person who does the wrong thing. Everyone knows the story of Macbeth. Macbeth was not a bad man. He was a great and splendid soldier, of lofty courage and unshakeable resolve. He knew the finer feelings of life, a warm generosity and a steady loyalty—a great man. What happened then? There was one weakness—vaulting ambition! Only one thing, but it was the root of the tragedy. Macbeth one thing you lack!

There is, it is a platitude to say it, no finer more sensitive character in all literature than Hamlet. Statesman, scholar, soldier, poet, man of piercing insight and great vision. Where does the tragedy come in? There is a flaw, that fatal indecision that ruins everything. Only one thing, but it was the root of the tragedy. Hamlet, one thing you lack!

Or if you want to be up-to-date, turn to the books of the psychologists where you will find there clever men giving one another PhDs for writing down what Shakespeare knew quite cold, except that fortunately for us, he didn't know the jargon. You will read case after case where one, often quite small, fault disorganizes a person's whole mental makeup and ruins his life. One thing you lack! Only one and yet perhaps it will be worthwhile to hear what even Jesus has to say on the matter. When we turn to the story in which our text appears we cannot fail to be struck, first of all, by—

The Problem of Good People

Don't misunderstand that; I'm not saying in the ordinary sense that good people are a problem, though that is true enough. If you doubt it, try being a minister for a time and have a lot of good people to deal with. But I mean something much more serious than that. I mean that good people are very often a problem to the themselves and a problem to the Church. I imagine that this rich man was a problem to himself. He knew his own achievements. He was prepared to tell Jesus, and there is not the slightest need to doubt his sincerity, that he had kept all the commandments since his youth. And yet he knew too that he lacked something. He wanted what he called eternal life. Never mind about a precise definition of that, I think we know fairly well what he meant. He had money, he had moral integrity, and he was not content. He is like Galsworthy's character of whom it was said "He doesn't know what he wants, but he won't be happy until he gets it."

I know people like that; people who have every reason to be satisfied with life and who aren't. I well remember how in one mission I shared in, a man came to me who said that frankly he was in the position of that man in the Gospel story (I don't mean that he actually made the comparison). He was well off, had made a success of everything he had tried, but he had never made a success of Christianity. He had seen in other people something that he did not possess. In effect, he was asking, "What must I do to inherit eternal life?" And it was not easy to answer him.

Good people of that sort are a problem to the Church. How are you to treat the people who are so near, and yet so far away? Suppose this man, prosperous and well mannered, came into one of our Churches. What should we do with him? He tells, with obvious truth, that he has kept the commandments, he has never murdered, committed adultery, stolen, borne false witness, defrauded; he has always honored his parents and done his duty by them. What should we say to him? I will tell you. We should say "My dear fellow, you must be a member here, and in due course you must come to the leader's meeting and the quarterly meeting, or you must go into the ministry." Don't think I'm exaggerating how often this happens or that I am speaking with the bitterness and stupidity of a young and ignorant person. I know something about this.

An older minister recently told of something that happened last year. At a service he conducted, a large number of young people came to the Communion rail to make a decision for Christ. After the service, he remained after most had gone home, and he was surprised to see a steward left alone with him get up and lock the vestry door. He said "I've been a Methodist 20–30 years. I am steeped in the church and circuit work up to the eyebrows. But no one has ever given me what these young people found this morning. Will you tell me what it is?"

I know it at clearer range than that. When I was a candidate for the ministry, I was a good young man. You who know me now may find it hard to believe but I was—too good. But I didn't know what being a Christian meant. As far as I can tell, I might still be in that state, if it had not been for a queer little group of people, two lecturers in the University of Cambridge and a professor (whom I have never seen) at Basel University. I don't say these things to pour scorn on our Methodist Church or its ministry. God forbid. I do say this to draw attention to the large number of people who are thoroughly good who keep all the commandments but lack one thing. What is it?

What Is the One Thing?

If you come down to details, the "one thing" is different for different people. But the general question, I hope, is clear enough. What is it that distinguishes real Christian faith from moral and ethical achievement? What more is required from, and what more is afforded to the person who has kept all the commandments? Let us be quite clear on a few negative points to begin with. What is wanted is not a stronger intellectual grasp of the situation. You know me and my history well enough to know that I am not likely to belittle that. I should like to see all Christians far better instructed than they are. But that is not the thing that is lacking. You must have notice how very unevenly brain power is distributed in the Church—Paul and Peter, Wesley, and Bunyan. Nor is it anything like a more elaborate ritual that is required nor even a stronger moral effort. What then?

For the answer, we must turn to our text, to see what Jesus had to tell the young man who wanted eternal life. His reply is of course addressed to a particular situation. "Go sell whatever you have and give to the poor; and come and follow me." I am quite sure that that is not a universal command, obligatory on all Christians, a command of absolute poverty. To take it in that way is to misunderstand both the meaning of the Gospel and the purpose of the Scriptures. It is not unlike the schoolboy whom the teacher asked for a text, and who answered "And Judas went out and hanged himself." "Good," said the teacher, "Now give me another." He replied "Go thou and do likewise." The command of Jesus is not in detail applicable to everyone, though I am sure of this, many people would find it easier to understand the Gospel if they were less comfortable than they are. The Gospel always presupposes the fact of human insecurity which it is easier to lose sight of when humanly speaking you are not quite secure. However, the command of Jesus is but an individual working out of a general principle. But what is this principle? We are sometimes so busy explaining away the literal sense of the command that we forget that there is a principle there at all. And the principle is a far more revolutionary thing than any amount of selling and giving would be. There is something more potent here than the Communist revolution or the Fascist one.

It meant for the questioner that he had to turn his back on the dearest thing in life and go with Jesus, in trust and obedience. It means that all the good things in life are not good enough without an act or attitude of complete surrender to God in Christ. Money is not enough; we are not surprised at that. We know that the Kingdom of God is not for sale. And we know that there is a limit to the satisfaction that worldly comfort can bring. Goodness is not enough. That is what we do not find it so easy to believe.

John Wesley did not find it easy to believe that. What was wrong with him? The good and industrious little boy with the redoubtable mother, the scholar of Charterhouse, the fellow of Lincoln college at Oxford. Surely there was nothing wrong with him? But he would do more than that. He too became a minister. He went overseas as a missionary. And then, after that, when he was 35 years old, he began really to know what it meant to follow Jesus.

The vital thing, the only vital thing is what John Wesley discovered it to be—a personal encounter in faith between God and a human being. All this lives not in some abstract world of speculation, but in things as concrete as selling your goods and giving away your money.

Round about 15 years ago there was a committee in Cambridge. There is nothing strange or new about that. I should not like to say how many committees I have been on in Cambridge, or how little they have done. This one consisted almost entirely of undergraduates—ordinary, healthy, sane, and not unintelligent young people. It had been constituted in view of approaching Methodist Union. It was to consider schemes for Methodist advance among young people. They were, they thought, well qualified to do it; they were not rich but they were good and they were clever and obviously, they were fitted to take the lead in the young Methodism of these days. They were planning how retreats should be conducted, and they had a memorandum by Dr. Platt to consider. On the first page came the inquiry—"Is the full rich evangelical experience God's purpose for everyone?" They knew the answer had to be yes, but it was an awkward answer, and the committee had to become a class meeting. With that week's meeting ahead, I want us to consider that question. And—is it God or is it me that stands between ourselves and the realization of God's purpose?

"Love Thy Neighbor"—Mark 2:31; Romans 13:9[1]

Before I come back to these words which are more important than anything else I shall say, let me say that the two of us who are sharing this service are very grateful for the privilege of doing so. We both feel this; the part of the service that falls to us gives me the opportunity not only to be the first to wish you well, but of saying what we feel. You will agree with me that one of the great things about Durham is that we do not divide up into us and them. Some of us can hardly help being a bit older than others, but this only means that we are like a family. And to this fact you have given the nicest and kindest possible expression. Now that I have mentioned Durham, I hope you will not think that I am simply taking up my lectures (as far as you two are concerned) where I laid them down in March of last year, though in truth what I am about to say is as much the theology and ethics of the New Testament as anything could be. "Thou shalt love thy neighbor as thyself." The words rise like a spring in the Old Testament and flow on into the New, and we have the highest authority for regarding them as (with the first commandment of love) the core of our faith. That they are of universal application in no way diminishes their particular application to you.

"Thou shalt love thy neighbor," you both know what neighbor means רֵעַ, πλησίον, "proximus" literally the one near or next to you, your companion, the one who stands beside you in the curious jigsaw or kaleidoscope of life. From this day onwards, each of you is that to the other. This is no new discovery, Luther said it, but I do not suppose he was the first to do so: "The Christian is bound to love his neighbor as himself. His wife is his nearest neighbor. Therefore, she should be his dearest friend." And I have no doubt

---

1   Editor's Note: This is one of the rare sermons or homilies that has no listing of where and when it was delivered. Obviously, it is a wedding homily delivered sometime in the 70s or perhaps early 80s since he seems to mention retiring from lecturing.

he would have been willing to put the sentences into reverse. It is easy to romanticize this and on at least this one day in your lives I am not going to say it is wrong to do so. But it is not itself romanticism. Marriage is a very serious school indeed for learning, and working out, and practicing the pattern of Christian relationships. There is no substitute for Christian marriages and homes. Double the number of Christian homes in our country and you will more than half the number of moral problems of our present predicament. And precisely because you love each other for each other's sake, you take up the responsibility of making your own contribution to the permeation of society with Christian values. You are so to live so that many will see what loving your neighbor truly means.

But there is another thing to say. I have quoted to you not only Mark but Paul and you will remember how Paul gives a new interpretation to the command to love, or rather uses a new word, to bring out its full depth. He who loves τὸν ἕτερον, the person different from himself, the "other" has fulfilled the Law. The real depth of love that goes beyond the general friendliness of the heathen, the love that is God's own, is disclosed here. He who loves one who may be physically close, but emotionally different! This too is marriage.

Today it is closeness, similarity you are conscious of. You have come together because, I suppose in the first instance, you both decided to read theology in Durham, and then because you liked the same things, the same tastes, the same basic convictions, hopes and plans. It is probably true to say that as you go on you will proceed to see the differences, how differently a man and a woman react to the same circumstances. A woman can seem a very strange sort of creature to a man; and to a woman, a man must seem far worse than that. Now this of course is a good thing, it is why God made us male and female. But it can sometimes impose a strain, create friction, work up a tension. Marriage is not always easy, and this is the place for really Christian love. It is easy to love the person who thinks and feels as you think and feel, who is always with you, and who wants to do and to have what you want to do and have. But to love someone who is different, sometimes different enough to be an irritant; this is really to fulfill the Law of God. There is one thing alone that makes it possible—the love for us all of the One by whom in his perfect goodness we were made different. "Beloved, if God has loved us, we ought to love one another." We love because he first loved us.

"Gethsemane"—Mark 14:32-42

[Preached nine times between 4/16/76 at Bondgate, Darlington, and 3/13/05 at Esh Winning]

I need not tell you that that paragraph takes you back to horrors far beyond the point that we should have gone on Good Friday. Many of you will have been here last night at the Maundy Thursday service recalling the last supper of Jesus with his disciples, possibly ourselves sharing in the bread and wine that he distributes to his people still from that supper he went out with his disciples to a familiar little estate, and there faced the future with prayer. Not a bad plan. We might imitate it more often than we do. But here begins a problem and I wish as a historian I could see to the bottom of it. This is what I mean. In the supper, in the accounts we have of it, Jesus speaks calmly of his coming death, calmly and with a composed acceptance. He speaks of the giving of his body and blood; he says he will never again drink wine until he drinks in the Kingdom with his disciples, he speaks with sorrow of those disciples who will deny, betray, and forsake him, but he accepts the situation, not only as inevitable but as willed by God. Now, however, as he comes into the garden all is changed, and he prays in agony that it may not happen, that God would take away the cup so that he may not drink it. What makes the change? What, if the new prayer is granted, will become of all those predictions he had made not only at the supper but before? What will become of the gift to people of his body and blood? Did he really pray that all this might not happen?

As I say, I wish I could answer all those questions, but a sermon is not a place for historical guesses. It is worthwhile to say that surely no one ever simply invented the story of the garden of Gethsemane. There are too many problems in it for that. What we can say is that the event is not inappropriately named "the Agony," and in a sense, it rather than Calvary provides the clue of what Jesus suffered for us. I do not say this easily. Physical suffering is a terrible thing, and I know that I for one am afraid of it. And death is an enemy that not many of us can put out of our minds with Caesar's Stoic apathy, seeing that death is a necessary end, and it will come when it comes. In fact, the real point, or the first real point comes here. Most of us can in fact take suffering when it comes, and we haven't much choice about taking death. It is knowing that things are coming soon, inevitably. This they say is the greatest horror of capital punishment, that the terror spreads throughout the whole prison as they know that there sits in the condemned cell one who will hear the next morning the strike of eight, but not the strike of nine.

Jesus was a real man. We are apt to forget it, but the New Testament says so and Christian orthodoxy affirms it. He was a real man and this was happening to him. And now everything was through. This was the moment. The only parallel which comes to mind, and you may think it trivial is the way in which one faces the end of school holidays and college vacations and the departure of one's children. There's supper brought, and then there is still breakfast, and then—nothing else. The time of separation has come. The time had come for Jesus, and he knew it, and he tried to pray it away. "Father, if it is possible, let this not happen. I don't want to drink this cup, take it away." Whatever else we say, here is a real man—"who was made man for us, and who was crucified for us under Pontius Pilate." Up to that point the choice was his; once he had made it events in the garden followed more or less automatically. All this is a beginning, an introduction. I think we can penetrate further than this. When we look at Gethsemane we can see—

The Failure of Humankind

I am not thinking of Gethsemane as the scene of the most disgraceful retreat in human history, or of Judas Iscariot who for the sake of a handful of money betrayed his Master to those who were after his life, of Peter who had boasted so loudly, "even if all others deny you, I will not deny you. Though I should die with you, I will not deny you." But then when the moment of decision, the moment of courage came, he turned his back like the rest, and ran like a rabbit. All this is true, all this important, all this is full of lessons for us, none of whom are in a position to throw stones. But I have spoken about it on another occasion and am not going to repeat myself today. I am thinking now not of the failure of the avaricious, the cowardly, the disloyal, the little minded, the mean; I am thinking of the failure of the good, no of the best; I am thinking of the failure of Jesus.

Had he not failed? Was this not part of the bitterness of Gethsemane? When he approached the city he had wept over it. "O Jerusalem, Jerusalem who kills the prophets and stones those who accost her. How often would I have gathered your children as a hen gathers her chicks, and you would not." He had done all he could to make his message plain. He had healed their sick, he had taught and preached, he had told them stories; and he had not got the truth across. Even those who stood closest to him did not understand. What a pale reflection of this it is when a teacher sweats away with his dullest student, works and makes him work, only to see him fail his examination in the end! For this is not the dullest student in the class, it is the whole class that has failed him. And this is not passing and failing (though that can be traumatic), but rather life and death.

I know what some of you are saying. "This is not the end, Easter is still to come." True; and we have not come to the end of the sermon yet. I am simply saying that though this is not the whole truth, that it is true. And I am saying it for a concrete and practical reason, in addition to the reason that because it is true, we ought to recognize it as part of the agony our Lord endured for us. There are people, no doubt people here today, who know for themselves this sense of failure and frustration. We are losing members, we are losing local preachers, we are losing ministers. We make a very small impact upon our contemporaries who are not greatly impressed by what we have to say. And it is not that we do not try. I can criticize the Church when I want to, and most of us can think of things we would do differently if we had offices in Westminster. But such criticism is beside the point. What matters is the past. We do all we can think of, I hope we do, and still we fail. At the moment let me say one thing. Jesus was in the same position. Perhaps the great Victorian and Edwardian days of packed churches correspond to Jesus preaching to the crowds in Galilee. We may be near to Gethsemane these days.

But what I want to do is say this to those who feel this personally—that life is getting nowhere, that you are a failure as a person and as a Christian. The friendships that meant most to you have broken down, the causes that were dearest to you have turned out to be lost causes. Death has robbed you of those you love most and what remains of life is bleak, and desolate and bare. For you too there is more in store before we exhaust the meaning of this day and of this text. But for the present, let me say simply this—Jesus was in the same position, lonely, friendless, a failure, and facing death. And this is not the end. Do we not also see here—

The Failure of God?

Here is the best of human beings. More, here is the Son of God. And he prays in agony that God will do something. Not, mark you, that God will let him go and drop the whole affair, but that God will do what he has to do, establish his Kingdom, at a less frightful cost than that which it seems he has to pay. And what does God do? Not a thing. The sky is brass. God might be like Baal in the old Elijah story—perhaps he is asleep, or out hunting or doing goodness knows what. But there is no indication that he is listening.

John tells us a different story of a different time when Jesus made a serious prayer, adding "Father, glorify thy name" and there was an answer "I have glorified it and will glorify it again." But now—nothing. I suppose this is partly what those people have in mind who tell us that the crucifixion means not only the death of Jesus but the death of God. Humanity is supposed to have now come of age. He must look after himself, as he no longer needs a Father, and there is indeed no Father for him to have. God is finished, an interesting idea, a relic of the childhood of the race, but no more. I can understand this thought. The story of the agony of Gethsemane suggests it up to a point. For all the response Jesus gets, God might as well be dead. You will remember his words (we have thought about them one Good Friday) spoken on the cross—"my God, my God why have you forsaken me."

Again, I am dealing with this aspect of the matter for practical reasons. Do we not ourselves encounter this kind of experience? I am speaking to Christians, to believers, not to unbelievers. I question whether there is one of us who does not know what it means to pray to a blank emptiness, to a God who might as well be dead for all the response that we get to our petitions. It is not the worst, but the best Christians who have known this. One thinks of Martin Luther's *Anfectungen*—the word defies translation. It is not temptation, though that may play a part in it, perhaps the nearest thing to it is Paul's "fightings without and fears within." Do people nowadays ever read G. K. Chesterton's *The Man Who Was Thursday?* There is a profound picture of the truth here that life is so conducted that many persons go through it knowing at least at times what it is to stand alone against the universe, meeting God and yet finding that when he does so that even God seems to deny himself. Hardy could write his famous postscript to his novel *Tess*—the direst of the immortals had finished his sport with Tess. Read the story of Gethsemane and you might feel like saying the same thing of Jesus. The president of the immortals had let him in, granted him this power to work miracles, the gift of a popular preacher, but now washes his hands of him. And in a pedestrian, un-tragic way we may feel the same. Economics, poetics, education, social and psychological pressures; these have made me what I am and are factors in our present situation. These are real, God is not. Is that the end? Are we to make a simple analysis of the situation using in part the New Testament story of Gethsemane as a framework, a vocabulary, leave it there? No. What is the lesson of Gethsemane?

The Lesson of Gethsemane

Or rather a few bits of the lesson of Gethsemane. First, and most simply, and assuming the story is true, we see more clearly what the Savior of the world was prepared to do and to suffer for us—what he was prepared to be for us, be one of ourselves, sharing all of our experiences right down the blackest and last. For consider—all this was worse for him than it can ever be for me. As a teacher, I have my failures. There is nothing surprising in this. I am not a particularly good teacher. But he was the greatest of teachers and his failure rate was 100%. That is one way of putting it. The truth is wider. As we look back on our lives we like to be able to think, though we may not talk about some little successes and achievements we have had. Here there was not one—"Simon could you not watch with me for one hour?"

Again, we sometimes complain bitterly about unanswered prayer. But what right have I in myself to have my prayers heard and answered by God? What have I done to deserve such goodness? You might well say that where we are concerned, the real problem is not in unanswered but in answered prayer. But here the Son approached the Father and sought a gift and there was no answer. "Which one of you," Jesus had asked, "when his child asks for bread will give him a stone?" But this Father handed out that kind of stony answer to Jesus. Luther once read out the story of Abraham's offering of Isaac in sacrifice to God and when he had done his Katie said "I don't believe it. God would not have treated his son like that." "But Katie," Luther answered, "he did!" All this for us.

Secondly, when all our resources fail, when we ourselves are failures and in despair, the one thing that counts is loyalty. It is there in the story and it is there from the beginning. "Nevertheless, not what I will but what thou wilt." Jesus does not hesitate to ask for what he wants, but he does not regard what he wants as the final criterion. He acts in absolute and unwavering loyalty and obedience.

I have spoken of our failures as individuals and as a Church. The one thing here that counts is loyalty. Of course, there is hard thinking and hard work to do, but these will get nowhere without loyalty. It is very easy, and in these days we see it happen on a big scale, to say: "We see that the Christian message is too demanding, too exclusive, too difficult. We cannot expect people to accept it. Let us water it down with a bit of Islam, Hinduism, and other odds and ends into a mildly religious view of life." Over against all this the lesson for us today is loyalty, plain and simple.

Thirdly, God has better answers than we think we can prescribe for him. Jesus in Gethsemane with the burden of evil, suffering and death, asked God to deal with the situation painlessly. And God in effect said No. How else will people be able to say "God forbid that I should glory in anything but the Cross of Christ, through whom I am crucified to the world and the world to me?" And if even Jesus could contemplate for a minute an answer, a way less than God's best, how easy for us to do so?

God is not dead. He lives and reigns in goodness and in power. But some of our little ideas about him would be better dead. That perhaps would be the best thing that Good Friday could mean for us—not the death of God, but the death of all our unworthy images of him and that we may come to see him only where he is most surely to be found.

> Jesus my God I know his name,
> His name is all my trust,
> Nor will he put my soul to shame,
> Or let my cause be lost. (Isaac Watts)

"No Room in the Church?"—Luke 2:7

[Preached once on 12/19/92 at Trimdon Station]

I am sorry for your sake that my presence at this service means that you cannot have the Chairman here to preach the sermon. But I will not deny that for my own sake I angled to have the privilege of being here in Trimdon on this day of thanksgiving and advance. If I have read my records rightly, it is just over 41 years since I was first at Trimdon. I put it a little vaguely because in that distant time it took me a year or two to clarify the relation between the Trimdons—Village, Grange, and Station. But I think I know where I am today even though the old landmark is gone and the tall dark brick building in which I have preached a good many times is there no more. With me there is a lurch of regret about it, for the old buildings have fine associations and many memories for us. But as Christians we are not here to become sentimental and emotional but to get on with the job, to live as Christians in the modern world. And that of course reminds me, I must get on with the job.

It is a job that is not without its problems. What does one preach about today? I need not say that this is a great Trimdon day. We have a new church building and the old church fellowship will meet in it and God willing more and more will enter the fellowship who were repelled by rather than attached to the old building. That is one theme that I dare not neglect today. But we shall have to admit that as important as Trimdon is to us, the world is a bigger place than Trimdon, bigger even than the Trimdons. And the whole world is busy celebrating Advent and Christmas, and there is another theme, less than a week before Christmas, that cannot be left out of account. But how do you combine the two? That is a question that requires a good deal of time and thought, and you may conclude my account of it is a bad one.

Luke 2:7—there was no room for them in the inn. There is no need for me to parse that line for you in the Christmas story. It is the logical basis of the most familiar of all pictures which you have already seen on countless

96

Christmas cards, in shop windows and elsewhere. Why are they not in the delivery room of a good Nativity hospital? Why is Mary not in a decent bed with clean linen? Because beggars can't be choosers. If there is nowhere else to go, your choice is determined for you. There they are in the stable because there is nothing better. There was no room for them in the inn. Of course, there is more in this than a matter of social destitution or Joseph's imprudence in failing to ring up to book a room in advance. This is an actual part of the divine paradox that finds the origin of salvation in the most unexpected place. This is where God chooses to begin the work of redemption. Here is the greatest conceivable outpouring of God's love. If you want to have the lesson in this pointed out to you, you must turn over the pages of the New Testament. Luke will give you the basic truths but he does not take them far. Turn more pages and you will find this—"who being in the form of God, thought life on the level with God not a treasure to be clung to, but emptied himself, took the form of a slave, and was made in the likeness of man." And so on.

Here in this great hymn, Paul is working out the truth about Christ. This is the core of Christian theology; and this place, this new building exists for the teaching of Christian theology. You know me well enough to know that when I say that I am not thinking of the dry bones of a dead as dust set of formal but lifeless propositions, a set of metaphysical oughts that people are expected to learn by rote. I mean the exciting, unparalleled message of God become human, and being like us in every particular except sin, sharing our weakness, and suffering and death in order that we might be able to share his nature, living in Christ as God's sons and daughters, born anew to a lively hope.

The same truths at the same time give us a moral basis for the Christian life. Why does Paul, writing to the Philippians, share this great and beloved Christian truth? To stop his readers squabbling, to stop them getting swell-headed, to teach them to live with one another in humble love. But maybe I am getting away from my text. Let me tell you what first made me think about it. There was no room for them in the inn. But that is where they expected to find room.[1]

---

1   Editor's Note: It is worth pointing out that the Greek in vs. 7 probably does not mention an inn. Luke uses a different word for inn, namely πανδοχεῖον, for instance in the parable of the Good Samaritan. When he uses the word κατάλυμα elsewhere it refers to a guest room in a house, for example, when Jesus asks for a guest room to be prepared for the Last Supper. There is the further point that Bethlehem was so small, and far enough off the main Jericho to Jerusalem road that it probably did not have an inn at all. Bottom line, Luke is probably saying "because there was no room in the guest room," hence Mary and Joseph were put in the back of their relative's house where the beast of burden might be kept at night.

That is what inns are for, to accommodate travelers as they pass up and down the road. The inn was where you would expect to find the Holy Family, but you couldn't find them there. They are making do in the stable. The place where you would expect to find them, the place where you would expect to find the Christ—that's the Church! Yes indeed, and that is the dreadful thought with which I started. Here is this new beautiful building, and sometimes there is no room for Christ—

In the Church

Does that sound extreme? Perhaps it is and I am not saying it happens everywhere and all the time. But it is a danger we must beware of, everywhere and all the time. You don't need to know a great deal of church history to be able to think of times when the church has been involved in all kinds of things, but had little room for Jesus. Prepared to mention his name with respect but not much more. There came into my mind a poem by Studdert-Kennedy, which is connected with Good Friday rather than Christmas but no matter.

> When Jesus came to Golgotha, they hanged Him on a tree,
> They drove great nails through hands and feet, and made a Calvary;
> They crowned Him with a crown of thorns, red were His wounds and
>   deep,
> For those were crude and cruel days, and human flesh was cheap.
>
> When Jesus came to Birmingham, they simply passed Him by.
> They would not hurt a hair of Him, they only let Him die;
> For men had grown more tender, and they would not give Him pain,
> They only just passed down the street, and left Him in the rain.
>
> Still Jesus cried, "Forgive them, for they know not what they do,"
> And still it rained the winter rain that drenched Him through and
>   through;
> The crowds went home and left the streets without a soul to see,
> And Jesus crouched against a wall, and cried for Calvary. ("When
>   Jesus Came to Birmingham")

Extreme? Yes, of course, but it makes the point I want to make. Another Calvary would overstate the matter. No room in the inn, no room in the church beyond formal, minimal acknowledgment does not. The trouble is that the accommodate is fully-booked already. Sometimes it is plain secularism, a secular outlook on life. Many years ago, my father was at a church in a circuit which I shall not identify for you. After five years, he said he was leaving. "No," they said, "Mr. Barrett don't go. The church has never been more flourishing, all the bills are paid, and the football club, and the tennis club, and all the rest of our organizations are flourishing." "I'm going," he said, "because I can't do the work I came here to do." Parties and socials, a hundred or more every Saturday night, and never as many as 20 at communion on Sunday morning. The church can become so worldly, that it has no room for Christ.

Sometimes we are so keen on running our institutions, sometimes it turns into a sort of power game in which each group thinks of nothing except getting its own way and party spirit rules. And there is no room for Christ. Sometimes we try to accommodate our message and our lifestyle to the world around us so that Christ is squeezed out of our preaching of the word, and out of the way we live. Forgive me, I am not saying I detect these things at Trimdon, or anywhere in this circuit, as I don't. But I know enough to know that these things are always threatening every church there is and to know that they sometimes win with the result that it is true as it was at the first Christmas that there is no room left, no room in the inn, no room in the church.

It's an old hymn, a hymn I haven't heard sung in decades that asks "Have you any room for Jesus?" And today we have to ask it of the church. But that leads us to what I must reach before we finish. I know you have room for him here and always will have. I hope you will make more and more room. Let me remind you of some of the great truths of the New Testament. "Christ in you, the hope of glory." We live in a world of people without hope. The BBC serves up what accounts of conflict it can find, perhaps there is a glimmer at the end—perhaps in Yugoslavia the next ceasefire will hold. Life is nasty, brutal, and short. But there is no message of hope.

Hope of glory? Pie in the sky? Well yes we are talking about the blessed hope that is full of immortality and we should be unfaithful to our calling if we did not say it. This life with its sorrow and suffering and indignity and pain is not the end. There is an end for those who come out of great tribulation and stand before the throne of God who wipes away every tear from every eye. But hope does not make us ashamed, for the love of God is poured into our hearts by the Holy Spirit who is given to us. The hope is secure because it is already realized in the love that transforms all our living. "Now are we the children of God, and it does not yet appear what we shall be." Love, God's love, transforms life as nothing else can do. "You are built up as a dwelling place of God in the Spirit." That is what you are, not the building as fine as it is. God does not dwell in temples made by human hands, even in Trimdon. But he does dwell in people. "I will dwell in them, and walk with them, and they will be my people and I will be their God." Being his people—that is your vocation and that is what you who worship in this place are to be. You in the building, and God in you. And if God is among you, you will be built up into the kind of fellowship the world needs. You will live, so to speak, with one another, that as Paul puts it a stranger comes in his conscience will be awakened and he will say "truly God is among you." Not that it will be just a matter of talk, that would be a mockery of the kind of fellowship Christ's presence creates. "By this shall all people know you are my disciples, if you have love for one another." It was as a fellowship of mutual love that the church made its way in the ancient world. It was as such a fellowship that the early Methodists made their way. It is as such a fellowship that we shall lead the world to Christ.

If you read the names under the hymns that stand in the hymnbook you will notice that the hymn we all sing at Christmas was written by Philip Brooks, who was a minister of a church in America and a very famous preacher. I once saw his church in Boston. Outside it there is a statue of the preacher, an impressive figure in his frock coat. If you look closely you see another figure. Brooks is standing rather like a soldier just astride his sentry box. The other figure is within the shadow of the sentry box and you know who it is—Jesus, who supports his servant the preacher, he indeed is speaking through the preacher's words. If Christ is truly in the church, the church's witness becomes his and is given with his power.

Have you any room for Jesus? I know the answer—indeed you have. Then be of good cheer. God has not called us to work and witness in an easy time and place, but the Son of God started not in a fine building like this but in a lowly cattle shed. And he will not fail you.

"The Anticlimax of Christmas"— Luke 2:10-12

[Preached twenty-three times from 12/25/55 at Bethel to 12/17/00 at Kelloe]

Luke 2:10-12 looks like the greatest anticlimax in all history and literature. The scene is magnificent, somewhere right on the moors above and around Bethlehem. The shepherds dazzled by the sudden glory of the heavenly host, before which mere mortals must quail in terror. Then the angel's message, of good tidings of great joy. The long-awaited moment of deliverance had dawned; the Savior, Messiah has come. And here is the token of it. What might the token not have been here! The wonderful Counsellor, Mighty God, Prince of Peace, Everlasting Father. What circumstances would befit his coming? What sign could be too inspiring and magnificent? Would it have been surprising if the angel had said—"the sun shall be turned into darkness and the moon into blood, the stars shall fall from heaven, the earth shall be rent with earthquakes, then shall you know that he has come?" But quite the opposite. The sign? Go to a stable in Bethlehem and you will find a baby lying in a manger. It is the humblest sort of powerlessness you could imagine. All the glory of the heavenly host—then this? And, of course, this was not the end. There was a yet more humiliating scene to come. A new born child has at least the promise of life and strength; a corpse has not that and the story which began with the plaudits of the angels ended amongst the cat-calls of the mob at Calvary. The Christmas story and the whole life of Jesus, the hidden years at Nazareth, and the rejection by his own people, follow on the opening scene as an anticlimax. Before I say more about that let me use it as a reminder of the—

Anticlimax of the Christian Life

This is expressed in many ways. Christmas itself provides an illustration. On what a high level of Christian charity and goodwill we live today! Our own homes are not spoiled by ill temper or selfishness. We are ready to open our doors to the needy and the stranger. We give to the poor and the refugees. And afterwards? How soon the anticlimax comes. Down to earth with a bump on Wednesday. But that is only an illustration. I can think really of the whole pattern of the Christian life. I don't know how any of you began to be Christians, nor is it my business to find out. I am quite sure that there are dozens of ways into the Christian life, and nothing could be more foolish than an attempt to standardize them. But there is at least one thing common to them all. We begin with a great burst of enthusiasm. Christ has made all things new and life will never be the same again.[1]

And then it turns out that it is pretty much the same. Let us be quite honest about this. With your new faith, you set out to work at your office, or your shop; and you don't fiddle the figures in the company ledger, but then you never did. That's a matter of what Wesley called plain heathen honesty. And at the day's end you come home sober, and treat your wife and children with kindness and consideration. But then you always have done, because you have always loved them, and never wanted to do anything else. What does this wonderful new Christian life amount to? Of course, you say your prayers and read your Bible, but after a few months, to say nothing of years, it becomes something of a routine. So magnificent a start when you set out on the new way; and then so great a climax. Is all this true? And is it the best we can find to say about Christmas and the Christian life? It is true, up to a point, it is the dangerous kind of half-truth, that needs to be set in a fuller light.

The Anticlimax of Christmas

The stable, the manger, the child look like an anticlimax precisely because they are what no one expected. They are anticlimax by our standards. But that is perhaps only another way of saying that God is different from us, that

---

1   Editor's Note: While this is usually true, one can think of notable exceptions to this rule, for example, C. S. Lewis who felt as if he was cornered by God in his rooms at Magdalen College, Oxford, and said "I was the most reluctant convert in all of Christendom." That doesn't sound like enthusiasm.

his ways are not our ways, nor his thoughts our thoughts. The anticlimax of Christmas means God's freedom, and God's freedom means God's grace, God's power to act independently of our judgment of what is right and fitting, our standards of what is and what is not meritorious. It means that God is at home with shepherds, that he is willing to share our stables, to eat and drink with publicans and sinners. And love like this transforms what it touches. "Things bare and vile, holding no quantity / God can transpose to form and dignity." That is Helena in *A Midsummer Night's Dream* and of course there is truth in the matter as Shakespeare put it. Human love can and does work strange transpositions in our estimates. But it is far more true of the love of God. Even Bethlehem is transformed and we listened gladly over breakfast to the bells of that obscure Levantine town. But I want to apply this especially to the—

Anticlimaxes of the Christian Life

It is easy to be a Christian at Christmas. It is easy to be a Christian when the great moments of enthusiasm and emotion come. What about the other times, so much more important in that they are so much more frequent? I want to say three things very briefly: (1) a point I have already touched on, the power of love to transform the commonplace; (2) if God is to be found in a manger, then there is nowhere where he will not go. This means: (a) that when we ourselves are in trouble, and need we can be sure to find him, and (b) when we minister to such people we are ministering to him and find him in them; 3) there is no proof that the babe found in the manger is a heavenly babe. We know him by faith only, and that is how we live.[2]

---

2   Editor's Note: At the very end of this sermon is a little preaching outline of the contents of what has gone before. Having worked through most of the 300 sermons in the sermon notebooks already, I can say this is a rarity. There are occasional outlines with no sermon, and once in long while an outline with a fully written out sermon. My own experience of hearing CKB preach is that he did not ever appear to be reading out a sermon. More likely he was following such an outline in the pulpit. Why then write these sermons out in long-hand? It could be so that the ideas of the whole were well ingrained in the brain before preaching them. I know for a fact that sometimes he wrote sermons during the week, which he would preach the following Sunday, so perhaps that was not the main reason. Perhaps, Penny his daughter has given me a clue to another reason. He hoped, especially late in life, someday to publish at least some of these sermons.

"Savior, Christ, and Lord"—Luke 2:11

[Preached nineteen times from 12/25/58 at Langley Park to 12/31/00 at Trimdon Grange]

Quite apart from any good we might get out of it, it seems to me a right and important thing that the Christian Church should hold a service on Christmas Day and that as many of us as can should attend it. It really is far more important than getting the turkey on the table at 12:30 prompt, for our presence in this place is a testimony that Christmas means Christ. It is a needed testimony. For all too many, not simply in Russia, China, or the Congo, there is no Christ in Christmas Day. More and more, Christmas becomes an international feast; less and less is it a Christian festival. A BBC program like that yesterday on Children's Hour is in a way a most disturbing fact.

But we, well we are little better than the rest, but at least like the wise men in the story, we have come to worship him. We know how much we owe to the Maker of Christmas, and we are seeking his blessing on our homes. But—to worship whom? Who is this Jesus whose birthday we celebrate? The words of the angel are so familiar that we tend to ignore the fact that they contain a quite precise account of who the new born child is. Let us attend to what he says.

A Savior

If we had only thought about it, it is there in the very name Jesus, which Matthew explains "you shall call his name Jesus, for it is he who will save his people from their sins." It is all in the Hebrew root from out of which the name comes. Jesus is the Savior. To go further afield, the Nicene Creed hits the nail on the head—"who for us and for our salvation came down from heaven and was incarnate by means of the Holy Spirit of the Virgin Mary." We find it hard to remember that the earliest Christians made nothing of

Christmas. They never kept Jesus' birthday for the reason that they didn't know any more than we do when it came. The Bible tells us nothing of the 25th of December. The earliest celebrations were of Good Friday and Easter, and when Christmas came in too, it came into the same circle of ideas and meaning. It helps to complete the story of God's wondrous love in saving lost humankind, for the whole story is a tale of God's love on behalf of human beings in need.

We shall not be so stupid as to set Bethlehem and Calvary over against one another, but there are some ways in which the manger makes clearer than the Cross, God's love in stooping to human need. It does so just because it is the beginning of the story. It is where God stoops down to lift up the lowly and minister to the needy. The best comment on it was made by Mary: "He has showed strength with his arm, he has scattered the proud in the imagination of their hearts, he has put down the mighty from their seats, he has exalted the humble and the meek, he has filled the hungry with good things, and he has sent the rich away empty."

This day is not only the birthday of Jesus, perhaps it is not even his birthday, it is the birthday of hope for all the sinful and sorrowing, the downcast and the humble. There is no doubt now about what is going to happen. Some of you can remember D Day in 1944. I think that after that we all knew what was going to happen. The world still had things to come. Von Rendstedt's counter offensive in the Ardennes, the menace of the rockets. But day by day, victory was being won. And so, with God's invasion of our world, God's victory is being won. Evil, sin, death, suffering are being overthrown and the lowly, the oppressed, and the poor are being raised up. The angel continues. Jesus is—

The Christ

There is one quite special thing this says about Jesus. He is the one who fulfills all the promises of God in the Old Testament. For centuries, people had been looking for the coming deliverer, the redeemer, the savior. And this was he, the Christ who fulfilled all his people's hopes and more. This suggests a great many true and valuable things that I shall not try to say this morning. One thing only will be enough. It means that God watches over his Word to perform it. If he makes a promise, he keeps it. He picks his own time which may not always fit with our calculations, but he does bring his work to fulfillment. That was true with reference to the past. What God has planted in the minds of the great Old Testament prophets he fulfilled in his Son. It is also true with reference to the future.

Start with the babe in the manger and you are already on the way to the rest of the story. For if he really means to live a human life, he will have to die a human death, and if he provokes Herod to a fruitless massacre, Caiaphas and Pilate between them will probably be more successful. And the babe in the manger who is Christ crucified is also Christ risen. For God did not let his Son come to earth through oversight, only to find that he could not look after him. And the babe who came in the manger is the Christ who will come to be our Judge and Redeemer. What God begins, he also finishes. This applies to us too as persons. If God has begun something with you, you can be sure, he will finish it. There may be many setbacks and disappointments, for him perhaps as well as for you. But he is a God who keeps his promises, and all his promises to you are sure. The angel continues—

Jesus Is Lord

This means two things and I want to put them to you simply, sharply, and directly. He is the Lord in the sense that he is the person from whom I take my orders. This is what "Lord" means. It is a strong word, so strong that the earlier Roman emperors would not have it used of themselves, and it made quite a stir when first Domitian brought it into regular use. "Our Lord"— indeed! People thought it was no proper word to use. It was the term for a slave owner. But 50 years and more before Domitian, Christians were using it of Christ; because he was the Lord. "It's no use calling me 'lord, lord' and not doing what I tell you."

This is the point where I begin what I never like to leave out of a Christmas sermon. Can we suppose that we are in any sense doing honor to Christ the Lord if we spend the day feasting without any thought for the poor, the suffering, the lonely, for all those for whom today there is no room in the inn? He has bidden us to love all people, even our enemies. To love them in deed, not in word, and I wonder what your deed is going to be. Is there some lonely person in Langley Park you could befriend in the name of Christ? Is there anything left we could spare, for say, the Children's Home, or Inter-Church aide for the refugees?

He is Lord, and he is the babe in the manger. This then is what God means by being "lord." It is not what the Emperor Domitian meant by it. It is not, let us be frank, what the Kings and Queens of England meant by it. It is not what Church authorities have always meant by it—Popes, and bishops and (let us be honest) Presidents of Conference, secretaries of connectional departments, and even District Superintendents and circuit Stewards. But it was what God meant by it. "He that would be chief among you, let him be servant of all." When God was about to establish his Kingdom among us he came as the child of a peasant, born in a stable. And here are we—petty, pompous, self-important, standing on our own dignity, when he "thought it not robbery to be on equal terms with God, but made himself of no reputation and took upon himself the form of a servant."

Our stable has a low-pitched roof. You come in on your knees, and you have to leave your pride outside. If only we, all of us, this Christmas could lose it altogether and never find it again! Here is he whom the angel bids you to worship—"a Savior, which is Christ the Lord."

"Let Us Go to Bethlehem"—Luke 2:15

[Preached twenty-five times from 12/25/49 at Calverley to 12/22/96 at Wooley Tee]

It would surprise me greatly if there were many people who had come to Church for a long highly wrought sermon today. Yet I am also sure of this, that no one would have come to Church at all this morning who did not, in his own way, wish to do precisely what these shepherds did. Let us go to Bethlehem, and see what it is that happened; let us go see this thing. In some ways, today it is harder. Not just a few miles tramp across the fields to a stable, and a mother and a child plain to the eye. Blessed are they who have not seen in that sense, and yet have believed.

And in some ways, it is easier. A babe lying in a manger is not a very impressive sight, nor is it a self-explanatory sight. But we have to guide us the whole story of his life, and with that the story of his work through the centuries and the people called by his name. It is, maybe, easier for us to know something did happen. But what did happen? What was this thing that came to pass? First—

God Became Real

This was what, for more centuries than we can compute, human beings had sought. This is the meaning of all the history of religion. Human beings sought to make God real by prayers, by sacrifice, by sacrament, by mysteries, by asceticism. This is the meaning of the age-long quest of mysticism. If only humans could strip off the gross outer trappings of their nature, see through the mists that surround the throne of God and grasp him in an unlimited devotion of spirit, and so make God real. This is the meaning of the progress of theology. If the being and nature of God can be pinned down, in a tight logical structure so that the mind of a human being can grasp by reason as well as by intuition the being of God—if this could be done, then perhaps God would be real.

None of these quests was in itself a bad one. None of them was a successful one. And now, without anyone noticing it, the thing had happened. The far-off dream, the desperate hope, had come suddenly to birth, and that birth at Bethlehem is the center and crown of history. It is a center to which we still look, for this question of the reality of God, the substance of religion, is something that concerns us still. For many people, God is simply not real. I am not speaking of people who profess to be atheists, or even agnostics. I am speaking for example of these youngsters who pass through our Sunday Schools and seem never to pick up anything they can cling to, never to learn something in such a way that it becomes an unforgettable part of life itself. We know them. Some of them have shown me a shelf full of Sunday School prizes. But while they were learning the kings of Israel and Judah, while they were learning the missionary journeys of St. Paul, they never learnt to know God in such a way that he became real for them, a part of their lives. Again, there is that constant leakage of members in our societies who "cease to meet." Why do they cease to meet? Is it unfair (for I want to do nothing but help them) to say that it is because their faith is never really real. How can they persevere?

If you only started going to Church because there was a football club, and never found a deeper reason for doing so, of course you give it up when you are past football. If you only went to Church because a certain girl went there, then of course you give it up when you either marry her or find another. Or deeper, you go to Church because the teaching of Christ is the one way to reform the world, and then you find that the Church itself needs to be reformed; until it is filled in every part with the charity that thinks and speaks and wills no evil. In these circumstances, only a real hold on God will keep you there.

This affects us all. It is extraordinary how frankly the greatest saints confess their barrenness in prayer, the times when God seems remote, unreal. And there are not a few for whom Christianity is true, but not real. "O that I knew where I might find Him, could find the place where sin and sorrow, suffering and death are completely and radically and finally dealt with, could find the place where I could lay my own burden down."

God becomes real, not on account of our search but in a process of his own. No matter what happens, no one, nothing can take from us the fact of Jesus, and if there is a God at all, he is as real as the babe in the manger. There is something here that side-steps organized religion and mysticism and theology. This is the solid ground of faith—neither our organization nor feeling nor our rational thinking. God himself has acted, God has found us. God has entered humanity and taken it to himself. It is Christ alone who is our hope. His faith, his goodness, his righteousness, not ours, are the reality of our faith. But that is not the last word. We cannot leave things there because God did not and does not leave them there. God became real, but also—

Human Beings Reached Their Goal

Not of course this particular person; not St, Paul, who knew he must still be pressing on. But the life humankind had all along been intending to live had now begun and was to be lived out. It was a life in which humankind was completely and inseparably joined to God, in constant and uninterrupted communion with God, a life in which a human will was willingly obedient to the will of God. A life which, consequently, showed every goodness—the faith, the love, the righteousness of which I have spoken. It was life as God had always intended for it to be, and it began there in Bethlehem. God had become real, and humankind had become what God intended he should be.

This was the beginning of a new day. For just as through Christ we can become sure of God and the reality of God, so also through him we are built up into a new humanity, reproducing his virtues, however imperfectly. For in Jesus, God is not doing something apart from the human race, he is doing something to the human race, to us and in us. Whatever he does he must do in us, or else he fails, which is unthinkable. You must know what it is to try and get a child to do some task which calls for a little skill and thought. You show him how; you explain, you let him try and fail. And then—it depends on how much time and patience you have. If you run short of either, you do the job yourself; it is perfectly done, but you have failed. You have failed unless and until the child is doing the job himself.

Now God has done something for us; whatever else Christmas may mean, it does mean that. But he is also waiting, with untiring patience, to do something in us. We do not begin by reproducing all at once the goodness of Christ. We begin by trusting in his merits, when we have none of our own. But the next thing is that God waits until Christ is formed in us. The coming of Jesus means a new day for humanity. It is like the day when the Wright brothers flew the first airplane. People had been much higher in the air, on mountains and hills but now they were in a new element. So, with us.

It is quite true that the great heathens, and many of the not so great, have climbed higher up the path of virtue than the worst Christians. But the worst and youngest Christians, if they really are Christians, are in a new element, a new world, and only heaven is above them.

Christ comes, says the New Testament, to be the elder of a large family. The story of God's people comes to its blazing focus in him. But the beacon of light which converges to its focal point diverges again and spreads with nothing to limit its scope. That broadening beam of light includes even us; we are part of it today. In Christ then, God became real, and a real human being, and the new humanity of which Christ is the head, reached its goal. This is the thing which has come to pass. But we must tackle one question more. Let us now go even to Bethlehem and see this thing, but how do we get there? Easy in a rough and ready sense for the shepherds. But for us?

How Do We Go?

And how do we learn the reality of God and the life of Christ? In the end, there is only one answer, it is one we do well to remind ourselves of today. "Unless you turn and become as little children, you shall by no means enter the Kingdom of God." If we today are to visit Christ at Bethlehem and enter into the inheritance which he has brought, that is the way.

There is no room for pride. You cannot be proud in a religion whose focal points are a cradle and a cross, the powerlessness of childhood and the impotence of an ignominious death. The work is God's not ours. We depend upon him, not he on us. We come simply with open hands to receive what he will give. We do not dictate, not even the form our religious experience shall take. We simply accept. We accept and love Him and offer our simple adoration. We love God in his children, and we worship him in his Son. We minister to the least of Christ's children and in so doing we offer him ourselves. Hungry, naked, sick, in prison, he is always there, always waiting for us. We go out of Church today to our comfortable homes, and to a world of want and sorrow. Let us go to Bethlehem? We are there, and in ministering to Christ in the souls and bodies of his brothers and sisters we shall find him and worship him. Bethlehem, as it turns out, is all around you.

"Pondering over Christmas"—Luke 2:19

[Preached eleven times between 12/25/91 at Framwellgate Moor to 12/30/07 at North Road]

What a good example! That is what we will do this morning, as Mary did—ponder. There is no need for me to tell once more, except by way of allusion, the familiar story. You have heard it in Luke's words which are better than any I could find and long before you heard this morning's lesson you knew it all. And carol singers and Christmas cards have reminded you of it. The thing for us to do now is to ponder them, to turn them over in our minds, to ask—What is the meaning behind the story? What does it offer me? What does it require of me? And perhaps most important of all, "How can we keep them in our minds as Mary did?" Think of them not just on one day of the year, but every one of the 366 until next Christmas comes?

"Mary kept all these things." We know from Luke's own story what all these things would mean for Mary. For her it all began nine months back, in a moment that neither she nor anyone else could understand when she responded to the amazing challenge with "Behold the handmaiden of the Lord; be it unto me according to thy word." Then the waiting, the embarrassment until she and Joseph married, the cheery visit with her relative Elizabeth, herself awaiting the birth of John the Baptist. Then the decree of Augustus coming at precisely the wrong time, and the painful journey to Bethlehem, ending not at the inn but in a stable. The moment of birth and the wonder and mystery of it enhanced by the entry of the shepherds struck dumb by the glory of God. Let us analyze it all if we can. There was—

A Gift to Be Received

Such a gift! Paul came as near to describing it as anyone could when he said "thanks be to God for his inexpressible or unspeakable gift, for what can you say about it?" If anything is going to be done about a world in which the proud put into practice the imagination of their hearts and work their wills, in which the mighty sit on their seats and grind the faces of the humble poor, in which the weak never get a taste of the good things because the rich have sent them away empty, in such a world if things are to be put right, God will have to put them right—who else could do it? But how? Will he blow up the mighty and wicked with an atomic explosion (which I presume he knew all about before the scientists did)? Will he simply turn a switch and turn all the blacks into whites? No, he has found a way to come himself into the human scene, to live in it, to die in it, and to take away the evil of it.

God gives a good many gifts, but his unspeakable gift is himself. And it is a gift, a free gift. But there are free gifts which it costs something to receive. If we leave out gifts that relate specifically to Christian life and faith, by far the most wonderful gift my father and mother ever gave me was to let me go to the university, to Cambridge. Looking back, it is not easy to know how a Methodist minister could manage it. In those days, there were no complaints about the inadequacy of grants, for there were no grants. And even a college scholarship did not make all that much difference. But even as an 18-year-old, I knew what that gift meant; it meant that I was going to work. And I did work—no credit to me; I loved it. It was what I wanted. The gift was free, absolutely; but I could not accept it, make it mine, without committing myself.

It is there of course, most plainly in the story of Mary herself. "Behold the handmaiden of the Lord." The gift was free; but it did not exist, it was meaningless without commitment. For this is what the story really means. It does not greatly worry me if someone tells me he has difficulty over the idea of a virgin birth, I didn't find it easy myself. And what matters is this—if you think, and there are no difficulties in this, of a world that has gone wrong, there are two ways of putting things right that simply would not work. One is that God should simply step in and stop all the folly and wickedness at a blow. Of course, he could; but to do so would mean that we human beings were not being treated seriously as moral and responsible beings. The other is that we should simply get up and put things right ourselves, and of course we couldn't. The right way to do it is God's way, and that is that he does what only *he* can do, but in doing it associates humanity as an associate partner with himself—"conceived of the Holy Spirit, born of the virgin Mary.' Thanks be to God for such a gift, and thanks be to God for taking us seriously. What else? There is here—

A Song to Be Sung

We are accustomed to speak of Methodism as born in song, and it is true enough; Charles Wesley set the people singing with the greatest hymns. But the whole church was born in song. We don't sing these as frequently as some Christians do, but there they are in the open chapters of Luke, so old in Christian use that we still call them by their Latin names—even if we are not particularly good at Latin. Mary's *Magnificat*—"my soul does magnify the Lord." Zachariah's *Benedictus* "Blessed be the Lord God of Israel." Simeon's *Nunc Dimittis* "Lord now let thy servant depart in peace." Maybe they were taken up almost at once from the Gospel. Many think they were in use as hymns even before the Gospel was written.

They all follow on the gift; for they are all hymns of thankfulness. They are not solicitous, they are not intercessions, they are pure gratitude for what God has already given, has already done. "He has regarded the low-liness of his handmaiden . . . He that is mighty has done great things for me"—all Mary's gratitude for the child that is already there, waiting for birth. Zachariah praises God for what has already taken place—"he has visited and redeemed his people, he has raised up a mighty salvation for us." And Simeon thanks God for the fulfillment of the promise—"my eyes have seen thy salvation."

They are all hymns of thankfulness and they all begin with God. That is how most of the greatest hymns begin. Work it out yourselves; pick out the Top Ten from the hymnbook and see. There is good advice here for anyone who wants to set about writing hymns. But there is more than that. This is the spring of all Christian living. The New Testament is not a book of rules. There is a rule or two, here and there, but these are not what kindle the flame. I must have told you sometime in the past about the great Heidelberg Catechism which works out the whole system of Christian ethics from the proposition—how I am to be grateful for such a salvation. For though hymns play a fine part in the experience of Christian gratitude for God's unspeakable gift, it is at best a limited part, and I cannot truly express my gratitude if I am not doing my best to live in accordance with his mind.

The trouble with hymns that consist of words and music is that even the longer ones are soon over. So is gratitude sometimes. "Oh I do want a puppy!" says the little boy. And soft-headed parents give him a puppy and he is so grateful for it. And before the end of January the poor little four-legged creature is starving and sick, locked out, driven away. The gratitude that would have seen to it that someone had fed and cared for the little dog had melted away. Bad enough when it's puppy dogs, worse when it's God. Oh may we keep and ponder in our minds, God's wondrous love in saving humankind. If we live out our gratitude we learn the way to sing even in the dark, for even though we pass through the dark places, the love of God is there to kindle our song, not as a matter of keeping our courage up, but because we know we have nothing to fear. This leads to a third thing. Among those things which we keep and ponder there is a—

Commission to Fulfill

If these things are true, they are worth pondering, more than that, they are worth proclaiming. Years ago, I read an article by Karl Barth with the Title "The Basic Focus of Theological Thought." Those, he said, are these. First is exposition, by which the Christian goes to Scripture and works at it so as to bring out and make available the truth that it contains. The second is criticism, a word Barth used in its sense of passing judgment. You put the truths you have learned from the Bible alongside of what you see in the world about you and in your own heart; and what you see in the world and in your heart is judged by the Word of God. And the third focus is proclamation. The truth you have discovered you must tell the world. There is no proper Christian theology that does not come to voice in preaching; not necessarily what is done in pulpits on Sunday, also what is done on street corners, and what is done when man talks to man and woman to woman.

It is there in the story, one more reminder of it before we finish. It would be hard to find in the New Testament less likely candidates to be fully accredited preachers, but look at the shepherds "the first apostles of his impact and love." But it is true, before Peter, Paul and John, they are at it. "They made known concerning the saying about what was spoken to them about the child. And all that heard it wondered at the things which were spoken unto them by the shepherds." If the shepherds could do it so can you.

How? Not by pretending to be Professor Karl Barth, but by keeping and pondering these things. Living in the humbleness of a stable, sharing in the love of the indescribable gift, leaving to give the news, to live as God's child in God's world; this way you will find a message to proclaim, a commission to fulfill.

"The Parable of the Feast"— Luke 14:15-24

[Preached eight times from 12/31/39 at SHABC to 7/14/63 at James St.]

There is little need to remind you either of the details of the passage which has just been read or of the circumstances to which, speaking at this time, I have to relate it. During the last few years we have been running from one crisis to another, until at length the pile of them grew too high, and the whole of life tumbled into confusion. Standing at the end of 1939, it is comparatively easy to trace the course of events which has brought us to this current time, but we look to a future more obscure than ever. We hope that this next year will bring peace again, but there can be no certainty of that. All that we do know is that this is a fateful, decisive period, a time of crisis, a time when bad may turn to good, or turn to worse.

Now this parable is a parable of crisis. Many people think that the parables of Jesus are the easiest of his sayings to interpret and for that very reason are frequently misinterpreted. Jesus never thought of his parables as easy and obvious, and the reason that we think that they are is that we have turned them away from their original purpose and meaning. They were not told to inculcate general moral principles, for example that we ought to use the talents God has given us. They were told to apply to a very particular and acute crisis in human history, a crisis of which Jesus and his friends and enemies were at the center. It is only when we read the parables as Jesus spoke them that we see how deeply they entered into that supreme crisis of human life when God spoke and acted in Christ. And it is only when we see their relevance to that crisis and cease to harness them to our own petty moral platitudes that we see how tremendously vital they are to our own situation, how full of judgment and salvation.

There can be little doubt about the meaning of this parable in relation to the particular days in which Jesus lived. He had got himself a bad name by reason of the bad company he kept—the friend of publicans and sinners they called him, the friend of those folk that pious people thought would have no share in the Kingdom of God. That Kingdom was the prerogative of the Pharisees, the holy people who would have nothing to do with the common folk. Jesus was now in the company of such people and he made his reply to them.

It was indeed true that these were the days when the great Feast of God's Kingdom was ready; the invitations had been sent out and the Pharisees had indeed been invited. But by their very rejection of Jesus himself, they were turning down the invitation, rejecting the Kingdom they thought was theirs by right. They were too busy to find time for it, and the horrible truth is their business was religion. They were so busy being religious, being pious, preaching their rites and customs they had no time for Jesus. People use many things to keep a distance between themselves and God, but the most dreadful, because the most insidious, is religion itself. There are no more dangerous people than Pharisees. "Cause the Holy One of Israel to Cease from before Us."

But God was not to be deprived of his guests by the folly and blindness of the Pharisees and for that reason, if not others, Jesus himself went out into the highways and byways to seek and befriend the poor, the sick, and the outcast. The coming of Jesus was the time of God's call and God's testing. Jesus was and is both savior and judge. The Jews required a sign or proof that he was God's Son. The Greeks wanted wisdom, metaphysical speculation, and Jesus had no time to give either. Those who were too preoccupied with their religion and their cleverness to hear the Word of God could find only foolishness and weakness. But to the saved he was the power of God and the Wisdom of God. And they knew who they were—not many wise, not many mighty, not many noble.

Now all this is the revelation of God worked out in the supreme crisis of human life and it is a truth of universal relevance. It is a fact that speaks as much to us as it did to the Pharisees and publicans in the first century. And the first thing it says is—

Come

That is a call which is made to you all, not to one or two particular people or one or two saints. It is an appeal made to all sorts and conditions of persons.

The worst mistake I think I have found in the opinions of people about Christianity is that it is all right, a very good thing, for the very religious, the people whose nature it is to enjoy services, and sermons and singing; but to others it just does not apply. All this sort of excuse is ruled out by this parable. The Pharisee, the religious person is indeed invited to God's Kingdom, but he is not the only one. God calls those who have had to drop out of the race of life. The sick, the lame, the blind. And he also calls those who are doing the ordinary work of life, just as he called people doing their fishing, making up their accounts at the customs office, on duty as soldiers, so now he calls people who are working in their homes, buying and selling, making things with their hands and their heads. Do not make this mistake; Jesus did not come, and does not come to call saints; he came to make them; not to turn the ordinary activities of life into the endless pursuit of an egotistic, priggish, piety but to flood the whole life with laughter and gaiety and power.

Consider the work of George McLeod on Iona. He and his men are studying, preaching and building as a sign that God through the Church must claim the whole of life for Christ. Why are Protestant pastors imprisoned in Germany? Because they insist that the whole of life belongs to God against a political insistence which says to God—"Hands off, politics is not your business."

And so, this parable means the universal call to every one of us no matter what our personal ideas and habits may be. God's summons rings out across all such human divisions and classifications with its command to come for all things are now ready. Come to what? To a dinner, a feast of good things. Is that how you think of Christianity? Or do you think of it as something in which all the good and pleasant things are rationed? Is your fear that of Augustine's who used to pray that God would save him—"but not now"? Not until I have seen life without its restrictions and exactions.

I don't want to make out that the life of a Christian is a bed of roses. It is no such thing. In this very Lukan passage we shall see that the Cross is well in sight. But surely you cannot miss the meaning of this parable, of this feast, of the shepherd calling his friends to rejoice with him over the found sheep, of the Father who has received his lost son back home, killed the fatted calf, brought out the best robe, and put the ring on his son's finger. To come to God means the end of wandering, the end of selfishness. Your life is newly oriented towards God in reliance upon and in service to him. There is another word here for us—

Go

Just as God calls us to come to us, he also sends us out to call others. We are his servants and he depends on us to go out into the highways and hedges and call people. He calls us to his own work to befriend the sick and the needy, the downcast and the despairing, the outcast and the despised. He sends us to plead with them, to urge them, to compel them to come to the feast. There is room for them, there is room for them with God. He wants them and he loves them; no matter what their sin and wretchedness, he is able to save them. And they are his, they belong to him and he is only calling home his own.

There is no need for any circumstances to get in the way of this. It is our duty in this year and in the years of peace. In one part of Hankow [China], there is only one stone building—the Methodist chapel. When the warning goes off, the people rush in and the pastor preaches while the bombs are dropped. The Chinese colonel, wounded, converted, brought 163 men wanting baptism. There is no reason why that should not happen in England. God wants Englishmen as much as Chinese. The trouble is that you and I are too often Pharisees. We are too busy, too busy with our work, with our war, with our hymn singing, to listen to the voice of God which summons us to the joy and service of the Kingdom. "Come for all the things are now ready . . . and yet there is room."

"The End in Time"—John 1:14

[Preached ten times from 12/31/44 at Bondgate, Darlington, to 12/31/75 at Framwellgate Moor]

I spent some time considering what I should say this evening. The Watch-night service, later tonight has been easy. Watchnight is Watchnight, you know where you are, it is not confused with anything else. But today is not only the last day of the year, it is also the first Sunday after Christmas, and that is a fact we ought not to neglect. Yet we are looking back, it is *after* Christmas. That is one reason we have gone to St. John's Gospel. John has, as the other Evangelists have not, a backward look. He does not tell in detail the stories of the birth of Jesus, as Matthew and Luke do. Why tell again what anyone can read for himself? Instead, he looks back and sums up the significance of it all, so that in this Fourth Gospel, you have no Nativity story but in its place eighteen of the most pregnant verses in the whole New Testament. But how are we to combine this last day of the year feeling with a backward look at Christmas? I can tell you best by plunging at once into the first point. I am going to begin with—

The End

I do not mean by that that I am neglecting the logical arrangement of my sermon. I mean that at the end of the year, I am thinking about ends—ends in general and the End in particular. You will have noticed that we use the word *end* in two senses. In one it is simply an extremity, the end of the book, the last page. The end of the rations is when there isn't a scrape of butter or a grain of sugar left, the end of a journey comes when you have arrived. But end can also mean purpose, intention, goal as in the phrase "ends and means." The end of a book is the thing it was written to achieve. Our Fourth Gospel was written (see the last verse) that "you might believe that Jesus is the Son of God and that believing you might have life in his name." Marx's *Das Kapital* was written to foment a social revolution. The end of rations is to keep you alive and see that everyone gets a fair share. The end of a journey is not merely the place you get to, but what you do when you get there, and most journeys of intelligent people have ends of both sorts.

Now what I am coming to is this—you can only really understand a thing from its end. That is easily enough illustrated from journeys; once a month you may see me cycling furiously out to the lonely and (if one may whisper it) not very attractive village of Eppleby. If you ever saw that you would doubtless say, justifiably, the man is off his head. But when you see a little group of people gathered around God's book, reading and praying together you see the real end of the journey and you understand. Or, to take a more topical instance, you see an old man of 70 or so jump into an air-plane and fly some thousands of miles over war ravaged Europe to spend a few days among bullets and draughts, and you say again, how stupid. Then you notice that the old man is Mr. Churchill, and he has gone to Greece on a vital mission, and then the whole picture is different.

Of course, this is true about a year. You can understand at the end as you cannot at its beginning or in the course of it. We can understand the plans for D Day and the invasion of Europe today as we could not under-stand them 6 months ago. I will use a very personal illustration. This year has been a fateful one for me (as many of you know) as I have been married in it (I said fateful, not fatal). I understand now what I was doing, as I did not understand it on August 16th. You understand the year when you can look back on it as a whole.

Now this is why, in the Christian faith, we are constrained to talk about the end. We are always concerned with ends, intentions; and especially we are concerned with The End. We have begun with a text about the Word of God and our well-known verses. Word is really expressed thought, reason. It is the Christian faith that there is a reason or a purpose of God. Now that could be seen clearly if we stood at the end of time. That is a point I often put to people in grave trouble, and who are perplexed about life. The pat-tern of life is too big and noble to see it at this close range, we could only see it, when we stand back and view it in perspective, in God's perspective. God has a plan and we mustn't think our loved ones are outside it, whatever hap-pens. They are not. Only it is too much to expect that we should understand the design with our noses pressed close up against the canvas.

At this point in my sermon I am asking you one thing. To cultivate, as far as you can, the habit of viewing things, as it were, from the end. I want you to look back to the end of your own actions, that is to examine your motives and intentions, and to consider carefully what the things you are doing will result in. I want you to look on life in this way, not with the shortsighted gage of one who picks up this detail and that, but from the end. Look on your sorrows that way, and see if perhaps they will fit into a plan. Look at yourselves like that. I thought for a time to preach on the Last Judgment tonight, but I've taken this wider subject. I may have been wrong for I am sure the Church is suffering from the lack of this viewpoint.

So far, I think, two things have been said, but nothing specifically Christian. Here to introduce it boldly is the Christian paradox—

The End in Time

The Word became flesh. The whole meaning for life, God's meaning for life became a human being. Of course, nothing like this had ever happened before or could ever happen since. It is the sort of impossible thing that no one would have thought of if it had not happened. It means now that there are two places where human life can be understood, one is right at the end of time, the other right in the middle of time, in Jesus Christ, who is God's truth in the flesh.

I told you just now one of the two things I tell people who are very troubled and grieved. I will tell you now the other. One is that we cannot expect to see now exactly how the pattern of life runs, we can only see that from the end when we look back on it all. The other is that we can look at Christ to find out what the pattern is like, because he is the end, the meaning of the whole thing, dropped into the middle of the story. In the same way, he is the judgment of life, and if we are to see ourselves as God sees us, we should for one thing put ourselves at the end of time, at God's judgment then. Alternatively, or as well, we should put ourselves in the presence of Christ to await his Word.

We see our sin when we look back to see how we have strayed here and here and here from the line, the pattern God marked out for us. In the same way, we can see where we sin when we look at the pattern of Christ. There is nothing else that can enable you to go through life with so sure a sense of understanding, and so sure a conviction that life is understandable. There are few things in the world so tragic as the number of people one meets for whom life seems to have no meaning. Some of them are just superficial butterflies who flutter from one flower to the next, aimlessly, irrelevantly. Some of them are genuinely tragic characters who have suffered one hammer blow of fate after another. There are the light, brainless, thoughtless, empty-headed good for nothings who are the problem and the failure of all educational systems, and there are shipwrecks of life, men and women like King Lear, fighting blindly with the stars of the universe.

Here is the key, would people take it and turn it. I can illustrate it this way. Have you ever seen a play twice? A play with something in it, I mean. The first time you are anxiously waiting to see what the end will be, the end that will supply the meaning of the whole story. The second time you know the end from the beginning, and everything appears in a new light, apparently simple events take on a new humor or a touch of dramatic irony. It is worth getting to know a great play for the sake of this experience. I, for example, have seen *Macbeth* three times and my reading of it probably runs to seven. That means I can be to that play (if this is not irreverent) almost what God is to life. I see the bearing of each speech, each line as the whole thing, so marvelously constructed moves to its close.

Now Christians should be in a position like that with regard to life. Every single datum should be eloquent with meaning and Christians themselves should be eloquent as they see, what no one else can see, the unfolding of God's purposes. Through our faith in Christ we see how joy and suffering are woven into the pattern of God's redeeming love. Look back now on 1944, look in the light of Christ and see how God works. It is necessary to add a further point. I have taken account of the end of time and the time of Jesus, God's Word made flesh. But what of 1944–45? Are we to speak of—

The End of Our Time?

There are many New Testament texts that speak of Jesus in language which elsewhere was reserved for the end of the world. This is one of them—"we beheld his glory." I cannot now go into all the allusions which make it fairly clear that John was thinking about the glory of God that people believed would shine in the last days. But so he did think; and so thought all the New Testament writers. Jesus brings into the midst of life, judgment and salvation, so that now there exists over against one another a Kingdom of light and a Kingdom of darkness, the kingdom of evil and the kingdom of grace and truth. And God's eternity enters time whenever the Holy Spirit moves a person to step out of darkness and into the light.

Christ came into our world; because that is so, you stand under the judgment of God. In the presence of Christ, you have no cloak for your sin. "Our secret sins are in the light of thy pure countenance" (J. Greenleaf Whittier). But Christ came not to judge the world, but to save it and you, if you will, may pass from death into heavenly life. The Gospel puts the clock on. There is no waiting. You do not wait for physical corruption to die, you are dead now in trespasses and sins. You don't wait to go to heaven, heaven is open now, if you receive Christ.

The year is running out. How much time have we to make up our minds? Do you know the story of the ancient general who could not make up his mind whether to attack his adversary or not? The war dragged on, men were killed, villages were pillaged, crops were burned. At last the opposing general demanded a parley. The generals met, one stepped out, spear in hand. With its sharp point, he traced a circle in the ground about the place where his lethargic enemy stood. That done, he cried "I charge you, for God's sake, for humanity's sake, and for your own sake, that you decide before you step outside that circle."

I charge you, for God's sake, for humanity's sake, for your own sake, that you make your reckoning with Christ before you step out of that pew and into 1945.

"One Thing I Know"—John 9:25

[Preached twenty-one times from 9/17/44 at Bondgate, Darlington, to 6/18/89 at Billy Row]

Those of you who were here last Sunday, and whose memories are not too short-lived will probably have surmised that this sermon is intended to follow that of a week ago. If you have so guessed, you are quite right. I preached then on the text "one thing you lack." Today, a positive word "one thing I know."

We began last week by reviewing a number of considerations which show how one deficiency in a person's life can lead to tragedy and ruin. It will not be amiss to make a corresponding beginning tonight that illustrate the statement that great achievements in the sphere of life, are commonly made by persons with one dominant aim. Few people have reached the heights without having one over-mastering purpose, one driving impulse. Again, we may start this on quite a low level though I will not in my earlier examples vouch for my facts.

I understand however that it was a passionate longing indeed a necessity to eat the fruit of lofty branches, that gave the giraffe a long neck. Evolution has always apparently gone that way. The giraffe that couldn't reach the food soon died and the long necks soon prevailed. So with the rhinoceros, those who couldn't develop the thick skins they needed just got scratched to bits and didn't survive. It was the giraffe who said "I will have a long neck" and the rhino who said "I will have a thick skin" who survived. All this is true on a much deeper and more important level. The really great pianist was not the boy whose parents said, "Now I think you ought to learn the piano, you shall go to so and so" and he went to Mr. So and So but during the week he forgot and practiced a few scales except on the days when there was something more interesting to do. No, the one who became the pianist was the one who said "I am going to play the piano if all the world tells me to be quiet. I'm going to play the piano if I starve in the process. I'm going to play the piano if I die at 35 like Mozart or at 39 like Chopin."

The great scholar is not a person who has a multiplicity of interests in life, who dips into this, looks at that, tastes one enjoyable thing after another. I have known these sorts of people, and I know the single-minded intensity of thought and labor which makes them. We are apt to think of the very learned as unemotional, dull; far from it. No one would ever do such work without a dominating passion, an all absorbing thirst driving him. The person who can say "one thing I know" is a person who gets things done. It is the person who says "I know the world is round" who gets in a boat and sails around it. It is the person who says "I know there is a way to the top of the mountain or to the Pole" who gets there. It is the person who says "I know I can succeed in this job" who does succeed.

And the one who succeeds (if the word may be allowed) in Christian life is not the person with a variety of religious opinions, but the person who knows, really knows—one thing. It is real conviction which is, I think the "one thing" lacked by so many people; they are interested, they are sympathetic, they are fairly well informed, but they cannot say "I know." Now I said quite enough last Sunday of a negative sort; tonight, I hope I shall be as positive as can be. What do we know? I hope you will bear in mind that I should be happier on this subject with three hours not 20 minutes.

What Is the Fundamental Christian Conviction?

Here is the answer the New Testament gives which was proclaimed forcefully and continually by Martin Luther, John Wesley and a million less known persons. It is not easy to put it in a single sentence but perhaps this will do. The God who did such great things for us in Christ is utterly and absolutely to be trusted. Let us talk about that for a little while and then come to the point again. The blind man in our story was quite willing to confess his ignorance about a lot of things. There are a lot of Christians we would like a lot better if they were equally modest. Don't you always feel a little uncomfortable when you hear some of our enthusiastic brothers and sisters proclaiming exactly when our Lord will come with the clouds of heaven? Don't you share my revulsion for someone who can give you a neat mechanical theory of the atonement, explaining in half a dozen glib sentences the ineffable mystery of Christ's death? And to take a different set of people, are you not suspicious of those who have a cast iron plan for the reorganization of society on Christian principles? It would do many of us no harm to confess our ignorance of the unknowable.

So, our blind man is ready to say he can't really explain who Jesus is. In this chapter, we find him gradually learning more and more about him, but here he admits that he doesn't know. Nor does he know just exactly what Jesus has done to him. It must have been a bewildering process to the blind man. He knows only this: that on account of Jesus, because of what Jesus has done, his whole relationship to life is different. Moreover, his human relationships have taken on a different alignment. There is no avoiding the facts. The religious leaders are distinctly unpleasant to him; even his own parents are scared and suspicious. In place of that, he will at first and at last hear no evil of Jesus, and in the end, comes to set his faith in Him.

Now let us turn back to our main theme. Our primary Christian affirmation is that God has done something for us in Christ, and by that "something" he is known. It is, I think, right and proper that people should use such brainpower as they have in explaining what was done; but the explanations will always be far short of the facts. Somehow God's love broke into the wheeling fabric of stellar space, settled upon our planet, and out of our kind of evil, made possible the great release. Christ died on Calvary and explain it how you will (or don't explain it at all) human life thereafter was never the same. The balance was changed. Not that the world was wiped clean as a slate with a wet rag. It was not so simple as that. There exists an illustration that is not a bad one, but perhaps one may use this.

Just four years ago was fought the battle of Britain. The R.A.F. won it. It didn't end the war. There remained even four years to go. The German armies were still to march nearly to Moscow. We were still to be called on to spend blood, sweat, and tears. But there was something decisive about the battle of Britain. So here, the decisive battle has been won; even though the blood, sweat, and tears of Christians are needed yet. Now what a Christian knows is that this is true, and because it is true, God is to be trusted and loved, and trusting and loving God makes a difference to life, to all its human relations, to its whole appearance. That is what being a Christian means. This is the glorious privilege that is open to you. God knows you and loves you with an everlasting love, that is true whatever you do about it. If you will take him at his word and trust him, for life and for death, it will change life, as so many of you know.

If our love were but more simple,
We should take Him at His word;
And our lives would be all sunshine
In the sweetness of our Lord. (F. W. Faber)

It really means waking up to the reality of the love God has for you. As I wrote this, this came into my mind (memory is a queer thing), a story I read fifteen years ago, in my old school magazine. I don't know who wrote it but it really is not bad. Two men were looking for a lost tribe of people in the Pyrenees and to their surprise, found them. They found themselves caught in a unique mountain fortress that offered no escape. Pillars of fire threatened them. All around was a precipice and a canyon thousands of feet deep. There was no escape. Then one accidentally knocked a pebble over the edge and the sound showed only a little drop. That removed their fear and set them investigating. What looked like fiery pillars were cold and clammy stalactites. They clamored down the precipice, all of ten feet. They leapt a mighty river, a stream of a few feet. How many people live in a world like that? A world of false fears and apparent dangers that aren't real dangers. I don't criticize them, I'm sorry for them. "One thing I know, I can see!" Put your trust in God and see how much of the care and trouble of life is lifted. I will quote again a text I have often quoted before, it is one of the keystones to life for me—"casting all your cares upon Him, for he cares for you." He cared enough to die for you, can you not trust him with your cares? There are two consequences of this which I want to mention very briefly.

This "One Thing" Co-ordinates All Our Other Knowledge

Don't think that the Christian who says "one thing I know" is shutting his eyes to the rest of life. It is like the fact that John Wesley called himself once, *homo unius libri* referring to the Bible. Actually, he probably read as many books as any person in the 18th century. What he meant was that the Bible gave him the standpoint from which he understood everything else—including all other books. So it is here. By all means let us know and love and be interested in all other sorts of thing. But this one thing, if you are really sure of it, will give us our standing ground.

The Christian sees a lot of things that other people cannot see and know. You remember Saul Kane in Mansfield's "[The] Everlasting Mercy"—"the shorter brook, to my new eyes, was bubbling out of Paradise" and so on. The Christian can go out in nature and see God's loving care of his creatures, and he can go about the world of human beings and know them all as his brothers in Christ, and so indeed he must know them. He sees too the things everyone else sees, and he can understand and know them as no one else can. He too can see the bombed cities and the bloody battlefields of Europe. But behind them he sees no mere psychological necessity of fighting, no mere economic determinism, he sees the immense rebellion of humankind against God, and sees behind it the patient suffering love of God and therefore he knows and understands as no one else can do. He sees the pleasant things of life too, as everyone else does, home and friends and books and music and art; the joy of work and games. And he can understand them too because he is grateful to God for them, and does not so enjoy them as to forget the Giver. The Christian is not like Nelson at the Battle of Copenhagen making use of his blind eye to disregard something he did not want to see "He clapped his glass to his sightless eye, and I'm damned if I see it" he said. Our knowledge of God means not the disregarding but the understanding of everything else. Lastly,

This "One Thing I Know" Involves "One Thing I Do."

Years ago, when I was taking Cambridge scholarships, my headmaster said to me "you know it must be 'one thing I do.'" He was dead right about scholarships. You don't get them any other way. But do you think a boy who wasn't really keen on his subject, and keen on going to the University could take it? Could cut out so much of what a boy enjoys? So here. It is no good expecting service where there is no motive. And, the other way around, real strong motive will find its way out. You remember what St. John says "if a person claims to love God and doesn't love people, he's just a liar." The New Testament doesn't mince its words. The Christian way, you will understand this, is a way of absolute rest, and of unresting service. It is rest because it is faith, and faith means you cast your care upon God, you rest on him—the sin and wrong, the "experience" or the lack of it are his show entirely, and it is service, service in a life poured out absolutely unto death, unstinting, unreserved, spending and being spent, because—because what less can the servants of Christ do, who gave himself for us?

"The Way the Truth and the Life"— John 14:6

[Preached thirty-four times between 6/29/41 at S.H.M. to 7/5/70 at Cockfield Camp Meeting]

Jesus was talking to a rather slow and stupid set of men. He was about to leave them; his work with them was finished. And still they were asking all the wrong questions and revealing a quite exceptional inability to see what he was driving at. Most of them were frankly puzzled by him. They did not know what to make of him and they did not know where he was leading them. But in spite of this bewilderment, there they were. When he called, they had left all they had and followed him and they had stuck to him. There was something about him that would not let them go. And some of them at least had made up their minds to stay with him even if it meant dying with him.

Many of us are in a position not unlike that, for this same Jesus is still collecting followers. He stands in our 20th century world as he stood in the first century world, and calls people to himself. And he is still a stranger, still a puzzle. He is no more at home in our world than he was in that world. He refused to be fitted easily into our conventional standards, to be fitted into our pigeonholes. And there is none of us who will fairly look at Jesus who does not know that his presence means some sort of challenge, and provokes some sort of decision. He must have some meaning, some significance for our world, for ourselves. But what is it? Can he ever be more than a strange, perplexing figure outside ourselves? Shall we ever get further than the blundering disciples? Therefore, we take his own words to them—"I am the way, the truth, and the life." And we may take them one by one.

The Way

And let us say at once that unless the world will speedily get a little nearer that way we are all together on the merry road to Hell, and it won't be long before we get there. Of course, there are other ways. We have tried a good many of them. Christianity is not one of the ways that have been tried and found wanting. It is a way that has always looked difficult and has been left untried. And for lack of it the world is perishing. I don't think that is an exaggerated or pessimistic view.[1]

What is the way of Jesus? It was this same Jesus who said that the first commandment was love God, and second was love your neighbor. And that sounds disappointingly feeble and elementary. We have heard it before, we have made jokes about it, we have even made a song of it. We want a bigger, more definite, more vital tougher thing than that. Very well. Remember that Jesus did not say he was teaching the way, he said that he was the way. If we are to know what it really means, we must look at him, and it might be well to do that before we are so quick with our criticism.

First of all, it was not for him a soft, easy way. Jesus had a good, comfortable job, as a carpenter. And he gave it up for uncertainty, for homelessness, for loneliness and poverty. His loving of people and of God meant in the end that he was ready to die for us and in faithfulness to God. He went through with his way, his way of love, and that was the end of it. Not so soft and easy as we thought. Nor again so unpractical either, for after all if there is nothing else to show, there is at least the Christian Church, still looking back to him, still confessing its loyalty to him and still trying as best it can to spread the same truth. It is not for nothing that one of the earliest names for Christianity was "the Way." It is a way that can still be followed. There is nothing more definite, concrete than Christian love, nothing which can get more done in the world.

About 30 years ago, there was a boy in a Lancashire town. He was very poor, and his home was the most miserable of places. In his spare time, he used to sell newspapers. Sometimes it rained and people hurried past and did not want a paper, and he would creep into the shelter of a doorway to get out of the rain a little. And as he sat on the damp stone, he would review

---

1   Editor's Note: There is marked out here from the original sermon a paragraph about the Socialist exhibition in Cambridge and their confident proclamation that a New World Order was forming. It was used to contrast with Jesus' way, and the implication in regard to such bold claims was that "this too will pass."

the placards he carried and take out a pencil and draw. It was always the same thing he drew, plans of buildings, buildings where boys like himself could go and find home and find friends and happiness—and Christ. Then he went away to war and came back with many of his dreams broken; but one was still there. He went to London and started work. He started with six boys in a cellar. When a policeman appeared, they were off in a flash. But it went on, it grew into the place he dreamed of. A place where lonely and wretched boys and girls would exchange their miserable existence of their filthy homes for real living. That particular piece of Christian love is no more. It was bombed out on May 10th. But that is not the end of the story. There is another "New Order" to put over against Hitler's. But all this is only scratching the surface of what the text means. For Jesus is the way to God. And that is not the end but the starting point of all we do. Because Jesus brings us to God, he is—

The Truth

Years ago, as an unhappy man lay dying he said "I have not understood the world, and the world has not understood me." Curiously enough, that man claimed to be the Pope of Rome, but he was not a Christian, or at least, since it is not our business to judge him, if he was a Christian he had not received from God all that was due him.

"I have not understood the world." There are not a few people who have to say that. The world is too big, too complicated, too contradictory for them to make sense of it. And some of them go further and say it is not our fault if we don't understand it—there just isn't any sense in it to see. The whole thing is a blind ugly machine, like those automatic men one has read of in stories, which get out of order and out of control and go about looking like human beings but performing the most outrageous acts of appalling and senseless cruelty.

Is that all that life is? Just a series of events of incessant sorrow, interspersed with odd moments of equally unreasonable happiness? Is the world just a mad, sadistic monster? Is history just one darn thing after another? Or is there a way of understanding it? Is there truth behind it, and a way of getting at that truth? Jesus said "I am the truth." Again, you will notice, not "I teach the truth," though of course he did, but "I am the truth." Jesus is the truth about the world, about life, about history because he is the truth about God. The world does not make sense of itself because by itself it is incomplete. History does not make sense by itself, because by itself it is without its own key. It is only God who can make sense of the world and of life.

And the truth which Jesus brought is that God has given us the meaning of life not by abolishing or explaining away its sorrows and troubles nor by taking his people out of themselves by a mystic rapture, but by himself coming into them and using them for his own purposes. The evil of the world has a meaning—it has a meaning in relation to God. Its meaning appears in the Cross of Christ, where it is shown to be the world's attempt to get rid of God, and to live for itself. And God's meaning for the world is that by his presence he can turn its evil into good, that he can turn a Cross into a resurrection, that he can take humanity's darkest deed and use it for our own redemption; that he can still cause the wrath of human beings to praise him.

And it is because of Jesus that we see the mind and movement of God which turns chaos into order, which gives meaning and purpose to our lives. It is through him that we know that we stand within the plan and purpose of God. Through him we know that even when we least understand his ways, God has set his love upon us and chosen us for his own purposes. He is the way to God, and so the way by which we find reconciliation to God, and reconciliation with life. Through him we even become sharers in God's plans, fellow-workers with God. That leads to the last point.

The Life

Cycling between Cambridge and Birmingham I passed a spot which is reputed to be the center of England. And now we have got to the center of Christian faith. Jesus is the life. He not only shows us how to live, and how to understand life, he is the life. That is the center and core of it all. That is the spring from which all the rest flows. That is what the disciples found eventually, that is what the Church has been testing and asserting for 1900 years. Jesus is the life of humankind, he refills us with power to do the work to which he calls us. There is no higher thing to say.

But to go back to my cycling journey, when I reached that point it was about 4 p.m., the sun was still high in the heavens. I was very hot, very dusty, and very thirsty. There was nothing on earth I wanted so much as a cup of tea. I stopped at one place that advertised teas, but they no longer made teas. I went a little further, the same answer. At last I found a place. It was a rather dirty, disreputable looking little pub, but it had some tea and bread and butter; it had a table and a chair. So, I'm very grateful to it and I'm not going to say anything against it. But I'm going to say something against this.

There are some of us who are within reach of the center of Christianity, of Christ's life, and we are content to sit in the filth and squalor of our own disreputable lives. I know of course that our lives look a lot more respectable than that. But appearances are not much to go by. You often see tobacco shops nowadays with a great pile of cigarette boxes in the windows. You go inside and ask for cigarettes. "Cigarettes, oh no, we haven't any cigarettes." And the window of course is full of dummies, just dummies. There is no reality behind them. They are a sham, they pretend to be what they are not.

In Scott's novel *Ivanhoe,* one or two try their hand at being fake friars, monks. It is quite easy. You mumble a few appropriate Latin phrases, you cover your head with a monk's cowl, and you can deceive the world. We don't use Latin phrases but there are plenty of choice phrases in English that will do. We go to Church and Sunday School, and all the time we are like a set of people who come off pretty badly in the New Testament, those who keep up religion as a form, but have nothing to do with it as a power.

It's not good enough. "Martin Niemoller in a conversation I had with him 5 months before his arrest on July 1 1937, insisted that the life of a Christian was life with an obligation. To the National Socialists, he said their National Socialism was a primary obligation and all other things were secondary; but he remarked that too many church people were lukewarm and put other things first, while their churchmanship was secondary."—George Kennedy Allen Bell, *Christianity and World Order* p. 144.

Let us get out of the foxholes we have dug for ourselves around the real center of Christianity. Let us accept for ourselves the offer of life. As he gives us power, let us live for him and for his Church. Let us serve him and let us die for him, if he should call us to do so. If we really know him we shall not need to be called upon to do so, it will follow inevitably. For he is the way, the truth, and the life. Must we then live forever at this poor dying rate?

"St. Philip and St. James"—John 14:8-9

[Preached twice once at Darlington Synod 5/1/91 and 5/1/94 at Bishop Auckland]

When the chairman asked me to preach at this service, my first reaction was to take out my diary to see what excuse I had for absence from this year's synod. Unfortunately, the space in the diary was empty. I had not yet got down to that important task. The space, that is, was empty of any entry by me. The diary itself reminded me that May 1 is one of those days which the church calendar devotes not to one saint but to two. It is the day of St. Philip and St. James. There is one other such day, on October 28th we celebrate St. Simon and St. Jude. And, of course, I remembered that hymn (not a Methodist one, so perhaps ecumenical, though it has failed to gain a place in Hymns and Psalms) and I believe I quoted it to the chairman: "Let us emulate the names of St. Philip and St. James, let us try to be as good as St. Simon and St. Jude." This of course is a joke. But the time came when something had to be prepared for this service, and the question occurred to me, why not take it seriously?[1]

St. Philip and St. James were doubtless good men, why not emulate them? At least why not learn from them? So we have two texts, but you will not get them both at once but seriatim. I had no doubt about St. Philip— John 14.8-9: "Philip says unto him, Lord, show us the Father and that will suffice." Jesus says to him, "Have I been with you so long, and yet have you not known me Philip? He that has seen me has seen the Father."

---

1   Editor's Note: American Methodists may be surprised to find British Methodists observing saints' days, as they may assume that British Methodism is more low church and a-liturgical than many American Methodist Churches. This generalization however is not entirely true, and much depends on what sort of Methodist Church one is in, both in the U.K. and in America.

"So long"—how long? It depends of course on what you make of the chronology of the ministry of Jesus. One year? Two? Three? Three years anyway is a maximum for Philip's discipleship. I have been at it far longer. I became a member of the Methodist Church, and I hope that has something to do with discipleship, in 1933; quite a long time ago. Yet I find myself asking the same question. It was not that Philip did not believe in God, of course he did. How could he be a first century Jew and not believe in God? I believe in God too. I have had some sort of theological education and probably believe more things about God than Philip did—the Trinity and so forth. Philip was not asking to be convinced that God existed. He wanted to be shown the Father, to have some sort of direct unmistakable apprehension of God. It is what religious people have always wanted, and some of them, I suppose, have had. And others of us, plain, unmystical people wonder wistfully what we are missing. I say "some of us" in hopes that there may be one or two others, in addition to me, and that looking at Philip may help us.

But Philip got a rough answer. This we are apt to miss because we do not expect Jesus to answer like that. But he does say some hard things in this Gospel. And here he says to Philip, "you'd better be content with what you've got, because you aren't going to get any more. If you have seen me, and obviously you have, you have got all there is, you have seen all there is to see. He that has seen me has seen the Father. How can you say—Show me the Father?"

Philip has seen and heard, I take up the language of John 14, the deeds and the words, the ἔργα and the ῥήματα, and these are of course the deeds and the words as they appear in this Gospel. There is no need to go in for historical criticism; this is the apostolic testimony to Jesus. This is what is meant and this is what we have. And this should suffice, though there is no verification and no credentials are presented. These were those who saw and heard, and there are millions who have read the testimony and found no trace of the Father—do not even believe that he exists. But—"he that has seen me has seen the Father." He that has detected in that figure goodness and truth, he that has taken up his cross and followed. . . .

I have never yet met anyone who has read what to me is the most profound theological novel I have ever read, and first rate entertainment into the bargain. It is Chesterton's *The Man Who Was Thursday.* I don't know how to summarize what it says, but I want somehow to share it with you. The anarchists are threatening to overthrow civilization. To fight them, the poet Syme infiltrates their high council. Its leader is Sunday, and every other conspirator bears the name of a day of the week. Syme is Thursday. It is of the highest importance that he should conceal the fact that he is a police-man in disguise.

Syme's commissioning to his task has been surprising. The chief of oper-ations he met in total darkness. He heard his voice but could see nothing. "But I am really not fit. . . ." "You are willing, that is enough," says the masked man. "Well really," said Syme, "I don't know any profession of which mere willingness is the final test." "I do," says the other, "martyr. I am sentencing you to death. Good day."[2] Then came the meeting with Sunday and the rest of the anarchists. But the story unfolds with the discovery that all of them—Monday through Saturday were policemen in disguise. They set out in search of Sunday, the one anarchist. They find he is the voice in the dark-ness, the power that sent them out.

"I sat in the darkness where there is no visible thing and to you I was only a voice, commanding valor and an unnatural virtue. You heard the voice in the dark, and you never heard it again. The sun in heaven denied it, the earth and the sky denied it, all human wisdom denied it, and when I met you in the daylight, I denied it myself."

"I see everything," Syme cried, "everything that there is. Why does each thing on the earth war against each other thing? Why does each small thing in the world have to fight against the world itself? Why does a fly have to fight the whole universe? Why does a dandelion have to fight the whole universe? For the same reason that I had to be alone in the dreadful Council of the Days. So that each thing that obeys law may have the glory and isola-tion of the anarchist. So that each man fighting for order may be as brave and good a man as the dynamiter. . . ."

"It is not true that we have never been broken. We have been broken upon the wheel. It is not true that we have never descended from these thrones. We have descended into hell. . . . " "Have you," he cried in a dreadful voice, "have you ever suffered?"

"As he gazed, the great face grew to an awful size, grew larger than the colossal mask of Memnon, which had made him scream as a child. It grew larger and larger, filling the whole sky; then everything went black. Only in the blackness before it entirely destroyed his brain he seemed to hear a dis-tant voice saying a commonplace text that he had heard somewhere, "Can ye drink of the cup that I drink of?"

2   This is C. K. Barrett's rephrasing of a passage in Chesterton, *The Man Who Was Thursday.*

Why go on telling tales? Paul has it all in plain language. "We walk by faith, not by sight, carrying around in ourselves the killing of Jesus." And all I am saying, Philip is saying, to myself and perhaps to a few others is, the doubts, the loneliness, the fears, the disappointments, the rejections, the defeats, the despair, that can mark all Christian living at its greatest depth, and somehow focus themselves on the ministry, have beneath and above them the peace that passes understanding and are the way to creative life. The summons you have heard in the darkness sustains you.

It is time, and the right time for James to come in. There really isn't much to choose for James. I could go back to "can you drink of the cup which I drink of?" Instead I will go to its fulfillment. Herod the king, killed James the brother of John with the sword. And though you may not think much of the hermeneutics of this, I am reading that as a word to those for whom the ministry has not fallen out as they hoped and expected that it would. Did James hear the words—"You will be my witnesses in Judaea, and Samaria and to the ends of the earth" and imagine himself sharing in a great world-wide evangelistic mission, founding churches in Italy and Gaul and Spain— even in Britain? Well probably not, but did he think that in the year 43 A.D. he would be gone? Of course, he had had a pretty good hint—"you will drink my cup, and be baptized with my baptism, but what I cannot promise is the best seats in the kingdom." But it didn't happen to his brother John (unless you are among those that embrace the conjectured emendation to Acts 12, but we will discuss that another time). Why should it happen to him? The ministry he dreamed of in Galilee when he responded to the call of Jesus and undertook to become a fisher of human beings, was not to happen. The dream fizzled out, ended with an executioner's sword.

I suspect most of us have dreams of what the ministry is going to be. I don't mean we think we are going to be President of the Conference. Anyone who dreamed of that would need to have his vocation examined, and have his head examined too. But we do dream of a full effective ministry, of some, of hundreds, won to the faith, built up in the life of holiness and love, and we spend God knows how much time filling in the forms, attending the committees, raising the funds, keeping the same old wheels barely turning around. I am not defending all this. It may be right to fling down the gauntlet and say "Down with the administration, let the thing administer itself." I am simply saying this—I don't think James liked having his head cut off. I don't think it is what he would have chosen. But it made him the supreme kind of witness—the martyr, μάρτυς, the witness *par excellence*. And there are ministers flogging away at the jobs they didn't really want to do who are superior witnesses to the truth of the Gospel.

I cannot think that I shall ever again preach at such a service as this, and I can only hope that you will forgive me for taking this opportunity to speak for my odd position, inside the ministry and yet in a sense outside it too, to my brothers and sister who are real ministers, circuit ministers, to speak a word of intense admiration and I hope of encouragement. There is Philip, there is James, Philip who longs for a more intense, a more personal awareness of God than he has, and gets the reply that he must keep his eye on Jesus, Jesus who calls the unlikely, and not only calls them but disciples them, and so he does what he is told and goes through his ministry looking unto Jesus, the author and finisher of faith. James who finds out that his ministry turns out to be a bit different than he expected, but giving his life for Christ becomes the supreme witness. "Let us emulate the names, of St. Philip and St. James."

"To Us Not to the World"—
John 14:22-23

[Preached nineteen times from 4/22/73 at Langley Park to 3/14/96 at Coxhoe]

Judas was puzzled, and well he might be. It was hard enough to take in the fact that the Messiah must be humiliated and suffer before coming to his glory, but after that surely, the moment of glory will come. All will see him shining in his true colors, dazzling all beholders as he descends in triumph on the clouds of heaven. He may have lived a life of humble obscurity on earth, but then the whole world would see him. But now Judas has to learn that even after crucifixion, there is to be no largescale manifestation of Jesus to the whole world but only to the little group of disciples. "Why?" he asks. "How is it that you intend to manifest yourself to us and not to the world?"

We know that this is how it did happen. On the whole, it was two little groups that Jesus manifested himself at the first Easter. There was Mary in the garden, and Peter. There was the two at Emmaus. There was (so Paul tells us), James. There were the ten without Thomas, and the eleven when he was present. The one exception was the group of 500 to whom Jesus appeared, but even this was very different from a manifestation to the world.

Judas has a real question—Why not to the world? Why not put them all in their place, stagger them with a show of power that would once for all put right the tragedy of the cross? What is the answer to this question? It is all embedded in the paragraph in John, but for convenience we will take it to pieces and look at it in parts. First, it is God's way to deal with human beings—

As Individuals and Not in the Mass

"He who loves me shall be loved by my Father; and I will love him and manifest myself to him. . . . If anyone loves me, he will keep my word." Of course, we can imagine a wholescale manifestation of the risen victorious Jesus to masses of people; it is easy to imagine this, because it is the way we should have worked the business ourselves. Indeed, it is the way that from time to time Christians have sought to work it out, and the story of Christianity is littered with the record of mass conversions which have, for the most part, been worth nothing at all. The King decided to adopt the new faith, and thereafter all his subjects adopted it too—or else. This is a carryover from secular life. There, almost inevitably, it is the method we practice, in political and in economic life. The candidate for parliament or local government may do a bit of door to door canvassing in the fortnight before the election, but I have yet to meet one who kept it up afterwards, though some of the best do make themselves available to individual constituents. They are part of a big machine. An employer will deal with a union rather than with individuals. Demonstrations, as we call them, are demonstrations of the masses for the masses.

This is the way we adopt, it was not, and it is not Jesus' way. True, he preached to thousands of people, but preaching that is real preaching is not mass communication, as the Holy Spirit takes the divine Word and applies it to heart and mind. Could anyone claim that it would have been in character for Jesus to climb up on the Temple roof and cry out to the crowds in Jerusalem "Look at me! Here I am—I've won!" But it was in character for him to seek out one weeping woman, and say "Mary, Mary don't you know me? It's not the gardener, it's me." This was the same old Jesus, a supernatural showman might have been very impressive, but it would not have been Jesus.

Note what John says—"he who loves me." Love is an individual thing, a relation between persons. We talk sometimes about loving humankind or the destitute and poor and what we mean is very proper and creditable, but I question whether it is a proper use of the word love. I doubt whether I can love humanity in the abstract; I can love X and Y and Z. So Jesus says "he who loves me . . . I will manifest myself to him." And it is love that counts. Jesus does not say "he who believes everything in the Athanasian creed, or he who belongs to a church with the apostolic succession, or he who can recite the Bible from cover to cover, or he who is of perfect rectitude and purity." He says "he who loves me." Read it in its context: "He who in the life that I have lived sees something he can recognize as utterly right and good, even though like the Twelve he may be in many ways a failure in following, he who looks at Jesus as he was and is and says 'that is the man for me'; he is the man to whom the risen Lord will manifest himself, the man who in the crowd will say with doubting Thomas—'my Lord, and my God.'"

Of course this love is not a sloppy affection—"if a person loves me he will keep my word. He will take seriously what I have said and practice it." But we shall come back to this later. For the present, the point is this—the manifestation of the risen Jesus is an individual thing, it must be because it is made in the context of love.[1] We can develop this in a second part of the answer—

It Is Not God's Way to Coerce

Logically it amounts to this. If God had been intending to coerce all human beings into accepting the risen Jesus by a manifestation of unmistakable supernatural power, he might have saved himself the trouble and pain of the Incarnation. Why go through all the motions of the ministry of Jesus if in the end all people were to be dragooned by main force into the right camp?

Practically, and that is not quite the same as logically, you cannot coerce the love we have just been talking about. As I write this, a pleasing memory comes into my mind from the distant past. It must have been in 1938 that the plans for the Cambridge Evangelistic Campaign fell through, and some of us joined in an Oxford mission in Stafford. I remember how we teased a huge and very gentle rowing blue, 14 or 15 stone of him, as he stood on a soapbox and brandished a huge fist in the face of the crowd, declaring with the greatest vigor, "my friends this is a Gospel of love." He knew, I am sure, as well as any of us, that you cannot make people love by shaking your fist at them. You cannot coerce love. If ever God tried it, the response would not be love.

I do not mean that the time will never come when God will draw a line under the sum, and bring the patient process to an end. But Easter means that the pleading with people, the waiting for the response of love that

---

1   Editor's Note: I think this claim can be made without exception if we are talking about first appearances. It seems the later appearances of the risen Jesus could involve considerable groups, but the first ones were to Mary, and a couple of other women, to Simon, to James, to his inner circle, and lastly to Paul. The appearances to the 500 or all the apostles, seem to have been secondary events.

marked the ministry of Jesus, goes on and is extended to cover all persons of all ages and places. "We love," said John in the First Epistle, "because he first loved us." Our love is a response. God's love is not. It is as Anders Nygren said, uncaused, unmotivated love; or as Charles Wesley said "he hath loved, he hath loved us because he would love." There is no charm, no attractiveness to elicit his love. But ours is response. And it is in some respects the supreme miracle of Easter that the response is still possible and the offer is still open. "Well" we might say, "I gave him his chance, I was willing to be friends, but he wouldn't have it, so I have finished with him now." How natural and how common. But it is not the way God asked. God could have, on Good Friday, closed the offer with a bang. But Easter means the offer of love stands open yet; "and he who loves me shall be loved by my Father, and I will love him, and will manifest myself to him." This still open offer leads us to a third and last point—

A New Way of Manifesting Himself to the World

"How is it," said Judas, "that you will manifest yourself to us and not to the world?" Henceforth he will confine his attention to the sweet selected few. The world has made its bed and now it can lie in it. But that is not true. As we have seen the whole story of Easter cries out against it. For Easter perpetuates and expands the love of Jesus for the world. What then? There is to be, for the present, no wonderful manifestation of the Son of Man riding on the clouds of heaven; no mass conversion of the human race by the compulsion of supernatural splendor. But that does not mean that God no longer loves the world he sent his Son to save. He has not washed his hands of it. He has found a new means of manifesting himself; he will do it through those who love him.

Turn over a few pages to John 17 and you will read the at first surprising words "I do not pray for the world." What??? Does Jesus not care for the mass of humanity? Is he only interested in the pious few, the people of his own generation? No for you go on to read his prayer for those who will believe through the disciple's word. He cannot pray for the world because the only hope for the world is that it should stop being the world. But he prays for those who convey his message to the world.

In the same way, he does not manifest himself to the world, but to those who love him he commits his word, and they in the power of the Spirit are his witnesses to the world. This is our share, and I do not forget that this is not only Easter but Church Anniversary on Easter. It is not where Easter begins, it is not where Easter began. It began with Jesus coming to his own, and then were the disciples glad when they saw the Lord. But very soon it turns to this. "As the Father sent me, even so I send you." Out of the Church's Easter faith and joy springs the Church's mission, the very existence of the Church and its mission is proof that Jesus is alive.

For us too, Easter begins between ourselves and Christ; "if anyone loves me, I will manifest myself to him." Not to all persons in the same way, but to each in his own proper way. But this [is] not where Easter ends. Each of us leaves this place as a fragment of the Easter message. The love that is kindled and nourished, the word, the message that Jesus gives us, we carry away as our share of manifesting Christ to the world. "He that has my commandments and keeps them, he it is that loves me." And the all-embracing commandment he had just given was the commandment to love, and of it he had said "by this shall all people know that you are my disciples, if you have love for one another." "If anyone loves me he will keep my word," the word is the message and it is the sort of thing you keep by giving it away. So, Jesus asks us as he asked Peter, not a theological examination question, but simply "Do you love me?" And to those who can say some sort of yes, comes the Easter message—"not to the world, but to us, and then to the world through us."

"Grief, Joy, and a Little While"— John 6:19-22

[Preached six times from 1/30/83 at Elvet until it appeared in the Methodist Recorder in 2000][1]

It is doubtful I would be preaching on this text this morning if I had not been asked to do so, because it marks today's stage in a course that you, or some of you are following at Elvet in your Bible study. Not of course that it is in any way an improper text; quite the reverse of that. It is found in Holy Scriptures and in what has often been described as a Holy of Holies within Holy Scripture, for it is part of John's account of Jesus' last evening with his disciples before his death, chapters which contain some of the most profound things we have in the New Testament. But I hesitate a bit over these verses, and I think I know why.

For one thing, I am a bit hesitant about the image that stands at the center of the text and is the cue of your Bible study. It is one that no one can really enter into. He may know it, of course, from the outside, especially if he is a husband and a father. We know that child birth is normally attended by pain and that normally it is followed by an infinite satisfaction. We have seen the look on the mother's face. But from within—that's a closed book.

That is only the initial problem. What does the image refer to? There is embarrassment there too. Here are puzzled disciples: "What is this 'little while' of which he speaks, during which we will not see him? We don't know what he's talking about." They were soon to discover it. Within a few hours, Jesus was taken away from them in death. A couple of days later, he was with them again. So, the most obvious meaning of grief and a little while and then the inalienable joy is simply Easter. Death and resurrection.

---

1   Editor's Note: As the note in the notebook says, this is a rewrite of an earlier sermon on the same text.

The three sad days are quickly sped;
he rises glorious from the dead.
All glory to our risen Head.
Alleluia! (F. Pott translator of old Latin hymn)

That is not all. Another meaning lurks within this, brought out in the surrounding chapters. After the resurrection Jesus was again with his disciples. But then "I ascend to my Father and your Father, to my God and your God." Here was a new separation, a time in which the disciples would no longer see Jesus. But again, after a little while they would see him again. At the end of this, the Son of Man would come and every eye would behold him.

There is, I think, no doubt that these two things are in mind here—resurrection and return. And are they not an embarrassment? What happened at the resurrection? What became of his body? Where is the body now? It's hardly open for you to say—somewhere up in the sky. In what sense is Jesus alive? The second coming is even more embarrassing. Can we really expect to see Jesus, the Son of Man, coming with the clouds of heaven? It is perhaps easier today than at some times in the past to believe that history will come to an end in a cataclysm that destroys the great globe itself, but a nuclear explosion would be a very horrific end and not at all what the New Testament has in mind. And in any case, in 1983, we have gotten a long way beyond "a little while" of John 16. The travail pain has been going on for an inconceivable while.

I said embarrassment, and you know why. We find these things embarrassing, because we cannot explain them, and it is always embarrassing, especially to a don, to have to admit that there are things he cannot explain. But embarrassment is not the last word of the New Testament would think of using about the resurrection or the return of Christ. Quite the reverse. They both meant victory, life. And whatever the explanation may be, they were right about the resurrection, so they may well be right about the rest too. You remember Swinburne's "Thou hast conquered, O pale Galilean; / the world has grown grey from thy breath; / We have drunken of things Lethean, and fed on the fullness of death" (Hymn to Proserpine).

Pale! Gray! It would be hard to think of a greater historical inaccuracy. Of course, the Church, we, have often made a muck of things, but even so the burst of life into the world that springs from the resurrection cannot be hidden. There was no pale grayness but a many splendored color. It was a fulfillment of Ezekiel's prophecy. Everything shall live wherever the river, this river comes. And whether or not you care or wish to picture the Parousia, to know that history is not in the hands of the Hitler of 50 years ago but in the hands of Christ, that he will reign wherever the sun does his successive journeys run, that the kingdoms of this world shall become the Kingdom of God and of his Christ . . . embarrassment! What a joke! But what has the New Testament to say to us about this? Your study notes point expressly to the theme of—

New Birth

But we must see how we got there and what it means. I think I detect a logical defect in the notes. The passage before us compares the disciples to a woman who passes through a period of pain into a time of joy; it does not compare them to the baby that is born after this process. For a long time, this gave me some hesitation about taking this text and this theme. I am not here to defend bad logic, but we will do the best we can.

Let us note two things. John does elsewhere speak explicitly about the new birth. "Unless a person is born anew from above, he shall not see the Kingdom of God." "Unless a person be born of water and the Spirit he shall not enter the Kingdom of God." Undoubtedly we have here a Johannine, a Christian, theme. The second thing to note is this—in the image, indeed in the whole passage John is using Old Testament language.

> Before she goes into labor,
> she gives birth;
> before the pains come upon her,
> she delivers a son.
> Who has ever heard of such things?
> Who has ever seen things like this?
> Can a country be born in a day
> or a nation be brought forth in a moment?
> Yet no sooner is Zion in labor
> than she gives birth to her children.
> Do I bring to the moment of birth
> and not give delivery?" says the Lord.
> "Do I close up the womb
> when I bring to delivery?" says your God.
> "Rejoice with Jerusalem and be glad for her,

all you who love her;
rejoice greatly with her,
all you who mourn over her.
For you will nurse and be satisfied
at her comforting breasts;
you will drink deeply
and delight in her overflowing abundance." (Isa. 66:7-11)

You will remember, some of you, how Brahms puts these words together, with perfect rightness. The theological point is this. Language used for the end of time is brought into the midst of time. The resurrection of Jesus was not a happy incident in an unfortunate series of events, the lifting for a moment of the clouds that had hung over the lonely disciples. Nor is the other world, the age to come merely the promise of pie in a remote sky. The restoration of all things has begun in the restoration of human lives. The resurrection of Jesus not only puts right the story of Jesus, it puts us right too. Tennyson speaks of "one far off divine event towards which the whole creation moves" (In Memoriam A. H. H.). There is truth in that. It depicts the world moving like a railway train along its track. But the picture is inadequate. This is a fantastic railway and the terminus is flying madly towards the train, and already you can get a book from the station bookstall, here it is, and a meal of bread and wine from the station buffet.

It is not my fault that the metaphors get so mixed, and with so many of them about, it can do us no harm to say that this means for the believing participant a new birth. Another embarrassment? Some of us at least react against the expression "born again Christian." Yet there are no Christians except born again ones. We have already heard John say so. The question is what born again means. Birth means a start in life, and born again means a new starting point, and that can make all the difference.

In a month's time my wife and I are going to Australia, generously provided with around the world tickets. The airlines make play in there advertisments; go where you like, stop when you like, stay as long as you like. And it sounds splendid until you work it out. Then, if you want to get there, you can't start here you'll have to start somewhere else. So it is in life. If you are to get back to the right goal, you'll have to start in the right place and this is it. There is far more to say about this. Read Wesley's sermon "On the New Birth," but this must do for today. This is where you start.

Christian Grief

You therefore now have sorrow, but you must be clear what this is. It is not grief for Christ in his suffering. The time for that is the first Good Friday and the Saturday that followed. Since then, it is out of place. I hope the new hymn book is dropping this hymn.

> O come and mourn with me awhile;
> O come ye to the Savior's side;
> O come, together let us mourn;
> Jesus, our Love, is crucified. (F. W. Faber)

Much better is . . .

> Weep not Him who onward bears
> His cross to Calvary;
> He does not ask man's pitying tears,
> Who wills for man to die. (T. B. Pollock)

On the grand scale, you will find things done properly in J. S. Bach's "St. Matthew Passion." Here the story of the Passion is simply told in Matthean words. The narrative is interspersed with comments, some as it were put into contemporary bystanders, others the remarks of the Christian Church as it looks back on the event. So you have

> Oh grief! Now trembles his agonizing heart,
> It sinks within, how pale his countenance!
> They lead him to judgment hall
> None is there found to comfort him.
> But almost immediately this gives place to

> O man thy heavy sin lament,
> For which the Son of Man was sent
> To die upon the Cross.

So far in poetical terms; but you will understand what I am saying. New birth, the Christian new beginning with penitence, my sorrow for my sin, my recognition that not only have I been going the wrong way, but that the burden of this rests not on me but on Christ. He has borne it for me, not that I may continue on the old way of self-pleasing, the old way of despair, but that in him I may start again. I don't see how any thoughtful person can escape this starting point. It is in itself incomplete. With Christian grief we must put—

Christian Joy

"Your sorrow shall be turned into joy." It is not a psychological reaction. It is the transforming power of the divine might which broke creatively into the world on the first Easter Day, turning death into life, defeat into victory, sorrowful despair into joyful achievement. It is forgiveness that turns penitence into joy. God takes us seriously. He does not say "Oh well, it doesn't matter." For it does matter, the measure of how much it matters is the Cross. But when he has taken it, and taken it in with full seriousness, he still loves. This is the message of the first Easter, for few can have failed more comprehensively than the first group of disciples. No wonder Peter wept bitterly. But Jesus had not given them up and he has not given us up. Forgiveness turns penitence into joy.

Birth turns suffering into joy. Let us get back to John's own picture and understand it as well as we may. Sorrow is forgotten as new life comes into the world and is established. Penitence never ends; it is unlike the pains of childbirth in that. Every day I must pray, "forgive me my trespasses." But by the mercy of God along with penitence, a new productivity of goodness comes to light and the joy of loving and giving mingles with penitence. Loneliness is ended by the presence of Christ. Did you notice how John transforms his Old Testament allusions? In Isaiah God says "You will see, and your heart will rejoice." In John, Jesus says "I will see you again and your heart shall rejoice." I am glad he puts it that way, for I am not a visionary. I am glad it does not depend on my seeing him, for I do not think I do—my fault, of course, my weakness, but so it is. It depends on his seeing me, and I believe he does. Wherever I go and whatever I do in my weaknesses in my strengths, in my sin and in my penitence, he never loses sight of me. And even if I cannot see him, I rejoice in that.

"The Fellowship of His Sufferings"— John 17:19

[Preached twice on successive days 4/6/50 at Behurst and 4/7/50 at Brandon Trinity][1]

A reminder of the contrasted theme of last night—loneliness. It is important that tonight's subject be viewed in the light of the last. This is not a more cheerful opinion of the same matter—not so bad as it seems. The Twelve did forsake, deny, betray. There is no reason to think ourselves any better. It is not a matter of greater effort. If there is to be a new situation, the initiative must come from Jesus, and so it does.

For Their Sakes

Jesus does not die merely to satisfy his own sense of duty. He consecrates himself to death so that his disciples may be *one in Him*. This too is something that may be traced through his life, and indeed further. The Incarnation is not a matter of self-display. It is disclosure too, God's initiative to seek and save the lost. Behind it is love, God so loved the world. This means that if people are not to be united in Christ crucified, then the plan of God fails. If Jesus is always to be deserted, to suffer alone, the Incarnation is defeated. The lost have not been found and saved. But this is not so. The Cross is victory. In fact—

It Alone Makes Fellowship Possible

Nothing else so unites people and nations. We can see why: (a) the Cross deals with sin which is the real disruptive force. The root of sin is pride. "And when I survey the wondrous Cross. . . . I pour contempt on all my pride."

---

1   Editor's Note: This is an expanded preaching outline, rather than the full sermon itself.

Pride makes wars; Christ destroys it. But not "moral influence" only. Jesus went out to wrestle with the powers of darkness and overcame them. The Cross is atonement, it deals with guilt; (b) on the positive side the Cross is the birth of love, and love, the opposite of pride, is the essence of fellowship. Remember the footwashing by Jesus, the humble service as Mark 10:45 makes clear Jesus came to give? This also takes us to our next point.

Fellowship in Suffering

Not merely in sorrow, but also in joy. But fellowship with Christ can only be fellowship with the whole Christ—who suffered and rose. One cannot pick and choose. This involves service of one another in love. This is the essence of the Church. And also, it involves love of the world. This must have broken Jesus' heart. He sees the souls for whom he dies. It may break our hearts too. But this is also the essence of the Church. The measure of the Church is precisely in these things. There is no Church apart from the Cross. This again leads forward.

Entry into the Church

It is by baptism into Christ's death. There is always value in recalling one's baptism (Luther). There is the symbolism of death, burial, and resurrection in baptism. But there can be daily renewal and remembrance of one's baptism. "The death he died, he died to sin."

The Life of the Church

The Church's life is represented in the Lord's Supper. It was initially enacted at the very time Jesus said these things. Note that the bread and wine are by Christ's word made to take their place in all that befalls the body and blood of Jesus, the sufferings and the subsequent glory. Thus, those who take the elements take their own place in the redeeming process of suffering and glory. By faith, and in his own appointed way, we are united with Christ crucified. In the contrast of loneliness and fellowship both spoken of in this text is expressed the miracle of grace. In ourselves, we are without hope and without God. By his love we are united to him forever. It is all of his mercy. We love, because he first loved us.

"Ashamed of the Gospel"—Romans 1:16

[Preached eleven times from 8/26/45 at Bondgate, Darlington, to 11/30/69 at Lumley]

I want to tell you why I have taken that text for tonight. I had planned, before I knew I was leaving Bondgate, to preach on it in three weeks' time. For this reason—in a Bible of mine you will find an inscription bearing the date Sept. 18, 1935. It was the Bible given to me when I was received as a fully accredited local preacher ten years ago. I had been preaching for sometime before then, but I made up my mind that on the Sunday nearest to that date, I would preach on the first text I used, and it was this one. I have the notebook yet, and I have read up the sermon—this is a new one, by the way. Then when I needed a sermon for my last service as minister of this Church, I decided that this text would do admirably. To it then.

"I am not ashamed of the Gospel" says Paul. That is odd because we are, and for an adequate reason. I shall return to that later. Paul on the other hand, you would have thought, had abundant reason for being ashamed of the Gospel. He was writing to Rome, and I started my old sermon on this text by contrasting the tremendous resources, authority and reprobation of the Roman Empire with the ignominious littleness of Paul and the Church which he represented. Now in the last few years I have had the opportunity of learning a good deal more about the Roman Empire, and I must say, the more I have learned about it, the more magnificent does it appear.

I cannot put the picture into a sentence, I haven't that gift; but in my own mind, at any rate it is very clear. Rome, meant no second places in anything, it was first all the way along. There was no better army, no better legal organization, and it is on these things that a state is built. And Paul, the feeble-bodied preacher of a struggling obscure sect. When later he came to Rome to which he was now writing, the people said "We have hardly heard of this Christian Church, but all we do know is that it has a very bad reputation—it is everywhere spoken against." It wasn't long afterwards that Christians were being put to death for their especially depraved superstition and, a curious charge, their hatred of humanity.

Paul had been on the top side of life once; Roman citizen, sharer in the greatness and majesty of Rome himself. Rabbinic scholar, educated under the great Gamaliel himself. He had thrown it all up, and come down in the world with a vengeance. And yet—"I am not ashamed of the Gospel." We must spend at least a few minutes on Paul's brilliant epigrammatic definition of it. It is—

The Power of God

An easy phrase to use, but think what it means. Think what it meant for Paul, remembering him to be a man of his age. He read the first chapter of Genesis and he saw chaos, unutterable and indescribable, then the Word of God, his bare word, and order appears, and beauty and life. Hills and valleys, seas and lakes, vegetation and animal life, man himself formed out of the dust of the earth. He read the rest of his Old Testament, the story of his people. He saw especially God's power at work in the life of his people, most of all in the deliverances that he wrought for them. Here was a rabble of slaves in Egypt, and God by the might of his arm brought them out of the heart of a powerful military state, conducted them through countless dangers, and installed them in a land, attractive indeed, but in the hands of powerful enemies.

The power of God can mean as much and more for us. We see further into the secrets of the universe than Paul did. We can calculate the momentum, the kinetic energy of a distant star as it wheels its way through space, a power almost incomprehensible. We pry into that tiny thing that 60 years ago people thought was indivisible—the atom, and find the power latent there. For remember atomic energy is not something that the scientists bring to the atom, they release it from the atom.

God the architect of the universe and the artificer of history. The power of God—who can search it out? But see this—a man who can talk about the power of God need not be ashamed even when he stands before the might of the Roman Empire. We have not yet begun to understand what Paul is talking about. All this power, he says, is aimed at one end, it is the power of God directed towards—

Salvation

That is a suspect word with some of us, so we will start from scratch. It means rescue. It means in simple Greek putting things right that were wrong, for example curing a sick person. It means getting somebody safe out of a place of danger, for example people on a ship, or in a shipwreck, or attacked by pirates. Now see what Paul is saying: all this power we have thought of, the power of creation, the power of history, the force of the atom bomb, all is direct along one channel. God has set it all at work for the deliverance of human beings from evil. I am not telling you that that is easy to believe, I am telling you that is what Paul says. Once God poured into human life the full stream of his power, that was the life and work of Jesus. From Jesus, as from a power station, there streams out throughout all the world a force that revolutionizes human life and human society.

Of course, Paul presupposes there is something wrong with human beings that needs to be set right, that people stand in danger of ruining their own lives through their own folly. Most of us are coming to see that in these days, and that some people fail to see the danger by no means proves that it isn't real. When we were down the mine at Oldham, we saw a man sitting on the ground, having his dinner. The manager (for no reason we could see) told him to move. Unwillingly the man did so; what did the manager want now? When he got up the manager pointed silently to the wooden beam under which the man had been sitting. It was cracked nearly in two; there might have been a roof fall any minute. I have often thought how like that we are, lulled into our false security, and impatient of warnings.

But in this state of things, Paul has no hesitation. All God's power is at work to set things right. He bases this opinion on facts. It was God's power which raised Christ from the dead. What else could? You remember Br'er Rabbit's sage remark: "Dead men don't rise up on their feet and say Yahoo!" And it was impossible to doubt that Christ was alive and at work, why Paul knew him! Knew too that this power was still working. It had taken hold of him, turned a preventer into an advocate. And he had blazed the trail of the Gospel across the Mediterranean world with a track of changed lives. He had seen them changing. He doesn't mince his words when he talks of sin as some of us mamby-pamby preachers do. "Fornicators, idolaters, adulterers, willful homosexuals, abusers of themselves with men, thieves, covetous, drunkards, revelers, extortioners, and that is what some of you were." Note the past tense "were" but not "are." For there is a new power sweeping through the cities of the Empire, cleaning up the filth of sex perversion, lust, avarice, dishonesty and the rest. How could the man of God doubt that the power of the living God was at work delivering people? One thing more. Who was to get this deliverance? It must cost a lot. We think quickly of our atom bomb again and remember the 500 million pounds it cost. No doubt this Gospel too is for the wealthy, the privileged. It must be for millionaires or high officials. No, it is for—

Everyone that Believes

Believing, that is a strange price. And the average person's reaction is to say, "Now what am I being asked to swallow?" The answer is nothing. It isn't believing in that sense. What is it? You believe in your friend? It is like that. You believe in the floor of this chapel for you walk on it. It is like that. They don't let you down in either sense. And this believing means you trust yourself to God, trusting that he isn't going to let you down. In a way, it is like putting yourself in the hands of a great surgeon, who you trust to put you right when you are under an anesthetic. And yet again it isn't because with God you have to keep awake, and put up with the pain sometimes, and cooperate. It means you are willing to try him, to trust him, to let him have his way. To everyone who will do that the power of God is sure.

On most Sundays, what I have said so far would serve for a sermon. Today it is really only the introduction to a sermon. I have set forth very briefly, and inadequately what it is. I am now going to exercise the Methodist preacher's right to say—What about it? I shall put this in two short points.

Is the Church Ashamed of the Gospel?

I am bound to say that it looks like it sometimes. When you examine both what we do and what we do not do, it often seems that we are quite happy to push the Gospel into a back seat. We practice what has been cleverly called "evangelism by proxy." We pay our subscriptions to home and overseas missions, we have our missionaries and evangelists and we let them do their stuff. We sat down with complacency in the face of the most appallingly dangerous situation we have been in for 500 years. When we do wake up to the situation we try to deal with it with palliatives, short sermons, or game clubs or the like. The one thing we do not touch is the Gospel. I am a

Methodist, and Methodism lives not on its ministry, not on its local preachers, but on the evangelists who sit in the pews.

Forgive me for speaking plainly, and do not put the cap on unless it fits you. For I believe, at least I think, there is reason to hope that a new day is coming, when the Church will recover its first love, when we shall return to the Bible and our Gospel. I see signs of new life stirring in the country and I see them here too. I see a new concern for the Gospel and a new recognition of the Church's mission. I hear the President of our Conference calling us back to the New Testament, to the Reformation, to the Evangelical revival. I see Commando Campaigns—not converting England, but revitalizing the Church and its Ministry. I think that there is just a chance that we might rediscover our place in God's purposes.

I don't want you to be out of it. If I have prayed for anything in the last two years, I have prayed that Bondgate might become the center of evangelistic work in this town. It might mean losing something. Jesus said that the Church would be poor, that we would have nothing but the Gospel. But it would not mean losing anything that matters. This is the mother Church of Methodism in Darlington. It is our heritage and our privilege to lead the forces of the Good News of Christ here. I can see no other future for us. But there is here a magnificent high calling in Christ Jesus. There must be one other point only. I repeat the text, unworthy though I am to do it—

I Am Not Ashamed of the Gospel

I am not attempting any self-praise. All the praise is Christ's. I am a shy, timid person really. Yet I have been in more factories in Darlington than in Churches; in pubs street corners, and the like. I have not done it for pleasure. I have not done it because it is my job. I have been pounds out of pocket on it. Only, Christ died to make the Good News of God's saving power possible for me. And I wish before God I had done ten times more than I have. It is the Good News which is so wonderful.

George Adam Smith told how he once traveled in a train with a young Roman priest, hardly more than a boy. They talked. The young man was going to Africa as a missionary, to a part where (at that time) a European's life was reckoned not in years but in months. He was going home to say good-bye to his mother. He knew he would never see her again. Smith pleaded with him—of course he must serve Christ, that was right, but could he not find some work he could do longer at less cost? Smith was so moved, that when the priest got out of the train, he lowered the window to urge him still. The lad only smiled, took the cross he was wearing, and said "He gave himself for me, and what less can I do for him?" For you and me he died that we might know his power for goodness against evil, life against death. It comes through faith. Is it nothing to you?

"The Law Established by Faith"—
Romans 3:31

[Preached once in Durham at the
Institute of Education 9/5/62]

Romans 3:31 is a large mouthful of solid Pauline theology. We shall deal with it before we have finished, but I think we shall do better with our meal if we begin with something lighter by way of aperitif. If I am rightly informed, you have all within the last few weeks, come into residence in one or another of the educational establishments in this region. It may be that you have already noticed that these institutions have rules. Too many rules, some of you may think, and if you do, I shall not go out of my way to disagree with you. You are probably right. But even if you are, you will allow that institutions must have rules if they are to function at all. To come a little nearer to Paul's language, society must have a law or it will break down.

You meet rules as soon as you enter a college. It is only gradually that you begin to encounter people; you soon meet them, but it takes time to get to know them in depth. When you do, you discover that it is not rules but people that make a college. I am not engaging in propaganda on behalf of a Don's Trade Union! This is true and if you have not yet found it out for yourselves, you will. A rule may require you to be in a lecture room at a particular hour, but it is the man behind the desk who, if he has the learning and the character can make you want to listen, to read, to investigate, to find out for yourself.

You must understand that you come into the process too. It may seem a long way ahead, but before long you will be moving to other educational establishments—to schools. There will be rules there too, for in my old-fashioned conservatism, I hope you are not taught that you can do without them. There will be rules and they should be good rules, and you should see they are kept. But they will not make one a wise, inquiring, upright child. Only you can make that. Either you will or you will not have it in you to pull the best out of children, to make them want to learn because learning is worthwhile, and want to do the right thing because it is right, and to be pure because purity is better than dirt. Well perhaps the aperitif has had a moral flavor to it. But at all events we are now in a position to read Paul. He is talking about Law and faith. First—

Law

It is not a bad description of the world if we say that it is God's school, and we are, all of us, the children whom he is out to educate. He has provided his school with rules. We have seen these in different ways at different times, but when Paul speaks of the law he means the Old Testament Law, the Law by which Jews did their best to regulate their own lives, the Law which they commended, as far as they could, to the rest of the world. Paul was quite clear in his own mind that this was a good Law and that it told people the right thing to do. And the world has not had so notable a success in keeping the Ten Commandments that it can afford to despise them as belong only to an elementary stage in its education. If we could just manage not to steal, not to kill, and not to commit adultery, three only out of the ten, we might not have reached a passing grade, but the world would be a healthier place to live in.

The Law is a good law, the trouble is it is not kept. We can illustrate this again from school. Suppose you took a newly entered five-year-old child, and gave it a page of Cicero to translate, or a differential equation to solve. These are very worthwhile tasks, but the child couldn't do them. He couldn't do them and he wouldn't want to do them. And if you confront me with the order "Thou shalt love thy neighbor as thyself" then I'm like the child faced with Cicero or a differential equation. I can't do it, and most of the time I don't even want to. I am more interested in loving myself than in loving anyone else.

Because of all this, and he has worked it out in far greater depth than I have, Paul says "It's no good thinking you can get on right terms with God by keeping the Law; you can't. The Law is alright but it is weakened by the material it has to work with. The Law is God's Law but it is not the way by which to find him." Well then, what is? Here is Paul's other word—

Faith

Justification by faith says Paul. What does that mean. It means the way into God's presence is not that of keeping the rules, even his rules, but that of knowing him and trusting him as a person. It is no good my pretending to be something different from what I am. I can't keep the Law, I don't always want to keep the Law. There is no hope that way. All I can do is take myself as I am and take God as he is, and that is what faith means.

There is a supreme and sufficient reason for trusting God like this; the reason is Jesus Christ. Jesus Christ is the word God has spoken to us, and since this is his word, it is not hard to take him at his word. Jesus did not make a careful search for those who had been most successful in keeping the rules. The people most successful in keeping the rules had, as a rule, the least time for him and he hadn't much time for them.

The people he looked for were the lost sheep, the sinners; those who had not kept the rules, and knew they hadn't. He sought them because he loved them with the love of God himself. And because he loved them, they knew they could trust him. He taught, and Paul taught after him, that that is the way to God—not obedience to a law, but the trust which answers love.

This is where we catch up with Romans 3:31. What will become of the Law now? Are we not using faith to break it down? No, faith is the only way to keep the Law. This is the way to get the Law done. Let me use my absurd illustration again. Put your five-year-old in front of a page of Cicero or a differential equation, and what will happen? Nothing at all. But let the child live for ten or a dozen years in the presence of really educated men and women who have a genuine care for it and then you will find him reading Cicero and solving equations (or in these days of specialization, at least one or the other). It is living with people that counts.

Tell a person that he must love his neighbor and nothing much will happen. But let him live with and trust and love Jesus Christ for ten or a dozen years and you will find, in Paul's word, that the Law is being established by faith. That is the essence of the matter. In conclusion—

Two Practical Words

You have heard in the lesson the story of a person who had done more than most of us toward keeping the commandments. There are some good souls who seem to enjoy observing the rules, and the rest of us, I fear, enjoy pulling their legs. For all his rule-keeping, this person knew he had not achieved what he wanted; that was why he asked Jesus how to get hold of eternal life. The answer was quite clear—personal loyalty and obedience to Jesus Christ, trust in Jesus Christ. There is no other answer now. There is no escape from the obligation to come to terms with Jesus Christ and the answer you give now will make all the difference for the next three years and to the whole of life.

Let us go back to where we started. It is not your mission in life to see that certain rules are kept, that children hang their coats on the right pegs, go quietly to the right classrooms, and go home promptly at the end of the day. We are nearer to the truth if we say that it is your mission to teach children facts and ideas they need to know. But we don't really arrive at the truth until we can say that by being what you are, you are to lead children to love truth, and beauty and goodness. You are to win from them the faith that establishes law. This is God's work; and you will do it well, and you will persevere in it in the face of discouragement only if you do it as the servants of God.

"Our Reasonable Service"—
Romans 12:1-2

[Preached seven times from 7/22/52 at Shebbear to 1/25/98 at Sacriston]

"I beseech you therefore . . ." but why? To what does St. Paul appeal? I beseech you because you are the people and wisdom will die with you? Hardly; it was not true of the Romans, and of ourselves the less said the better. I beseech you because you are so virtuous, because you have never known what it is to break a rule, to transgress a law, to sin against your conscience? Again, I question whether that would work (unless the world and schools are very different from what I always thought they were). I beseech you because you are naturally religious? Because you take to hymns and sermons as ducks to water? Well, I should be surprised, so—why then?

Paul is appealing to something outside ourselves—something concrete, objective, perfectly real; in a word, to history. History itself, he argues, summons you to a decision, demands from you a particular attitude towards life. History of course is always doing that, that is if you know what history really is. Some of you will remember a blackboard that used to stand in the old VA room. On one side, it was an ordinary blackboard, on the other side were two spindles which could be turned by a handle and were connected by a long roll of paper, like the film in a camera. On this were written in John Rousefell's neat and beautiful hand, dates, which were as innumerable as the stars in heaven. This was the date list. A week or so before school certificates we revisited it. The first ten dates appeared and we learnt them; the sheet was wound on to the next ten, we learnt them and forgot the first ten, and so on. That was the date list. But it was not history, and it is no more than fair to say that J.R. himself was one of the first men to show me that that was not history.

I don't know that I can tell you what history is, but I think I can tell you what it does. Look back at some of the first things I remember from the date list. Here are men like Pym, Hampden, Cromwell, men to whom conscience and freedom and duty are more than comfort and home and life itself; men whose life-blood has entered the stuff of England. Here a little later are seven bishops in the tower and a jury of common Englishmen warned, cajoled and threatened to bring in a guilty verdict. And neither bishops nor jury men will give in, for they stand for the common rights and duties of free persons. What then? Once you know these facts, this history, you are required to live as a free and responsible person. Required, not compelled. Not seven nor seventy times seven bishops could do that. History summons you to a decision, demands from you a particular attitude to life.

There is time for one other illustration. When you come to a school like this, you enter into a tradition, you become heirs of a particular piece of history. Again, the names are perhaps not mere names to you—Ruddle, Pollard, Raab, Stone, and many a one more. The whole company of them will not force one decent, courageous, generous, honorable or kindly action out of you; but they shall require that you shall either deliberately and knowingly enter into the life of the Shebbear[1] they made; or deliberately and knowingly turn your back on it. History, our domestic history summons you to a decision, demands from you a particular attitude to life.

History; the history of England, the history of a school. But there is one piece of history that you enter into not as an Englishman nor as a Shebbearian but as a human being. You live, says Paul in a world where God finally and radically revealed his mercy in history—in the life and death and resurrection of Jesus. Of course, in the passing ages, there have been and are many who go from the cradle to the grave without hearing about this. What becomes of them I do not know; but I am satisfied with my ignorance and God's mercy. But you know that we in this chapel have had a Christian education, and we cannot escape the responsibility that that gives. We know the life Jesus lived, his care for the weak and helpless, his scorn for the proud and self-righteous, his obedience to his Father, and his certainty that in his person the new world of God's kingdom was springing to life and activity. And we know the death he died, rather than be false to his life, to bring it to a climax of judgment and mercy. We know this, for this is history, and history summons you to a decision, demands from you a particular attitude to

---

1   A private Christian school.

life. Can we say more than that? What kind of life is called for by the fact of Jesus? First—

Be Not Fashioned According to This World

I don't doubt that Paul knew well enough what he was talking about here, but I question whether he knew the weight of his own words much better than anyone who has lived in the kind of school this is, and left it. It is, I know, possible to talk a great deal of sentimental rubbish about "going out into the world" but at least of what the parsons and the schoolmasters say is true. A few weeks ago, the Conference of the National Association of Boy's Clubs included in its report a phrase to the effect that "many boys in their first few months at work learn from their adult companions as little as possible for as much as they can get" (*Manchester Guardian*). I think most of you will find influences rather different from that, but you will certainly find ideals and standards, not to say ways and means, which are different from those you have learned in the New Testament. And there are many of us who know how desperately easy it is to go slack, to let things go their own way; in fact, simply to take the color of the society one lives in. Of course, it is a rather weak-kneed attitude to life; if it were not commonplace it would be extraordinary that we all adopt it.

Of course, it is so much more comfortable, it is the easy response to the challenge of history. Away with duty, let us enjoy ourselves. Away with responsibility, the burden isn't worth it; away with Christ, his life is too hard, let us take the easy comfortable way, living simply to our own satisfaction, as if God had never come into the world at all, as if nothing existed beyond the sphere of our senses and feelings, this present moment of existence. What is the alternative? Not to take the shape of this world, not to adopt ourselves to the conventional molds of society, taking pains always to be square pegs in square holes (square pegs in round holes are bound to be incomplete, but they have greatness), but to be—

Transformed by the Renewing of Your Mind

This is the thing that is hard to put into words. The fact of the matter is this. The life of Jesus was not merely a fine example, showing us how we ought to live, by giving us a picture of life as God meant it to be. It was what Paul says it was—the mercy of God. It was God himself offering to a race which deserved little enough at his hands the possibility of a new kind of life. In Jesus, the kingdom of God (as the Gospels put it) came near, and ever since we have lived between two worlds, with the possibility of belonging to one or the other, of taking on the general pattern of our own world of self, being fashioned according to this world, or of God's world, and so letting all our thinking be transformed. It is not so much a matter of attaining or even of striving desperately towards something which we ought to be, as of recognizing something that already is, and living in the truth of it. Not painfully struggling up a mountain but taking off in a glider and knowing that the air itself will support you.

I wonder if that sounds too airy, even a bit gassy. Perhaps it sounds like auto-suggestion, convincing yourself something is true when all the time you know it isn't. Perhaps it sounds too easy. Well on one side Christianity is easy, just as on one side it is (whether we like the word or not) "otherworldly." It is a gift, and it does put us, here and now, in touch with another world. But I am glad that on the other hand, and to correct any misunderstanding Paul urges us to—

Present Our Bodies to God

Not our souls, not even our minds (though they are included) but our bodies, all the solid corporeal reality of life as we live it. This is the pure worship God seeks, and there is no substitute for it in any ritual, however elaborate or however simple. This is the way, and, so far as I can read the New Testament, the only way into the renewal of the mind, the revision of all the fundamental bases of life, of which Paul speaks. This is the response, the only possible response, to the challenge of the history of Jesus. It is the response humans made when first they heard the words "follow me." They left all—boats and books—and followed him. It is a response which can equally be made today.

I must have heard some seven or eight Special Day sermons in this chapel in my time. Of them all, I can remember one text, and this—and this is something I do not think I am likely now to forget. The preacher was Frank Dymond who went out as a pioneer missionary to China with Sam Pollard, a link with an already almost unreachable past, and he must that Special Day have had memories in his mind as he stood again in Lake pulpit, after 40 years of almost incredible hardship, suffering and devotion in the face of persecution, disease, and death. This is all I remember of what he said, but I think I can give you the words as he uttered them—"Some people will tell you that religion is dope (or it is true enough that they do); strange dope this, that has kept me in China these 40 years."

"I beseech you brethren by the mercies of God that you present your bodies a living sacrifice to God." Your hands to work with, your feet to travel with, your heads to think with, your mouths to speak with, your whole selves to suffer, to show with Christ the indescribable burden of the world's suffering and sin. That is the way, by God's mercy not our achievement, into a life so strong, that it shapes and is not shaped by the environment, into a life vitalized and renewed by God himself.

"Gifts and Graces—The Ministry"— Romans 12:6-7

[Preached once at Elvet on 6/5/55]

There are two subjects which are especially connected with this day—Trinity Sunday. One of course is the doctrine of the Holy Trinity itself. The other is the Church's ministry. The former we considered this morning. The latter has already been before us in our prayers. We should spend a few minutes more in thought about it now. There are several good reasons for doing so. One is that Scripture contains quite a quantity of material bearing on the subject, and it needs exposition. The second is that Christian people have a good deal to do with ministers anyway; they see them in the pulpit and in their homes, and it is no bad thing to clear up the misunderstandings, of which there are not a few, and understand who these queer people in white collars and black coats are. A Christian ought to know what he can expect from his minister, and what his minister has a right to expect from him. And thirdly, it maybe be that there are young persons in this congregation that God is calling into the ministry, and who ought to be responding to his call. Now since this is not a general chat about the ministry, but the exposition of a text, let us look again at what Paul says. The first point is that—

The Church Lives by the Grace of God

If we are Christians at all, if we are the Church, it is because of the grace of God revealed and conveyed to us in Jesus Christ. We are not Christians because we are good, virtuous or nice, but only as sinners pardoned through grace. By the grace of God, said Paul, I am what I am, and if we are anything at all it is "through the grace that was given to us." Of course, we know this; but we do not always take it really seriously. May I try to bring out the force of it by stressing my introductory sentences in different ways?

First the Church lives by the grace of God, not the ministry lives by the grace of God and the Church by the ministry. A few verses earlier, Paul has begun to use his great metaphorical description of the Church. It is a body and all the parts belong to it equally. They all need one another. A body that was all head would be as useless as a body that was all feet. In the same way, a Church that was all ministry, would be as bad as a Church with none. Of course, the ministry also depends on grace; and it is not just as an organization, a body of administrative officers instituted for our convenience.

People sometimes argue whether the ministry is (as they say), from below, that is, appointed by the Church and having only the authority delegated to it by the whole body of Christians, or "from above" that is appointed directly by God and exercising authority over the Church. The Methodist answer to this question is clear. The ministry is both from below and from above. It is from below because the minister is not a higher grade of Christian that the lay person. The whole Church is a Church of priests, and for example, at the Lord's Supper the ministry represents the Church, and it would be chaos if we all tried to celebrate; the one acts for the many. But the ministry is also from above, because it depends on God's call. God lays his hands upon individuals, puts his word in their mouths, and they speak to their brothers and sisters with his authority.

The Church lives by the *grace* of God. This is what we all, Methodists included, find it hard to believe. A candidate for a theological examination is reported to have written "we are justified by faith, but a few good works don't matter." Most of us live on the principle "we are justified by faith, and a few good works are tremendously important." We have not yet understood St. Paul. If everything depends on God's grace then nothing depends on our works, otherwise, as Paul himself says, grace would cease to be grace.

Our practical error lies in trusting to our institutions and organizations rather than in God's grace. Of course, we must have institutions and organizations; that is just part of the fact that we live in this world. The important thing is that our institutions should themselves bear witness to their own insufficiency and the all sufficiency of grace. All too often the reverse is the truth. It is the besetting sin of all ministers, stewards, and other officials, and in consequence it sometimes happens that our Church order has more experience of business efficiency (occasionally of business inefficiency which is no better) than of grace.

The Church lives by the grace of *God*. This takes us a step further. We live by the freedom of God, in the might and love of him who alone is unconditioned by the littleness of humanity. God is not bound as we are. He does not act in terms of precedent and convention but always in creative love. No one has emphasized this more than Paul in Romans 9. He is dealing with the problem of the Jews who remain untouched by all Paul's efforts to win them to Christ. The trouble is, that many think that just because they are Jews, in the line of descent from Abraham, they must be alright. It's not so simple says Paul. Abraham had two sons, Isaac and Ishmael, both his sons, but God wanted Isaac. Isaac had two sons, twins, Jacob and Esau, and it is written Jacob I loved but Esau I hated. There are problems there that maybe someday I can talk about, but the point for us to note is that for the Jews to depend on a physical line of descent from Abraham was blasphemy against the sovereign freedom of God, in love.

The moral for us is clear. Whenever the Church bases its own life and validity of its ministry on a line of succession connecting it with Augustine of Canterbury or Peter of Rome it is committing the same blasphemy against the sovereign freedom of God to choose his people in creative love, from generation to generation. Of course, the claim to an unbroken succession is bad history, but it is worse than that, it is bad theology. John Wesley called the so-called "apostolic succession" a fable. It was and is also a denial of the free grace of God which he preached and no Methodist has any reason to seek orders elsewhere.

I don't want to end this point on a controversial note. All our errors and sins have never prevented the Church from *living* by the grace of God. He is all victorious, he triumphs in spite of us. The full rich life of the Church in Word, and sacraments, prayer, fellowship, and love goes on—by the grace of God. This leads directly to the next point—

Grace Is Actualized in Gifts

"Having gifts differing according to the grace given to us." Gifts are acts of grace. In Greek, they are nearly the same word grace is χάρις and gift is χάρισμα. Gifts are not grace, but they are a parable of it, a sign that it is at work. A wedding ring is not a marriage, but it is a sign that a marriage has taken place. A book is not a brain, but it is a sign that a brain has been at work. In the same way, the gifts God gives his people are a sign of the divine life which inspires his Church. It is important to be clear about this. One can imagine a woman with a beautiful and very valuable wedding ring, which she prized highly and kept clean and sparkling, who also so failed to maintain proper relations with her husband that the marriage came to pieces on the rocks. In the same way, sometimes the Church is so busy with gifts, and so proud of them, that it neglects the relationship of grace and faith by which it is bound to God. This happens when we are so pleased with our religious experience, or our sound and accurate theology, or our rich and beautiful liturgy that we forget to be humble before God. There are two things to say about the gifts and graces here.

First, they are infinitely various and they are not bestowed on ministers only. God's gifts are for all, and they are not the same for all. At Christmas, I try, as every father does, to be both generous and fair. That means that neither son nor daughter goes without presents, but it also means that they don't get the same presents. So, it is, in God's family, the Church. None goes without, but we don't all get the same. One person is called of God, and equipped with gifts to do the work of a layperson—a steward, a caretaker, a musician; another is called of God and is equipped with gifts to do the work of a minster. One is not greater or better than the other, they are simply different. Nor are God's gifts simply designed for exercise within the Church. He gives us gifts of grace which enable us to do public service. The administrator, the doctor, the teacher, and every honest worker, acts as God's servant, equipped with gifts for his service.

There are two tests by which every gift can be tested and weighed. They are Paul's own tests, but they still apply, however changed the circumstances. The first is, do our gifts proclaim the lordship of Christ? The second is, do they make for the building up of the Church in love? The most splendid of gifts of mind or mysticism are nothing if they fail here. I may be a most religious person; if I do not obey Christ I am nothing. I may speak with the languages of humans and of angels, but if I have not love, I am nothing. Obedience and love, not glorious individualism, not pietism and emotionalism. These are what count. I have spoken in this way in order to lead us to the last point. What in particular is—

The Gift of Ministry?

I have tried hard all through this sermon not to give the impression that the ministry is a class apart, a group of priests who stand between the ordinary Christian and his God. All of us, whatever special gifts God may have bestowed upon us, are equally God's stewards and God's sons and daughters. Yet here in fact is a company of persons, separated in many ways from their fellows and given a special place in the Church. Why? What do they do? What are they? My last points give a clue.

The gift of ministry is an especially clear and articulate manifestation of the grace of God which lies behind all actual gifts; it is a proclamation of the lordship of Christ and of the love that builds up the Church. God uses many ways to speak to humankind, but the one "regular" way, the more guaranteed way is Scripture. He meets them in many places, but the place where he has promised to meet them, and where he may always be found, is the sacraments. The ministry therefore is a ministry of Word and sacraments. Ministers do not exist to glorify themselves, quite the reverse; they exist to point away from themselves, like John the Baptist in Grünewald's famous picture, and to Christ, the Christ who is revealed in Scripture and known in sermon and sacraments. For themselves they can claim nothing; in Christ's name, they must claim everything. Poor fellows! After all they are only human beings, and they get it wrong sometimes, and they fail to make things clear. It looks as if they are full of their own importance and sometimes perhaps they are; but in truth their only word is "we preach not ourselves, but Christ Jesus as Lord, and ourselves your servants for Christ's sake."

The minister of a Church has two jobs—or his job can be looked at in two ways. It is his task to see that Christ reigns in love in the community committed to his charge. He must see first of all that the Word of God, the Gospel of Christ, is made clear and commanding. He must see that the sacramental means of grace are available to all. He must know his flock, Christ's flock, one by one, and see, insofar as lies within him, that each one is committed to Christ and is serving him in love pressing on all the time (as Wesley said) to perfect love. He must see that the community as a whole is governed not by its own self-interest, not by the strongest members, not even by a democratic vote, but by Christ, the one head of the Church. He must see that all its members that mutual self-satisfying love which Christ himself said should be the sign of his disciples.

It is his job to see that Christ reigns in the wider society of which his Church is part. He must see that the laws of God are kept in daily life—in trade, in industry, politics, and international affairs; and when they are not kept, it is his business like the prophets of old to call heaven and earth to witness the human revolt against his maker. And he must see that Christ reigns by doing the work of an evangelist, commending Christ to all people and offering salvation through him.

Now to sum up, or rather to bring all this to a point, here is the life of grace in the family of God. Every one of you has some part to take in it. Every part is different and there is not one that can be left out. Are you playing yours? Better, have you taken advantage of the gifts of grace God waits to bestow on you? Through God's supreme act of grace in Jesus Christ the way is open. And one last special word.

Some of you, in two or three weeks will be going down from Durham; some of you for good. A university career has many purposes; one of the most important is that you should have years of quiet and leisure, yes leisure, in which to come to terms with life and find out what to make of it. For a Christian, that means having understanding, and obeying God's call. What his call is for you, it would be sheer presumption for me to say. Whatever it is, he will give you grace and gifts to fulfill it. It could be the ministry; if it is, think about it, and pray about it, and discuss it with your chaplain. And wherever Christ calls—follow Him.

"The Meaning of Work and Religion"— Romans 12:6-16

[Preached ten times from 1/20/57 at Shincliffe to 11/7/99 at Harrowgate Hill]

This 12th chapter of Romans is one of the great surprises of the Bible, that is if you study the Bible consecutively and pay attention to what you read. For eleven chapters, Paul has labored to give the greatest constrained presentation of the doctrine of salvation. The whole process depends, says Paul, not upon the exercise of human will, not upon his efforts as he runs like an athlete to his goal, but upon the merciful God. Salvation springs from the grace of God alone and the only contribution (though that is the wrong word) a human can make is the faith that is content to stand still and see the salvation of the Lord. All human beings, without exception are sinners, and they are ignorant fools into the bargain. They cannot by thinking discover the truth of God, they cannot by their virtue deserve his kindness. They are lost souls redeemed only by the incomprehensible love of God, poured out upon them freely. "God commends his love towards us in that when we were yet sinners, Christ died for us." For those who could do nothing, Christ has done everything.

I have just been re-reading Wesley's sermon "On the Death of Mr. Whitefield," a careful piece of writing, which should bring us all close together. It is all summed up there in burning phrases. "In the business of salvation, set Christ as high and man as low as possible." "All power to think, speak, and act aright is in and from the Spirit of Christ, and all merit is (not in man, how high soever in race but merely) in the blood of Christ." "But by what means do we become interested in what Christ has done and suffered?" "Not by works, lest any man should boast but by faith alone."

All this is the theme of the first eleven chapters of Romans and all at once we find Paul busy with this, that and other duty, like an over-fuzzy Sunday School teacher anxious to have all her class, each in his own small corner, busy about his own particular duties. Are you a prophet? Then do your bit of prophesying. Are you a teacher? Then teach as well as you can. Do you do good turns? Then do as many as you can, and as cheerfully as you can. And so on. The great sermon on free grace, which ends with an all-embracing picture of the full close to which the eternal purposes of God will come, continues in a stuffy moralizing conclusion, which indeed will get worse as it goes on, for Paul will tell us we must pay our income tax, and deal gently with vegetarians and teetotalers.

There is the umpire. Now what has happened? Paul was no fool; certainly, he was not the sort of person to forget in chapter 12 what he had said in chapters 3 and 6 and 9 and 11. What he is showing us is the crucifixion and the resurrection which all our human activity has to undergo when it meets the Christ and takes him seriously. Crucifixion, for we must learn that all our wisdom is folly, if Christ crucified is the truth, then all our virtues are sin if they lack the obedience of faith, that there is nothing we can do to merit God's love. And resurrection, for when we have met him at the Cross, Christ does not send us out into a desolate world, or into pious idleness. He fills our hands with his work, and our heads with his thoughts, so that our work and thoughts are renewed and transformed.

Look at that for a moment in terms of the theme of this Preterminal— Study and Bible Study. For most of us here, though not for all, study is our daily job, the ordinary stuff of existence. Others do jobs different and perhaps more worthwhile. In all this the same pattern is to be observed. Our world as a whole is trying hard to construct itself afresh on the basis of daily jobs—the jobs of the politician, the administrator, the scientist, the planner. And we look on it all with a jaundiced eye, or at least with the weary despair of the Psalmist. "Thou carriest them away as with a flood, they are as a sleep, in the morning they are like grass which grows up. In the morning, it flourishes and grows up; in the evening, it is cut down, and withers. All our days are passed away in thy wrath; we spend our years as a tale that is told." Or . . . "our little systems have their day, they have their day and cease to be" (Tennyson, "In Memoriam"). But no—weary despair is wrong. That is not the Biblical word. For the Psalm does not end with the tedious, boring failure of humans to achieve their ends. "Let thy work appear unto thy servants, and thy glory unto their children." "And let the beauty of the Lord our God be upon us and establish there the work of thy hands upon us; yea the work of our hands establish them."

Even the work of frail and sinful human hands can be established and made permanent by the Lord our God. We know at least enough of our studies to know that we shall never really know anything properly; but our poor few fragmentary scraps of knowledge, the will-o'-the-wisp gleams of insight and coherent perception, these, surrendered back into the hands of God, will be established; the labor is not lost. Through Christ, our love, our service, our devotion to the needy ones of humankind, is built up into a building that shall not pass away.

That suggests the other aspect of the Preterminal Bible Study, which may stand for all the religious activities we engage in. Do not suppose that merely because they are religious that they must needs fare better than all else we do. If you are in any doubt about that reread the 2nd, and parts of the 3rd, 7th, and 9th and 10th chapters of Romans. There is one hope and one hope only for the religious life of humanity. It is not that we steadily plough through a chapter of Bible study every day, and not that we go to Church every Sunday. It is that we surrender all things to God, not with the intention of reading the Bible and going to Church no more, but that we may receive them again raised from the dead.

Let me put this in the only picture I can use in this service. Here on this table are bread and wine. Someone has brought them to Church this morning—ordinary stuff; wheat that has been harvested in the field, kneaded into dough, baked in the oven; wine crushed out of grapes. In a few minutes, we will receive them again. I shall not attempt to define what will become of them then—there never has been and there never will be a satisfactory definition. But we know that they will be charged with a new divine significance; that by means of them we shall hold communion with Christ our Savior.

That is the pattern of which we have seen a part of in our Epistle; the pattern of Christian existence. God is our judge; but he is not a cynic. And all the poor broken and meaningless pieces of life which we lay before him, he unites into a living, active, creative organism, in which our work, our study, our religion are meaningful and alive. And the key? "I beseech you brothers and sisters by the mercies of God to present your bodies as living sacrifices, holy, acceptable unto God, which is your reasonable service."

"Receive One Another"— Romans 15:5-7

[Preached six times from 1/25/61 at Tynemouth to 1/21/80 at S. Hetton]

We may in this service humbly make the limited claim to have fulfilled what St. Paul in vs. 6 desired. We have, as Christians in this district, come together of one accord, and with one mouth to glorify God. We should be foolish if we claimed to have reached the end of the road, fooled indeed if we pretended no problems remained unsolved, that no barriers separate us, that there was nothing left to pray for in next year's Week of Prayer for Christian Unity. But at least we can thank God thank him jointly in a united service. And if some of us have found parts of the service strange, if not all are familiar with Anglican prayers, Wesley hymns, and free prayers offered spontaneously from the heart, then so much the better. We are learning something about our brothers and sisters. I hope we shall not immediately seek to ape them, but it is good to know each other.

This is a service of Thanksgiving and the very fact that it can take place at all is a reason for thanksgiving. But there is one comment on that that all of us would agree upon, and we should all be in this agreement with Paul. A service may be a good thing but a service that is isolated from Christian living is an appalling danger. To give thanks to God with the mouth is a right and proper act; but to praise God only with the mouth is not adequate Christian service. This stands out at once if you read through the verses I have given as a text, not to mention the whole context, and this is not the only place Paul makes the point here. You will remember how he ends the theological argument of the first eleven chapters—"of him, and through him and unto him are all things." To him be glory forever, Amen. But the next verse, 12:1 shows immediately what it means to give glory to God—"I beseech you brothers

177

and sisters by the mercies of God to present your bodies as living sacrifices, holy and acceptable to God, which is your reasonable service." There is no true worship which does not include the deeds of the body. This is stated in general terms. Chapter 15 gives a particular example. With one accord we glorify God with our mouths. What next if this verbal glorifying is not to be a mere hypocritical sham. What has Paul to teach us about this?

What Paul Does Not Say

He was dealing with a concrete situation of Christian disunity. It was not quite the same kind of disunity as ours, but it was real and had in it the bitterness of censoriousness and contempt. There were strong Christians in Rome, the adjective is Paul's, who knew that as Christians they had gotten beyond the old religious rules that were expressed in food laws and calendars. Does God love us any more if we eat this or don't eat that? And there were weak Christians who needed all the religious crutches they could find to help them to walk. The strong made sport of the weak, and the weak condemned the strong. It was a division not peculiar to Rome. It certainly was to be found in Corinth and probably split most of the churches.

I say this to make clear that Paul was not writing in a remote golden age or (as university professors are supposed to do) in an ivory tower. He is in a real and serious situation, yet he never makes the suggestion that the practical problem is to be solved, or even could be solved, by the application of ecclesiastical politics, or in terms of organization. I cannot but feel that there is a lesson for us here, and that ecclesiastical politics are in danger of proving more of a hindrance than a help. I know that the ecclesiastical politicians do not share this view, but I think an increasing number of ordinary Christians are getting impatient about this, just as a good many Englishmen and women are getting impatient with the secular politicians.

Some of you will have read Sir Charles Jeffries letter in the *Times* last September and remember his suggestion that what we really need between the churches is the simple recognition of one another as Christians, so that when any church holds a communion service, any recognized member of any recognized church would be welcome at it. Of course, Sir Charles added modestly "I am not a theologian." Well I am, and it seems to me that Sir Charles is right. Paul's silence about organization here is matched by the attitude of the New Testament as a whole and the instinct of a vast number of Christian laity that if Christians can live in love and fellowship that organization can be left to look after itself, is more soundly based than some of them know. This is not to say that Paul has nothing both practical and positive to say to us. He prays that we might be—

Of the Same Mind, According to Jesus Christ

Whatever else this means, it must mean that it matters a good deal what goes on in Christian minds. I have just said that in one respect I believe that the instinct of the mass of Christian lay persons is right. Let me now say that I think that this is a matter in which many of you are wrong. There is a widespread notion that it doesn't matter what a person believes. We all mean the same thing, we are all good chaps together, what does it matter if we all think alike?

This is a place where some careful distinctions have to be made and I have no time tonight to make them in detail. There are some areas where disagreement doesn't matter—indeed where it may be welcomed. We are all different, thank God, and we should not expect to see everything in the same way. A little earlier Paul, could say "let each of you be convinced in his own mind." You must think your problems through for yourself and it is less important that you should be in complete agreement than that each person should follow faithfully what his own mind and conscience tell him. Christians do not all think alike in all moral and political problems and if everyone thought identically on theological problems, some of us would be out of a job.

But this does not mean there are no standards, no objective truths. There are some aspects of Christian faith and morals where there is a standard of Christian belief. What this is, is encompassed here in the phrase "according to Jesus Christ." This means two things.

First, all Christian ministry is focused on Jesus. There is no philosophical orthodoxy that all Christians must embrace, but any way of Christian thinking that does not have Christ at the center is simply not Christian. He is God manifest. He that has seen him has seen the Father. The Holy Spirit is the *other* Comforter who brings to mind the truth of the first Comforter, Jesus. This is why (to put the matter in one way only). There is no better joint activity than Bible Study Groups, in which we can talk not about bishops or the Methodist Conference, but about the Jesus to whom the Bible points us, and perhaps learn from each other where we have dishonored him, by letting other interests and standards come too close to him.

Second, the words of Paul in Romans may remind you of others he used elsewhere—"have this mind in yourself that was also in Christ Jesus." The one mind we are to have is the mind of Christ, the mind that never sought power or glory for itself, that was always accessible to need, that was always ready to spend and be spent in the service of others. That is why (to take one practical point) the second great joint activity for Christians is practical service to the community of which we are a part. What form this should take is for those who know the local situation to judge. That it must be done is the plainest of Christian duties, for those who would be of the same mind in accord with Jesus Christ. Paul has one more point for us. If you mean to glorify God together then you must—

Receive One Another as Christ Received You, to the Glory of God

This is perhaps the most fundamental thing the New Testament has to say about Christian unity. For how did Christ receive you? Perhaps that is too personal a question to start with. How did he receive people during his earthly ministry? You know the answer to that. Outcasts, sinners, harlots, tax collectors, the unpopular, the irreligious, the scrupulous, the dead. He received them all as they were, he received them with no qualification but their need, he received them on the ground of nothing whatever except his own free, undeserved love. And each of us in the bottom of his heart knows that that is how he received you and received me, not because I am a good Methodist or my father was. Wesley may have written better lines, but he never wrote one nearer to the New Testament than "He hath loved, he hath loved because he would love." "All my hope is nowhere" said St. Augustine, "but in thy great mercy." He did not wait for me to be good, religious, orthodox. He took the initiative in love. "Receive one another, as Christ received you." Have I any right to pitch my demands in terms of virtue, orthodoxy, of church order, any higher than Christ pitched his?

To the glory of God; "a strange glorification is this," said Luther, "that God should be glorified when we welcome the sinful and weak. Yet it is the way God chooses to be glorified." And if this service is to end in the glorifying of God, if it is to fulfill its promise, then we go out of this church as witnesses to Christ and because of his Gospel, as evangelists to win the world for him, and as brothers and sisters to receive one another, as he received us all.

"Ordination"—1 Corinthians 2:2

[Preached once 6/29/97 at Sutton]

There, in 1 Cor. 2:2, is the model of an apostolic ministry, the sort of ministry to which you are called and which you will fulfill. "I decided to know nothing except Jesus Christ and him crucified." Can he really mean it? Can he be serious? Nothing? And in that nothing what we receive from him and take into our circuits? Nothing; so we have been wasting our time and our effort these three years in the Shedy Centre in Durham? Not only we but Dr. Luscombe and the college and university teachers have been wasting their time too? Can a ministry based on "nothing except" persist through 40 years or more? Should we not be content to make a respectful bow to the apostle and pass on? Well, in a sense we will, but only to find out what he means.

Let us make a confession. This is not the sermon I originally planned for today. I had a text, a good solid practical text in the Pastoral Epistles and on the strength of it I think I could have given you a quantity of good advice. I worked at it; the outline was there, a real classical three-decker of a sermon. And the more I worked at it, the clearer it became that it wouldn't do. I couldn't preach it. This is not an occasion that calls for good advice, for plain common sense. It is an occasion that comes once in a lifetime, like a wedding perhaps, an occasion that calls for unreserved and passionate commitment—

> Give me the faith which can remove
> And sink the mountain to a plain;
> Give me the childlike praying love,
> Which longs to build Thy house again;
> Thy love, let it my heart overpower,
> And all my simple soul devour. (Charles Wesley)

So we must have the passion of the Corinthians but the common sense of Timothy for, as I thought on about my responsibility in this service, I saw that I can use my Pastorals text to provide the framework for the exposition of Corinthians—discipline the passion of the Corinthians with the sober sense of Timothy. Let me tell you then the second text—1 Tim. 4:16 "Take heed to yourself, and to your teaching. Continue in these things, for in doing this you will save both yourself and your hearers." These are the three points, three points that determine the full circle—yourself, your teaching, your hearers. And each time it is Paul's nothing, nothing but Christ and him crucified that is the determinant. So then first—

Yourselves

But is that really the right place to begin? Does it not suggest putting the minister first, ahead of all other church members? The prime sin of the ministry and the direct contradiction of Jesus' teaching, "he who wishes to be first among you shall be slave of all"? Well it could suggest that, but it does not mean that. It is open to misinterpretation like that other Pastoral saying—"Let no one despise you." It is easy to take that to mean "right I'll show them who's boss, no one shall look down on me." But the people, Christian people, will not despise anyone for being humble and serviceable, for arrogance and self-assertion is a different story. And if it is true that a minister must have gifts of leadership and with them the potentiality with them for doing more good than most others, it is also true that if a minister goes wrong, and it can happen, he does infinitely more damage to the cause of Christ.

This takes us back to the original text. Nothing except Christ and him crucified. This belongs not only to Paul's apostolic preaching, we shall come to that in a minute or two, but to his apostolic living also; always carrying about in the body the dying, the killing of Jesus. We are weak in him. The life of a minister is itself, before he opens his mouth, a portrayal of the cross. He too carries the burdens, stripes, wounds, dies the death of those they serve.

It is easy to speak of this in terms of rhetoric and emotion. These are the wrong terms. The right word is *discipline*. There are many facets of it, including some very simple practical ones. I hope I shall never forget the words of that great and good man W. F. Howard in his presidential year. He had been shocked, he said, on his presidential rounds to find ministers at 9 o'clock, still unshaven, unprepared, and unshod. Pretty basic, but for that reason never to be neglected. But discipline means more.

Personal religion. How easy it is, I speak for myself if not for you, "it's all the Lord's work isn't it?" Yes it is, but filling in schedules is no substitute for saying your prayers, and reading the *Recorder* is no substitute for reading the Bible. It is as a man or woman of God that the minister goes into the homes of the people, knowing them not only as they sit in the pews but as they sit at their own firesides. There is no substitute for this. Some may think it old fashioned but in fact there is no substitute for constant regular pastoral visitation by one who is a true pastor.

Discipline in moral life; it would indeed be old-fashioned to take this for granted today. Sisters and brothers, be careful, be strict; give no occasion for scandal, even by misinterpretation of an innocent act. We know what the press can do when a minister absconds with the funds, or with a church member. When in preparation for the current Conference a paper was issued which acknowledged cases of abuse, it appeared on the front page of the *Times*. I do not blame the *Times* for that; I am glad that such cases are sufficiently unusual as to be newsworthy. But in all Conference conduct, no standards but the highest will do, and that not simply because of possible bad publicity, but because we are called to a life of holiness.

Discipline in study; you will promise in this service to be faithful in the reading of the Holy Scriptures and in those studies which will help you to understand and expound them. That is a task that could occupy all your waking hours. It won't, for there are many other tasks to do, but it ought to occupy a good many of them. If you know Greek and Hebrew don't let them go but understand these "other" studies in a wide sense. And to draw this part of my sermon to a close, let them include the lives of the great models of ministerial life, such men as Richard Baxter or Alexander Whyte or John Denholm Brash. They will show you what it is to live a life which as a life proclaims not wisdom, not ambition, not ruthlessness but nothing but Christ and him crucified. Next—

Teaching

What are you to teach and preach? Nothing but Christ and him crucified. Does teaching doctrine matter? Paul thought it did. There was only one Gospel and substitutes for it were not Gospel, were not good news at all. And to deny the Gospel, to get the Gospel wrong, was to miss everything.

It is not the ministry that validates the Gospel, it is the Gospel that validates the ministry. Paul accepted this for himself, and we must accept this for ourselves too. We must preach the Gospel of the cross, and we must teach it too. There are too many of our people, good people too, who do not know, because they have missed teaching, what Christians believe. They do not really know why they are Christians, not to say Methodists, and I am not so concerned about teaching them what we call the special Methodist emphases as with teaching them the great core doctrines of the faith, which we share with almost every other branch of Christendom. And the heart of this is the word of the Cross.

I am not going to set about a brief summary of the doctrine of the atonement. Let me rather share with you something I have only recently learned. I have often enough used, especially in speaking to preachers, Matthaus Grunewald's great picture of the Crucifixion, the Isenheim altarpiece. In the middle, Christ hangs on the cross, a ghastly figure, looking, unlike so many Italian masterpieces, utterly dead, blotched with sores and wounds, with the greenish pallor of corruption already upon him. On the right, stands John the Baptist. As you go on looking you can make out his gaunt figure (a shortage of locusts recently?), his cloak of camel's hair, his leather girdle. But not at first; at first what you see is his forefinger, pointing to Christ for Grunewald (who was a great painter and knew all about human anatomy and proportion), has drawn the finger disproportionally long. That is what John is—a finger pointing to the crucified. "Behold the Lamb of God who takes away the sin of the world." What a lesson, what an example for the preacher. And if you want it spelt you can just make out the letters *Illum oportet crescere autem minimi* (John 3.30—"he must become greater and I must become less").

But there is more. The Isenheim altarpiece was commissioned by the authorities for one of their hospitals where they gathered patients who suffered from St. Anthony's Fire, a foul skin disease, loathsome and lethal. There the sufferers might gather in the chapel and gaze on Christ dying, dead, with them in their disease, a Christ who had passed through it all and knew their pain, their vile appearance, their suffering, their fear, their death. The word of the cross—he takes my suffering, my disease, my sin, my death, even my doubt, for did he not cry out "My God, my God, why have you forsaken me?" He took them all he bore them all for me. Third—

Your Hearers

Faith, said Paul, comes by hearing and hearing through the word of Christ. Does listening to you, to me, generate faith? That depends on whether what people hear is the word of Christ and we are back with the old proposition—nothing but Christ and him crucified. This is what you have to give them, but they have much to give you; they are more than mere pulpit fodder. Let me remind them in this service, you are their ministers but they are yours, and again and again when you are discouraged, when you are baffled by the problems that can arise in any church, they will uphold you and guide you. But they can do that only if there is something more than a pulpit-pew relation, only if you know them and they know you. That is why for you, as well as for them, there is no substitute for regular pastoral visitation. I know I said it a few minutes ago. I repeat myself deliberately, because this is so important, and I fear so neglected.

What ties this all together is the word *saved.* You will save both yourself and those who hear you. "The word of the Cross is to them that are perishing, foolishness, but to us who are being saved, it is the power of God." Yes, of course it is your business to declare this to anyone who will listen. The old word is still true; you have nothing to do but save souls. But don't forget that you too have a soul to save. And remember the last terrible lines of *Pilgrim's Progress.* "Then I saw that there was a way to Hell, even from the gates of Heaven, as well as from the city of Destruction." There is, and we shall every one of us need the Cross until the day we die.

"God's Remedy for Sin"—
1 Corinthians 6:9-11

[Preached thirteen times from 11/14/43 at Bondgate, Darlington, to 11/15/81 at Framwellgate Moor]

"He who takes the highest and most self-respecting view of his own welfare, which it is in his power to conceive, and adheres to it in spite of conventionality is a Christian whether he knows it and calls himself one, or whether he does not." Do you agree with that? It is Samuel Butler writing in his novel *The Way of All Flesh*. It is of course a complete and venomous perversion of what Christianity is; and the fact that far too many Christians have read Butler and his like uncritically and that such views have got abroad, has done more than anything else to bring about the dangerous situation in which the Church exists today.

St. Paul was in a similar dangerous situation with his Corinthians. They were very good and clever people filled with the notion that, after all, is not so very modern, of expressing themselves and realizing all their own abilities. Of course, they were far above all the petty restrictions of weak Christians; they were not to be checked. And consequently, their unhindered impulses were leading them to a fine row of very questionable pursuits, and more. So, St. Paul found it necessary to give them a pretty sharp reminder of what they were doing and where they were going. And it will do us no harm occasionally to take an equally sharp reminder ourselves. So, let us find out what Paul has to say. He is insisting first of all that it is—

Possible to Miss the Kingdom of God

This is a thing we are fond of forgetting. If we do not exactly formulate our thought, we vaguely run on to the effect that in the long run everything will be alright for everybody. There is no need to worry. In the words of the old phrase of one of the fathers of modern heresy and unbelief, "God will forgive me, it's his job." Do you think I'm speaking too strongly? Or preaching to the converted? I wonder if any of you noticed a slight hitch in the first Communion Service which I conducted at Bondgate. It happened while we were saying the Confession together. I suddenly noticed that we were saying different words, but it was put right in a moment. But what had happened was this. You were using the old service books, which were printed before the Methodist Union of 1932, but I have a copy of the new Book of Offices adopted in 1936. The 1936 edition chose to leave out of the Confession the words describing our sins "provoking most justly thy wrath and indignation against us." I look upon that as a very serious matter. You may say it is but a straw; I say it is a straw which shows which way the wind is blowing. Is God no longer wrathful and indignant against sin? Does he regard it with complacency? Does it not matter? It does matter very much. And it matters very much that many of us have ceased to care about God's wrath, or even to believe that he can be angry at all.

I think that this failure to think seriously about God and sin is at the back of the moral disorder in our own day. That a weak, sentimentalized, humanized view of God is going about, there is no doubt. You can find the details in the newspapers. I shall not go into them. I am merely putting two and two together; and I am sure that the answer is four. A learned Jew in Cambridge, Mr. Loewe whose death a few years ago was certainly hastened by his labors for and his passionate sympathy with Jewish refugees once said "The trouble with the world today is there is not enough righteous indignation in it." Well, how do you expect to find righteous indignation in it if even God is not allowed to have any? Especially in these days when science can make possible so many social sins without social consequences what sanction can there be but—God?

I hope that no one thinks I am giving you stuff that is out of date, and obscurantist. For my own part, I am content to rely upon the Bible. But I can give you other authorities too. One of the most notable theologians in Methodism told me this story. He was preaching one day in Clapham, and on Sunday afternoon took a walk along the Clapham Common, a great place for open air meetings. He joined one rather riotous crowd. He found a woman on a box not getting a hearing at all. She seemed to be a rather queer sort of Christian, a crank of some sort, but she certainly was having a bad time. The crowds, mostly young people, were not heckling her, they were just spewing filth at her, and she could hardly get a word in. The theologian drew his scarf over his collar, that he might seem to speak as a layman, and went to the middle. "Let me have a turn, you've borne your witness" he said to the woman. "She looked at me as if I were an angel." Then he got on the box and started right away. And I should like to think that if I had been there, I would have thought of the same opening line. "What this lady says is quite right; you're all going to hell."

Now isn't this obviously true? How can anyone remain a member of the Kingdom of God who quite deliberately rejects its king? How can those who say "we will not have this man to reign over us" expect to have anything to do with the Kingdom of Christ? Again, St. Paul says that the Kingdom of God is righteousness, peace, joy in the Holy Spirit. How can the unrighteous inherit the Kingdom? It is possible, it is dangerously possible to miss the Kingdom of God altogether, and if we have broken one of the least of the commandments and have taught others to do so, may God have mercy upon us. But now let us ask—

What Sort of Things Exclude from the Kingdom and Why

I don't think I need to say much about most of the sins Paul enumerates in these verses; except perhaps to remind you that even if you do not commit them, they are not out of date or out of fashion. But I am sure that this is not the time and place to go into a general expose of modern morals. Paul took his list from what he had seen in the world of his own day; and not only from his own observation but from lists which were ready-made for him. A lot of contemporary literature is just full of such lists. In making this sermon I looked up a number of references and have been skimming over pages of Greek all full of this sort of thing. But it is not only that the philosophers saw the same sort of vices and condemned them. In fairly recent years an ancient game has been discovered, played with round objects rather like draughts. Unfortunately, we haven't got a complete set yet, and we don't know exactly how the game was played. On one side of each game piece was a number and on the other an address to the player so that you might pick the piece up and read "thief" or "extortionist" or something worse. Think of it, playing games with these things.

Paul took his sins from the customs of his own day. We may well do the same. At least, so I thought last Tuesday morning when I was writing this sermon, so I left my New Testament up in my study, went downstairs and picked up the *Manchester Guardian*. In a couple of minutes, I had picked out these. This was in a report of a speech. "The struggle for the freedom of small nations . . . the battle for democracy, the struggle for social equality, and *such empty phrases.*" I do not need to remind you who was speaking in Germany on Monday night. Then across the page to the *Guardian's* own leader: "It is generally agreed that there is excessive drinking among young people." And again, I do not need to remind you that that is true.

For not in our country only, England, as in Germany, there is a pervasive atmosphere of moral cynicism and a general trend of what Paul calls covetousness which has been well translated by Anderson Scott "insatiableness." It doesn't matter what happens to anyone else, so long as I get my way. It doesn't matter what happens to me, so long as here and now, I get my share of pleasure. If it be true that things are like that, then if no one else will ask it, you and I in the Church must ask the question—What can be done about it? I have spoken about the pagan lists of vices. Now in general, it is true to say that these lists however exact and however acutely analyzed, did nothing to stop the vice they described.

But St. Paul did know something that could stop them. Now I'm very much afraid, and especially on this Sunday, that in these days the Church has gotten down to the level of these pagan vice lists, the level of the mildly shocked conscience and the book of rules. Believe me, that will do nothing. They couldn't stop the sin of the Hellenistic world, and they will not stop the sin of the 20th century. Only one thing will do. The key to social problems is not in lists, but through—

Redemption in the Church

Such were some of you. But how is it that you are such no longer? "You were washed, you were sanctified, you were justified in the name of the Lord Jesus Christ and in the Spirit of our God." There is need for us to do some realistic thinking and some plain speaking here. There is no other way than this. The situation we have to deal with, when we confront the situation in which human nature exists, is not rightly thought of as parallel to that of a bud which has to be developed, so that we may hope to watch the human race, as a school of Christian teachers think they can watch children open like flowers to the sun (why not like a cabbage, said a friend of mine). The real situation would be more aptly compared to the Gadarene swine rushing to the precipice. There was only one thing that could save the Gadarene swine, and it was not that more little pigs should grow up to be big pigs. The only thing that would have saved them would have been for them all to turn around and go in the opposite direction. And that is what this generation needs to do.

To be more serious, life needs some authoritative treatment if it is to be put straight. Do you know of J. B. Priestley's play *Johnson over Jordan*. It is strange and very interesting. The whole play takes place after the death of Johnson, a man as ordinary as his name. In some very clever scenes, the conflict between good and bad in him is worked out. In a sort of nightmare sequence, the evil is worked out in all its loathsomeness. Next in a similar way the good is portrayed. And the play finishes without an end. The last scene shows Johnson, walking out, a tiny figure among the stars, walking into the unknown unbounded future, with all the tension of good and bad unresolved and with neither Johnson nor Priestley knowing when or how it will be resolved, only hoping that somehow, sometime it will be resolved.

As a picture of life, that is excellent. We are like that; every one of us has that mixture of good and bad impulses within him. But we, let us say it humbly, know more than Mr. Priestley. We know the answer to the problem he has set us. And the answer is that God justifies the ungodly by faith. This is the only thing that can set us straight. God can and does deal with sin. No one else can do so, but he does—

> Rock of Ages, cleft for me,
> Let me hide myself in Thee;
> Let the water and the blood,
> From Thy riven side which flowed,
> Be of sin the double cure,
> Save me from its guilt and power. (A. Toplady)

"You Are Not Your Own"—
1 Corinthians 6:19-20

[Preached twenty-seven times from 10/31/43 at
Bondgate, Darlington, to 8/18/02 at Howden-le-Wear]

A Definition of Sin

The train was in Rugby Station and I was waiting for it to go. I was sitting alone in the compartment until, shortly before the train was due to depart, two women came hurrying along the platform, flung open the door and joined me. For a moment or two they had nothing to say, they were too out of breath. Then they began to talk with low voices which I couldn't help but overhear, and I must confess that I was too interested to even try to close my ears. I will give you three things they said. They must have all come within five minutes. The first was "Yes I always manage it this way; if you do this, you do the railway company and save yourself shillings every time. They never find out." The second came quite shortly afterwards. "Oh no, he isn't living with *her* now, he is living with (name given)." And number three: "Church? Oh no my dear I never go to Church. Why I should fall asleep if I did."

Now that was no mere haphazard collocation of irregularities. If you will take the trouble to compare and analysis the three things involved, you will come upon a penetrating and entirely adequate definition of sin. In the first statement, there is the question of our relationship to the property of others. In that field, it is the tendency of all. Robbing the railway is but one indication of a tendency that breaks out again and again, the tendency to draw to ourselves whatever property we can lay hands on. The property is there, it is associated with someone else, but without regard for them, like magnets we drag it to ourselves. You may give this tendency a pretty name like "the

191

acquisitive instinct" but that does not alter the fact. The fundamental thing is that we idolize ourselves; *we* are what matters, and if the interests of others get in the way, they must suffer; they must lose that we may gain.

Take the second instance, the case of sexual irregularity. The same tendency is at work here. What matters is the satisfaction of my desire, my lust. This time it is not the material property of other people that may suffer, it is their own persons. No matter what may be the effect on anyone else, *I* must be satisfied; this pernicious ego of mine must be exalted over everything.

Or the third case, which to give it its proper name is simply contempt of God and of his Word. Again, the same tendency appears raised to its ultimate degree. First, I am more important than other people's property, second I am more important than other people's own persons, third I am more important than God. For it means no less. I presume to measure myself against God and to rate my own interests above Him. Think of that—Church too tedious and dull to go to!

I know preachers are poor and uninteresting; it is true most of us are. In many churches the singing is bad, second rate to worse. And perhaps in some places the people are unfriendly. But when all that is said, in this place God's Word is read and spoken, prayer is offered, the bread is broken and the wine poured out signifying Christ's death and its power in human lives. And that's not interesting enough, not good enough for me?

You see the definition of sin at which I am driving don't you? It is not derived in the first place from that very interesting conversation on the train, though that may very well have helped to clarify our thought. It comes from the words of St. Paul. He is talking to Christians and he says "you are not your own." Now sin means just this, that we fancy that we are our own, that we have every right to please ourselves. "You are not your own, therefore glorify God" he says. "I am my own" reply our sinful hearts, and I shall therefore glorify myself. In the world of property what matters is possession; and I will glorify myself by making mine the property that belongs to others. In the world of personal relationships, I am my own and what matters is 'I' and therefore I will glorify myself at the expense of someone else's personality. What does the effect on her or him matter, so long as I get what I want? Even in regard to God, I am my own, and God has no business to invade my rights. I matter more than God, and I will have my way, not his.

That is what sin is; it is really not a particular act so much as this essential egocentricity of the soul; though you can readily see how this spontaneously involved inward dispositions which issued in outward acts. "Now" says

Paul, "no doubt all that has been true of you Corinthians but if you really are Christians, it has changed now for—

You Are Not Your Own

You are not egocentric, but God-centered and in consequence a new life with a new direction is expected of you. You must glorify not yourself but God, with every part of your personality (that is what he means by "body"). I want to consider that in the same three terms we have used for the other side of the picture—sin. Of course, you can divide the subject in others way but this time this way will do. So first, in respect of material things. You are not your own and you must glorify God in your body. I know that that will sound to some people as if it has little to do with religion; if you think so, it shows you don't know much about religion.

God is to be glorified in the way we relate to material things. That means more than you must be scrupulously honest, but it does mean that. There are some businesses that would not stand looking into on that basis. It means a standard of not only honesty but godliness and that is far harder in business. But even that is not the whole picture. It is for every one of us to ask—Am I glorifying God in my job? Can I do so? Of course, that does not mean we must all be parsons or teachers or doctors. A minister I know once said something on these lines. A young woman came to him worried about her job. She didn't think it had any service in it and wondered if she should change. He asked her what she did. "Oh just ledgers and accounts for the N.C.H.O. (i.e. the National Health)"! And she could not see how she would glorify God in that.

This works on a big scale as well as on a small one. This is where we can and must talk about Christianity and politics, Christianity and the social order. We are commanded to glorify God in these departments of life. We are not to think of ourselves as our own. A sermon is not the place to work this out in the details of economics and I don't propose to lower my office as a minister of the Word. But it is well within my office to ask whether a system, whatever it be, which tolerates extremes of wealth and poverty, or which lives by propaganda and the suppression of the truth, or which has no sanction other than force, does glorify God or not. Whether it glorifies the God and Father of our Lord Jesus Christ, or some other god, Mars or Odin, blood or race. But there is more to say than that, for a system of complete equality and liberty, of freedom from want and fear, might nevertheless be the most idolatrous system the world has known. For we have to glorify not human-kind but God, so that we have not rightly understood the material things of life until we see them as parables of God's truth.

In personal relationships, you are not your own. In them all you must glorify God. That means certainly that you must not glorify yourself. You must not set up your own aims and purposes as the ultimate thing of greatest importance. Now again (and this is where the Christian parts company with most social workers) are you to take as your goal the highest good of other people and the community as a whole. That sounds very imposing and noble, and so it is. But it is a way that breaks down.

The question—Am I my brother's keeper, is as old as the hills. And as long as people think on these terms, Cain will slay Abel, or vice versa. Cain would not regard himself as Abel's keeper. He didn't care what happened to Abel, and that led to disaster. But it was not the only contributing factor. Abel apparently did think he was Cain's keeper. He was a superior person, he could go one better than his brother; and perhaps that was as much the root of the tragedy as anything else. This thinking one is someone else's keeper is mighty dangerous. You may say that you are not, and tell him to go to hell as he pleases. Or you may say that you are, and drive him to hell by priggish-ness and interference. The plain fact is that as Christians we must avoid this language and this way of thinking. You are not your brother's keeper, you are however his brother! And as St. Paul says he is your brother "for whom Christ died." That is to say that you have not understood your relationship to your brother until you understand that it is a theological relationship, a relationship which includes not only you and him, but also the eternal and infinite "Thou." Life does not go straight when you are glorifying yourself and it does not go straight when you are glorifying your neighbor, for he too is a mortal and sinful human being. It goes straight only when you two stand together as brothers and under the mercy and judgment of God, and thus glorifying God. In all our contacts with one another we must glorify God, we must set the Lord always before us. We must bring God into all our relationships of life. That does not mean stuffing religion down people's throats, far from it. It does mean living by faith, seeing our own deeds complete not in themselves but in God, in his purposes.

In regard to God himself, you are not your own. There are many excellent and unselfish people in the world, who lead exemplary lives of goodness and usefulness. They do not come to Church; they tell you they have no need of it. Without any assistance from minister and Church they can live as well and as serviceably as those who are in the Church three times every Sunday. In regard to material things, they recognize that they are not their own. They are honest and unselfish. In no circumstances would they take anything not their own. They would rather labor for the common good. And in regard to other persons they recognize they are not their own. They never consciously wrong anyone; they would not dream of infringing on another's personality. Their appetites and desires they never exercise at the expense of anyone else. On the contrary, they do good to others in a tactful and kindly way.

What more? It is when they come into the presence of God that they take possession of themselves. God alone has no claim on them that they will recognize. They will be independent of Him. And there, without any show of open wickedness, is sin, in its ugliest, bleakest form. The most dreadful Christian heresy, which is hardly even worthy to be called a heresy, so fearful a perversion of Christian truth it is, is summed up in the phrase that it "emancipates human beings from God." That is not sin that the world commonly recognizes as such, but it bears its own damnation upon its face. What but damnation can there be for people who have never suffered God to take possession of them and will cut themselves adrift from him, the fountain of all life and salvation? "We want"—it is so easy to stand up before God as the fine independent fellows that we are; we are at great pains to tell Him what fine persons we are, and we show anything but a broken and contrite heart. You are not your own, least of all are you your own when you stand before God; he claims you as his own, you have no independent standing, no power, no pride of place. Glory belongs to God alone. What right have I, has anyone to say these things? Is it all simple assertion which may be true or false? St. Paul has a reason. You are not your own because—

You Were Bought with a Price

Once for all, God invaded our world and broke down human independence. He bought us out, acquired all our rights, or fancied rights, at the cost of the Cross of Christ. He gave himself for us. Let us glory in that fact but let us not forget its consequence—that we are his. By his act of unparalleled grace, he broke into our lives and demanded unconditional surrender. He broke down and he breaks down the isolation behind which we shelter and by which we insulate ourselves from God and other human beings. He comes into our lives to dethrone the ego that sits in solitary glory there and to make us his own.

You were bought with a price. And if there is anything which can break down that pride and make us humble people of faith and trust it is that thought of that price, as the Holy Spirit brings it home to us. "Two things chiefly" said Erasmus in the *Enchidrion* "will keep you from pride, if you consider first what you are in yourself, filthy at birth, a bubble through life, the food of worms at death, and secondly what Christ was made for you."

> My worthless heart to gain, The God of all that breathe
> Was found in fashion as a man, And died a cursed death.
> And can I yet delay My little all to give
> To tear my soul from earth away, For Jesus to receive
> Nay, but I yield, I yield! I can hold out no more,
> I sink, by dying love compelled, And own thee conqueror. (Charles
> Wesley)

"Christian Marriage"— 1 Corinthians 7:16

[Preached once at Luddington on 4/7/69]

It is hard to imagine a more frightening and off-putting congregation than one whose eventual nucleus is made up of two of the most learned theologians I have had dealings with. For this reason, let me begin quite informally at the point where I know that I shall have everyone else in the church behind me. There is no one here who would not wish, in the context of this service, to assure you both of our affection, to tell you how warmly we wish you well, and how earnestly we pray that God's blessing may set upon you, not only today but all the days that follow it. We shall always be concerned for your welfare, and we shall thank God for all your achievements. Having said that let us fall back on St. Paul—1 Cor. 7.16: "Wife, it may be that you will save your husband. Husband it may be that you will save your wife."

You are doubtless too polite to show it, but I am sure you are, both of you, even on your wedding day, too alert not to be saying "But this doesn't apply! Paul is speaking of mixed marriages, between Christian and non-Christian." Of course, you are quite right, and yours is a marriage of Christians. I know that, not because of your firsts in theology, it is possible to have a first in theology and be a very poor sort of Christian, as no one should know better than I, not for that but for much surer reasons.

True; but what is Paul essentially saying here? *That a measure of genuine Christianity will always win.* The Corinthans said, "We can't risk marriages like this, the non-Christian partner is sure to swamp the Christian one." Paul says "No!" real Christianity will always win. And so it will. And this matters, because there are more things to beat in marriage. There is adversity. University teachers are perhaps not quite as badly treated as they sometimes think, but he would be a fool who thought the way was sure to be always easy. Christianity can beat adversity, not by providing an unending supply of jam for the head, but in deeper ways than that.

There is friction, there is boredom. You don't feel either today, but of course they can and do arise. Real Christian faith, forbearance, love, ἀγάπη not "eros" can and will overcome them. There are social pressures from without, that do not always make the way easier. But these too can be overcome. And finally, is paganism right out of the spectrum? Not quite, there is the professional theologian's brand of it, his blasé indifference to holy things, the descending line, gradual at first, then plunging of diminishing concern for the things that matter most.

"Wife, it may be that you will save your husband; husband it may be that you will save your wife"—each of you God's minister to the other, each a standing sign first, pointing out the Way, the Truth, the Life.

"Communion with What?"— 1 Corinthians 10:16-21

[Preached twenty-two times from 7/1/45 at Bondgate, Darlington, to 7/19/98 at Bowburn]

This is this month's communion Sunday, the day of our communion service. It is moreover a special communion service since there are some who will be taking part in it for the first time. That is why I especially want to raise the question which is raised by St. Paul in these words, summed up briefly in three words—"Communion with what?" The word communion, though it is not in our colloquial speech today, is a very big one. It does not mean merely that we share, have in common, the rights and privileges of the particular group to which we belong. It does not mean that we have an equal share in some common property, as we might divide a bag of sweets between us. It implies a union, a real and deep belonging to, and belonging together.

Now it is quite plain that that sort of communion can be had outside the Christian faith as within it. The question is the one I have raised— Communion with what? St. Paul is dealing with a special case, one which was vital in his own time and, we ought to recognize this, quite insignificant in our own day in this country. He is talking about sacrifices made to idols, and he doesn't find it easy to make his point clear. Of course, he says, an idol has no reality and we know that. Yet those who take part in their rites have communion with the evil powers—demons Paul calls them, who are behind the whole scheme of idol worship. We should say, they identify themselves with the whole evil and unreal framework of the pagan religion. Thus, he says they are sacrificing to and having communion with a no-God. That is how we ought to translate his rather clumsy Greek. Paul is quoting the Greek Old Testament, and the Hebrew which the Greek translators rendered means "no God."

As I say, Paul's special care is out of date, none of us is likely to run along to the Serapeum and offer a sacrifice to Serapis. We must leave this on one side (only reminding ourselves that in precisely these terms the problem occurs on the mission field today). Yet there is much to be said about—

Communion with a No-God

It is one of the commonest things in the world today. I have quoted to you before a very famous saying of Martin Luther's: "Human beings will have either God or an idol." You could put that in other terms and say human beings will have communion with God or with a no-god. A person will pledge himself to something. There isn't time to discuss this fully, to consider all the no-gods that are about in the world today, the unreal ends and causes, the untrue truths. It is a preacher's business to comment on sin and error but he ought to spend most of his time on goodness and truth.

There are however some examples that will occur at once. I hesitate to mention Nazism and Facism, because they have been talked of so often as pseudo-religions. But they do show up our special point very clearly and will serve to make plain exactly what that point is. Those, says St, Paul, who make their sacrifices in a pagan temple have communion with all the evil reality of pagan religion. They become intimately joined to it. Now see what has happened in Germany. I am making no excuses for anyone, I am merely stating what seems to be the fact. In the early days, many Germans threw in their lot with Hitler, they approved part, for example of socialism's policy (there was 1,500,000 unemployed in December 1931 in Germany). They thought that under him they would be more prosperous. But having once given their allegiance they were committed to the whole program and some of them, at least, were horrified by their own new duties. It meant communion, full communion with this no-god and there is no clearer illustration of what I mean (though there may be more personal ones). Just start playing with evil, even with something less than the best, and as St. Paul says, you will find yourself in a pledged union with it.

The old Faust role is a true one after all, true as an allegory. You know the story, that the very learned Faust, anxious for yet more wisdom, and still more wonderful experiences, sold his soul to the devil for 24 years, and that when the time was up, the devil, prompt to the minute, appeared to claim his own and drag Faust off to Hell. That is what does happen, what has happened again and again in human experience. If you want the devil's goods, you have to pay the devil's price. If you go part of the way, he will take you the rest. I am not thinking merely about going to Hell when you are dead. I mean that those who trifle with evil, find themselves in its power to a far greater extent than they dreamed when they began.

You cannot, as St. Paul says, "drink the cup of the Lord and the cup of demons." You cannot enter into vital, all-embracing communion with Christ and with something else at the same time. It is like Christian marriage. Christian marriage must be monogamous, because it pre-supposes such a complete union of a man and a woman that it is simply impossible for a man to enter into such a union with two women at the same time (and vice versa). So it is here. This communion with God is so radical and deep a thing that you cannot run it along with a similar union with something else. Other interests of course—books, music, games and so on; love for other people too; but always this dominant and guiding power.

I want to say this very plainly to everyone. It is possible for you to give yourself to something less than God, but that you cannot do that and have God too. I want to say it to those who are starting out on the Christian life. I want to remind those who have been living that life a long time, and who (like myself) find it easy to forget those fundamental things. I want to say it to any who have not yet made up their minds. It means that you must make up your mind. You cannot drink the cup of the Lord and someone else's. You cannot even be your own. But now let me be positive for some time as is left to speak about—

Communion with God

Let me say right at the beginning that I am talking to you all. I am not talking about a special benefit that a few especially good people may have. This is the privilege of all Christians, and since it is a privilege that all may have, it is a duty of all to accept it. Suppose your children were seen running about without shoes and socks, with ragged clothes and always dirty faces, unwashed and uncared for. People would not very much like the children, but they would not only dislike them, they would say "What a home they must come from! What parents they must have!" Of course, you would never let such things be said, but listen. We are the children of God. And there are so many of us who go through life in our poverty, our disease, our dirt that people say (in effect) "I don't think much of God, his folk aren't any better than anyone else's." I am saying this to myself as much as to anyone else. I read a sentence the other day that went into my mind like an arrow. It was in a book by Richard Baxter, that most saintly English minister of 300 years ago, who going to Kidderminster in 1640, in a few years had transformed the town. He said, "Happy the people who have a heavenly minister." And I thought of all the other things I spend so much time in trying to be—a friendly minister, easy to get on with, a clever minister, a good preacher, and how little time I spend in becoming a heavenly minister, daily and hourly in contrast with your Lord and mine.

How are we to practice such a life of fellowship with God? There is nothing automatic about it. A Christian life is not like a watch, wound up and set going from without, it is rather like a human body working from within through its own active energies. You are to remember that God is with you always, and that you know what he is like. You know from Christ, above all you know from the Cross. This God is in your life. He is saying to you—"your sins are forgiven." He is saying to you "follow me." He is saying to you "not everyone that says to me lord, lord . . . but he that does the will of God." He is saying to you "I am the Way, the Truth, the Life."

Seek him in prayer. Share your life, everything you hope and want and fear with him. You can tell him of everything, you can ask him for anything, provided that you can remember that love may say no as well as yes. Seek him in fellowship. Few things will help you more than the advice, or even the presence and affection of other Christians. Seek him in the appointed ways, in reading the Bible, in hearing it preached, in the service of communion.

You need not fear. Jesus said "seek and ye shall find." Venture on him, trust in him, and you will find how very practical all this is, how it brings a peace and joy into life that comes no other way, how it breeds love and gentleness, and strength in all you do. Truly—you cannot drink the cup of the Lord and the cup of demons. Choose, choose him and you will not regret it. In an election speech, Ernst Brown said "Mr. Churchill wants votes, not words." Christ has your word, I know, but does he have your vote?

"Proclaiming the Lord's Death"— 1 Corinthians 11:26

[Preached seventeen times from 2/13/44 at Bondgate, Darlington, to 3/28/91 at Billy Row]

Christian people are always proclaiming the death of Christ. They never do it more pointedly, more poignantly than when they break the bread and pour out the wine of the Holy Supper, the act in which it is the privilege and the duty of every Christian to share. Not every Christian can preach, but every Christian can eat and drink. Probably, St. Paul's words mean not merely that the symbolism of the supper is a vivid, dramatic portrayal of the broken body and the shed blood of Christ, but also that the narrative of the Passion of Christ was told in the course of the service. There are many indications that that was the case. Be that as it may, in any case Paul is here emphasizing the central theme of his preaching; Christ crucified.

I hope that theme has not become monotonous to any of you. I make no apology at all that I am continually referring to it. The Bible continually returns to it. A preacher has only one task; to expound, to explain, to compare Holy Scripture, and consequently if he is not continually speaking of the death of Christ for sinners he is not true to his own appointment. I have no right to stand in this pulpit to do any other thing than that.

There is a picture at Colmar which in artistic grounds is becoming well-known today. It is an altarpiece by Matthias Grünewald. In the central section is a picture of the crucified Christ. Christ hangs on the cross, contorted in the agony of death, painted with a grim, harrowing realism. On one side stands John the Baptist a tall gaunt figure, dressed in skins, a wild creature. One arm is stretched out, pointing at the cross. And Grunewald has painted his outstretched forefinger and hand as having excessive size, quite out of proportion, to symbolize the fact that John is a pointing finger, pointing to Christ crucified. He has no other function, no other meaning. That is the function of the Christian preacher too. Every other part of him may and must shrink, provided that the pointing finger swells and grows until it fills the spectator's eye. Necessity is laid upon us to proclaim in preaching, in the sacraments, and in our lives the death of Christ for various reasons, three of which I will now set out—

To the Glory of God

Certainly, the cross means no glory to anyone else. No one else comes very well out of it. There is nothing for human beings to boast about in their share of the crucifixion. As Dorothy Sayers has said: "All this was not very creditable to us, even if he was (as many people thought and think) only a harmless, crazy preacher. But if the Church is right about Him, it was more discreditable still, for the man we hanged was God Almighty." The story of the Cross, as far as our side of it goes, is not a very edifying one. It is a picture of people stretching the law on all sides with falsehoods to squeeze their way through so that they might do away with the man they hated. Yet it is a picture in which everyone of us may recognize himself. This is what we do. And by this means, God abates our pride. He shows us what sin means, he shows us the depth of inbred sin. The real consequences of our pride and sin are easily concealed from us. The sins which you and I commit, which you and I harbor in our hearts, are not such as plunge a world into war, such as ruin homes, and drive men to drink and women to despair. They are just little sins, apparently insignificant, until we see them in the light of the Cross. Then they stand out for what they are, our blatant denial and defiance of God.

There is no glory for us in the Cross. But it is God's glory. So much God endured for his children. To such lengths he would go. No one else would have done so. St. Paul, you will remember, says that it is not very likely that anyone would die for a person that was merely just; though perhaps someone could find it in his heart to die for a person who was really good. But God, says Paul, died for us when we were neither just nor good, but simply down right sinners. There is the glory of God and it is not our notion of glory. People generally think themselves glorious when they are getting, acquiring, aggrandizing themselves, and imposing their will on others. Not so with God. Do you remember the great scene of the revelation of God in Exodus? Moses asks that he may see God's glory, and God replies "I will cause all my goodness to pass before you." And as God passes by, a voice proclaims "The Lord, the Lord, a God full of compassion and gracious, slow to anger and plenteous in mercy and truth." The same thing is written in one of the greatest of hymns—

> Great God of wonders! all thy ways
> Display the attributes divine;
> But countless acts of pardoning grace
> Beyond thine other wonders shine:
> Who is a pardoning God like thee?
> Or who has grace so rich and free? (J. Stainer)

We glory in the Cross because the Cross is the glory of God. It is the death of all our boasting in ourselves, but it means that we have more than ourselves to glory in. We can no longer boast of our own achievements, for they are less than nothing; but through the death of Christ we know that God is for us, and therefore we exult in hope of the glory of God. We proclaim the Lord's death, therefore to the glory of God. We must also proclaim it—

To the Saving of Our Souls

There is no other salvation for us. If there is not life when we look at the Crucified one, then there is no life at all, and we are dying human beings. On one of his visits to Oxford, Dr. Johnson heard the official sermon preached for the benefit of those criminals who had been condemned to die at the assizes. A week or two later, the same learned preacher, preached the University sermon before the University of Oxford. He did a thing which is evidently not restricted to Methodists. He preached the same sermon. Dr. Johnson commented on this and received the usual reply. It was a good sermon and therefore worth preaching more than once. "Yes sir," said Johnson, "but the University was not to be hanged the next morning."

Do you preach a different sermon to those who are not to be hanged the next morning? No doubt circumstances can and do give extra point to a sermon, but as the old preachers said, "all sermons should be preached as by a dying person to dying persons," and we may add they should be about the dying God. Certainly, we are dying human beings. What does it matter if it is today, or tomorrow, or next week, or in fifty years? We are dying people who live in bondage to the universal sway of corruption. Moreover, we are already dead in trespasses and sins. Hence we must say

> His only righteousness I show,
> His saving grace proclaim;
> 'Tis all my business here below
> To cry Behold the Lamb! (Charles Wesley)[1]

We try from time to time to find life elsewhere. The Gospel of life about a dead Christ has never been a popular one. Yet at least it is the only radical one. It is the only one that takes into account all the facts of the situation and meets us where we are, that addresses us as dying human beings. For the last enemy is death and the sting of death is sin. The Cross is a drama of redemption in terms of sin and death, and it is the message of the triumph of life and love. I suppose some of us do find it hard to say "Nothing in my hand I bring, simply to the Cross I cling." That is because we have not really known what it is to cry to God out of the depths. But just suppose you were to be hanged tomorrow morning, suppose you were never to hear another sermon. Where would your thoughts turn? Would you not say "O Savior of the world, who by the Cross and precious blood has redeemed us, save us and help us we humbly beseech thee O Lord." That leads me at once to the third point. We proclaim the Lord's death—

For the Evangelization of the World

We have, I must make this confession on behalf of preachers, tried preaching a whole lot of other things. We have offered dying and starving people a nice variety of stones and scorpions instead of the bread they needed. The result is plain. They now believe the Church doesn't have anything to offer them at all. We have offered them entertainment at Church. I do not mean entertain by concert and social only; I mean we have offered them entertainment in the pulpit. And they find that they can get it better in the cinema.

We have offered false doctrines. We have fed them with the idea of evolution and progress. Some of them are simply disillusioned, as they have

---

1   Editor's Note: Here and elsewhere I have quoted the hymn directly and it is I who have added the parenthetical reference to the composer, as CKB rarely says whom he's quoting when it comes to a hymn. He assumes the audience will be familiar with it. It is interesting that in his later sermons from the 90s and thereafter he seldom quotes the old hymns, perhaps because he knows he is preaching to a mostly different audience less well schooled in Methodist hymnody.

every reason to be. Others have discovered that they can find all this outside the Church, and therefore do not need us any longer. We have offered them a romantic, superficial, kindliness and good will, with the same results. But there is only one message that makes Christians, and that is the Word of the Cross. There is only one thing you can talk about to people who are going to be hanged the next morning.

I am far too young, and I hope humble enough to criticize an earlier generation, but at all events we are learning this today. You will remember what Kenneth Grayston had to say on this subject only a fortnight ago. It is no good thinking you can bribe people with the hope of a new world, the only thing to do is to preach Christ, to offer life by his death. Such is the experience of men on the most recent Commando Campaign.

I am far from saying that you only have to preach the Cross faithfully in order to secure results; quite obviously, it does not work that way. There is nothing infallible about it at all. That is the nature of the case. The Cross is the denial of all human achievements, the extinction of all human power. It means that everything depends upon God's raising the dead, God's bursting in upon the chaos of human despair. And it is precisely to that that Paul leads us. "We proclaim the Lord's death, until he comes."

As you know, the Lord's Supper, in its origin, was clearly related to the Jewish Passover. It is very instructive to study the Passover service. That service too was built around a story, the story of the deliverance of the Jews from bondage in Egypt. And the instruction was constantly given that the tale was to be told "beginning with the shame and ending with the glory," from slavery to freedom, from darkness to light.

St. Paul takes up the rubric. You proclaim the Lord's death, he says, until he comes. You begin with the shame and end with the glory. Here we live by faith and under the Cross. But the Cross, the very bread and wine, are sign and symbol of the glory that shall be revealed.

> And now we watch and struggle,
> And now we live in hope,
> And Zion in her anguish
> With Babylon must cope.
> But He whom now we trust in
> Shall then be seen and known;
> And they that know and see Him
> Shall have Him for their own. (Bernard of Morlas, 12th century)

"Victory over Sin, Law, and Death"— 1 Corinthians 15:57

[Preached once at Undercliffe on 9/27/94]

This service has been announced not as a funeral, nor as a memorial service but as a thanksgiving service. That is what it is and that is what it ought to be. We are all different from one another, but it is safe to say we have all come to this service with some reason for thankfulness for Elsie Denison. That is what brings us here. We shall have different things in our mind, and some of you who know her week after week in this church, day after day even, could fill in more details than I can give, who saw her now and again. But I think I know enough. She sprang from, and I think she was always glad to remember she sprang from the Heap family which meant so much and contributed so much to Methodism not only in the West Riding but far beyond it. And she was a worthy member of the family; knew what it stood for and herself stood for what she knew.

I have often been told how good she was to her immediate family, and she and Arthur (which we cannot but remember as we remember Elsie) were a fine loyal couple, united in their service to this church as in the rest of life. It is not easy to find the right words to speak of that kind of loved and loving member of the family. Like most parents I think, who have normal or gifted children, I sometimes wonder how I should have reacted if I had had a handicapped child. I don't know. But we do know about Elsie and Arthur too, to see the unwavering patience, love, understanding, and appreciation—and the memories, the happy memories that lingered to the end.

In addition to loyalty and service to her family, there was the loyalty and service she gave to her church and through her church to her Lord. There was tradition in it, but there was more than tradition. We were able to visit her only three days before she died. We talked about this and that. And she

208

spoke of her appreciation of the care she was receiving from Hospice. After a half an hour or so, she was getting tired, and turned to me and said "can we have a word"? She knew, and she was quite right, that though when Christians meet they may chat about this and that, and she could do plenty of that, they have more serious concerns that can only find expression in prayer.

And she is dead, and now that is the end of all the good things we have been thinking of giving thanks for. Or is it? Death is a serious business. There is no room in Christian funeral for a panegyric (though I have heard that word used). Death, the ultimate human weakness means no panegyrics. But it is not the end of thanksgiving. Grateful as we are for Elsie, the real thanksgiving is in the text I gave you—"Thanks be to God who gives us the victory through Jesus Christ our Lord." Remember it all. The Pauline observation—the sting of death is sin, and the sting of sin is the Law. But we have sighted victory here—victory over sin and victory over legalism. We have not seen them complete. There is only one place where you will see perfect sinlessness and absolute freedom and that is in the power of Jesus.

But when you see a Christian you will catch glimpses, sometimes more than glimpses, of a life freed from sin and unfettered by petty limitations. We have seen this in Elsie. And because Christ has in us and for us defeated sin and law, we know that he will not be defeated by the death of the body, so that though death makes us sad, we know now that Elsie lives a life perfected, and that by the grace of God we too may share it. "Thanks be to God who gives us the victory."

"Victory and Endurance" — 1 Corinthians 15:57-58

[Preached once at Sherburn Hill 3/6/91]

In this service, we need to give thanks to God for all that he has given in the life and work, the service and example, of Jenny Cole. We are also here, in this Church which she knew and loved and served so well, that we may be reminded of the Gospel, the good news of Christ crucified and risen; crucified and therefore giving meaning to all our suffering (of which we have plenty to think of today) risen, and therefore giving life even in what we call death. It is the same Gospel which in the same act gives comfort, strength, peace to those of us who survive, and not least to those who feel the pain of loss most keenly.

There are of course many of us here who through the years have often met in this place for precisely this purpose—to bear in mind the message of Jesus Christ, crucified and risen. But we are doing it today in a particular context marked by sadness and shock as well, and all this adds weight to the problem we all must feel as we ask ourselves why it should happen not to one of the worst but to one of the best people; as we ask ourselves what we have to say in the face of death.

For there are few better, more loyal Christian families than the Coles of Sherburn Hill. It was certainly characteristic that Jenny should have been here at the Church Fellowship last Tuesday evening. It can't have been easy to come, but she came. The fellowship was her special care, how much she had contributed to it through the years, as week after week she found speakers for it, no one can estimate. So she was loyal to the last, for (as you will know) by Wednesday morning she was in Dryburn Hospital and early on Friday she died. This was no final showpiece, just part of the whole. Most of us here will have some idea of what the Coles, all of them, have done for this Church, and of how much suffering, not just physical suffering, there has been in the background.

I have never forgotten this. It was on Easter Sunday morning in (I think) 1984 that I had preached here. We came out and were talking in the bright cool April sunshine. And, with much already behind her, and I do not know what medical and surgical procedures already, she said to me, "I'm afraid." I recognized it as the fear that all sensible people will sometimes feel, and sometimes as the highest form of courage, which knows fear and yet refuses to be moved by it, even to as much as a whimper. And there was Christine, whom we all loved, so that we all know something, even if only a little, of what her loss meant to the family. All this; but unwavering in so far as physical weakness permitted in loyalty to her family, in Christian discipleship and service to the Church and in hospitality.

So, indeed we give thanks for a Christian example that we have had the privilege of seeing. And we think of Jack and Jean, who, whatever the memories of earlier years, have lived lives of patient loving service, and will therefore feel the gap most keenly. I know them well enough to know that they would not thank me or anyone for merely superficial comfort. It is time once more to recall Jesus Christ, crucified and risen and to go back to the words of Scripture from which we set out. Let me recall it to you; and let me point out two things.

"Thanks be to God who gives us the victory." He gives it after death and we are the more confident that he can do that because we have seen him give the victory before death, in the valiant endurance of suffering, and in patient, loving self-denying care. And second "be steadfast, immovable." The work of the Lord goes on and that means, since it is his work, that he will not fail those who do it. Your labor is not in vain in the Lord. He will support you and never let you go.

"Despair and Faith"—
2 Corinthians 1:9-10

[Preached five times from 10/31/43 at Bondgate, Darlington, to 11/19/67 at Langley Park]

"What is the only comfort in life and death?" That is, I know a personal question, but it is not I that ask it. It stands at the beginning of one of the great theological documents of reformed Christianity, the Heidelberg Catechism. It is a not irrelevant way of beginning one's theology. It would be an entirely good thing if more preachers would ask personal questions of that sort. "What is the only comfort in life and death?"

I may be wrong, but I suspect there is one word in that question with which some of us would like to quarrel; the word *only*. Are there not more resources of comfort than one? Do not many things combined to bring rest and satisfaction to us? We like the story of the great Roman dignitary who lay a long time dying. They gave him once the last sacraments, thinking the end had come. But still he lingered. He asked that he might receive them again. "No," they replied, it was against the rules to give extreme unction twice to the same person. "Very well," he said, "bring me Pickwick." Are there then not many things that are a comfort to us? Books, friends, beautiful things? But the reason why some of us object to this "only comfort" is that one does not really know.

Despair

Paul knew it, at close quarters. It lies behind our text. The exact historical situation is one that raises a number of difficulties, and it is hard to say precisely where Paul was and what he had been doing. There simply is not enough evidence, and what there is, is not very clear. But there is no mistaking the language that he uses. "I heard the sentence of death in my own heart" he says. He saw the judge and his court, he heard his doom; abandon all hope. It was like that. He despaired not only of his work but of his life. This was the end.

We should understand more about Christianity if we knew more of despair like that. In a recent book, Alec Vidler has a very penetrating chapter entitled "The Need for Despair." The people who have seen life must clearly know best the futility that lies behind all its most splendid achievements; they are not taken in by its showy success, because they know it is simply—a show. One of T. S. Eliot's very great but very difficult poems ends in this way—

This is the way the world ends,
Not with a bang but a whimper. ("The Hollow Men")

Despair means getting as far as the last ditch of life, and then finding out it is a hole; that one is not yet in hell, but is certainly in a deep hole. Alec Vidler, in the chapter to which I have referred, says that apart from the way of Christian faith, there are three ways of facing that position. He gives them names. The first is *suicidism*, that means just running away, saying that things are so bad that there simply is no solution. The second is *diabolism*, that is the deliberate choosing of the evil alternative, a process of which there are notorious examples today. The third is *indifference,* simply pretending there is no problem there, or at least not caring about it.

When they are analyzed like this, we see that none of these alternatives will do. It is when we have exhausted the other possibilities that we realize that "other helpers fail and comforts flee." The "only comfort" clause becomes tolerable because in spite of its intolerance, when we take a sufficiently long view. I think it has come home to me most vividly when I have walked alone in the backs at Cambridge. There you get long term gardening. My own gardening never gets beyond putting in seeds and hoping they will be flowers of a sort a few months afterwards. But there you are dealing with trees; you see the gardeners putting in tiny saplings which in 100 years time, will take the place of monsters now middle-aged at 2–3 centuries. And as you walk there, you think, I cannot help but think of the people who walked there when those trees were saplings. The 16th century undergraduates who were going to change the world—the mighty poets, the university wits, as they called them, of the Elizabethan stage, the scientists of the 17th century with Isaac Newton at their head, the smug self-satisfied 18th century and so on. And the people who in a few hundred years will see my saplings as gnarled and full grown chestnuts and oaks. What will those people be doing and thinking? Poor, clever, happy people! So full of brilliant ideas, which in the end turn themselves out a paper and never do change the world which goes on rolling out the old round of wars and rumors of wars, splendor and scholarship and sin.

What is thy only comfort? If all other helpers in this transitory life fail, and comforts flee, where shall we turn? To God, says Paul; that we should not trust in ourselves but in God. Who is God? What is God? God is not ourselves. God is the next step beyond every human possibility. God is the unplumbed depth. God is the unknown. All other possibilities are to some extent in our hands. But we are in God's hands.

Does that sound unsatisfying to you? It is not so to me, for it seems to me a necessary qualification for being God that he should be unlike me. But we are not left entirely in the dark. Paul goes on to say not just who God is, but—

What God Does

He raises the dead. He delivers from death. Now that in the first place has reference to what actually took place in the case of Jesus of Nazareth. That event is fundamental. The Gospels present us with a swift movement from life to death. They open in the fruitful and beautiful countryside of Galilee. As the story rapidly unfolds, Jesus moves down the map to the bare and barren hills of Judaea, to Jerusalem, the place of death, always a place of death, of sacrifice or of bitter battle and siege. Then, told in plain unemotional language, comes the story of the Cross; the movement from life to death, geographically adumbrated is now consummated.

But then, dramatically, God breaks in; God becomes the subject of the verb. "God raised him from the dead." So that the process is not described by life—death; we must say life-death-life.

That, I say, is fundamental; it is the unique act of God in history. But the same pattern or movement becomes visible in all God's dealings with human beings. When Paul wished to illustrate the meaning of faith (in Romans) he turns to the story of Abraham. Abraham and his wife were very old—90–100 years old. And it was promised them that should have a child. It was absurd; the whole situation was really laughable. But Abraham thought not of his own deadness but of God's power. And God brought life out of death. That, says Paul, is characteristic of faith. Abraham is the father of all believing persons. God enters the desperate human situation and there raises the dead and brings life where formerly there was none.

That is the meaning of faith. It means we take our eyes off of the deceiving show of human appearance, and look instead upon the power of God which raised Christ from the dead. But this is a thing that we only do when we come to the last ditch of despair of which we spoke earlier. While we are still pleased with ourselves and confident in our own achievements, while we are still surrounded by the many comforts of life and have not come to the blank new age of hopelessness. We do not see the necessity of looking to God. We may indeed talk long and loud about a god of our own constructing, our own imagining, a god who takes a kindly interest in our church work and who is a convenient subject for our lessons in Sunday School. We are not really concerned with the God who raises the dead until we have tasted the bitter taste of death. We are not troubled by what lies beyond the boundary of the world while there are areas of attractive countryside within them. They only know meaning of Paul's saying "who delivered us" who have stood with him on the edge of all createdness, and looked shuddering over the blackness of the abyss. All this leads us to see the—

Positive Value of Suffering and Despair

Such a state is again and again the condition of creative life. Goethe says, thinking chiefly of poets and poetry, that the person who never ate his bread with tears, who never tasted the bitterness of life, will not do much. He hasn't got it in him. Like the old fashion educationists against the moderns, I believe we learn best what is knocked into us. It is written even of Jesus that he learned from what he suffered. Certainly, Goethe was right in what he said about the world of creative art. That, we could illustrate at great length. Did you hear a radio play about Beethoven some time ago? I remember a most moving scene in which Beethoven sets aside the possibility of human love and happiness, because they would destroy the business, the agency of soul in which he alone could produce his music. Or to take a similar but different picture, there was someone who on the other hand made his music with a background of turbulent domesticity in which there were two marriages, 20 children, and a perpetual grinding struggle to make ends meet.

Now let there be under no misunderstanding here. I do not say that if you refrain from marrying you will write another choral symphony, nor that if you try to keep 20 children on a meagre income you will compose another set of Brandenburg Concertos, or a Matthew Passion. Something more is necessary for that. Beethoven and Bach produced their music because their melancholy situation was fertilized by a vital creative impulse, in their case, musical genius; and it was the interaction of the two that gave us that music.

In our case, that musically creative principle is not there, but what I want to say is this: that there is a similar creative influence that is available for us all. It will not necessarily make us musicians or poets, it will not cause our names to be written in the newspapers and history books; it will do something far bigger than that. It will take and transfigure our lives, and bring out of their emptiness and defeat something beautiful and good. That is precisely what God does. And faith, faith in the God that raised Jesus from the dead is the thing that delivers us also from death and is the answer to despair.

I do not mean that faith is just another psychological factor like a gift of music, which acts as an automatic panacea, calculated like the much-advertised modern patent medicines and foods to send you through life with a permanent smile and in invariable good spirits. Faith is at once something less and more than that. It *is* faith, and *not* sight. The new person who is created by it, is God's new person, of whom the only visible pledge is Jesus Christ. Our life is hidden with Christ in God. It is not a commonplace every-day affair that can be paraded about the streets. There is, I know, something difficult to understand, and there is no earthly means of making it easy. A later New Testament writer made no mistake when he said that St. Paul wrote things difficult to be understood.

Yet is it so hard to believe? Out of the chaos and desperation of your own life, the welter of worry and sin, you are to look by faith, not at some ideal which you hope to attain, but at Christ—look and live. For that, by grace, is what you are. You are remade in his image. It is true that the best of us show no more than glimpses of that character in the ordinary conditions of our present life. But that is our *real life;* that is what you are, by faith. The answer therefore to our despair is not in our ideals or idealism; but in Jesus Christ, the eternal word of God.

"How Can I Receive God's Guidance?"—2 Corinthians 1:17; 1 Corinthians 7:25

[Preached nineteen times from 11/25/56 at Elvet to 7/20/97 at Wheatley Hill]

I should not be surprised if that strikes you as a rather odd coupling of texts. On the whole, I should agree. Certainly, they were texts that took some finding. And now that I have found them and read them to you I am going to leave them for a moment and come back to them a little later. Tonight, I'm asked to deal with a question which falls in your series on personal religion. We shall come back to the texts for the answer to the question; there is no other place for a preacher to find the answers than Scripture. But we will start with the question itself. It runs—How may I receive God's guidance?

When I first got down to serious work on this sermon, about a week ago, I said to my wife "I shall preach a sermon of three words." She replied, "My word, won't Elvet be surprised." I shall have to spare you the surprise, but I will at least begin with my three words. How may I receive God's guidance? "Use your common sense." Too many people, when they speak of guidance, think they can short-circuit commonsense and other unromantic processes of human reason. But you can't. Of course, God is not restricted to speaking through human common sense. If he did so, he would find his field of activities sorely limited. But normally, it is by the work of common sense that we find out what it is our duty to do. Only, and this is why I cannot be satisfied with these words, it must be Christian common sense. And now we must go back to the texts and find out what Christian common sense means. They show us two ways of reaching a decision.

Take the passage in 2 Corinthians first. This epistle is one that provides a fascinating field for detective work. Evidently, all kinds of things had been happening in Corinth. Things had gone wrong in the Church. Paul had visited them, he had sent letters, he had sent his friends and we can only get at the story by piecing out the evidence from 2 Corinthians itself. Most of the details don't matter now. But it is clear that at some stage or other, Paul had changed his plans, and there were nasty-minded people at Corinth who said "Fickleness! See how unstable the man is. You never know where you are with him." Paul explains what he had really been doing, and what his intentions really were, then adds "when you really know the facts, does it look as though when I make my plans, I make them according the flesh, that is on the basis of purely human standards?" That is one way of making a decision and as we shall see, it is a very common way.

Now consider the text in 1 Corinthians. Here Paul is giving answers to questions and problems which had arisen in Corinth. Exactly what the problem "about virgins" was is a question on which a good deal of scholarly ink has been used. It is a very obscure question, and fortunately it does not matter to us for our present purpose in the least. What does matter is this. Earlier in the chapter Paul has been able to settle another matter by quoting a saying of Jesus. This time he has no quotation, no flash of inspiration. But he can and does give his view as one who, by God's mercy, is faithful. Here is the second way of reaching a decision—in faithfulness to Christ, by the mercy of God. The first way is the way of the world's common sense, the second is the way of Christian common sense. Let me try to answer our question by developing these two themes.

Purposes According to the Flesh

That is how most of our purposes are conceived. This is the natural way we all take when we are off our guard. In the whole of the study of theology, there is nothing more humiliating than the discovery that the Church, in the person of many of its leading members, has practiced just this kind of plan-making. Our fathers and mothers risked their lives to assert that it was possible that even general councils of the Church might err. When you read the history of these councils, the record of all the sordid bickering, back-biting, place seeking, the toadying, fear and the use of fame, you marvel not the councils sometimes erred but that they ever hit upon the truth. But I am not talking about councils and the obvious machinations of the princes of the Church who wangled ecclesiastical politics to feather their own nests. I am talking about ourselves. How often do we make our plans according to the flesh in the same way that worldly people make theirs? What sort of common sense do we apply? Let me be precise and particular.

Suppose you have to choose between two jobs. On what principle do you decide? Pay, prospects and conditions, or opportunity of service? How do we choose our friends and associates? Do we simply pick out those who are wise and congenial, whose company pleases us; or do we give first consideration to who needs us most? Suppose you live in a circle, social or political, in which things are practiced which you know to be wrong. Do you for convenience hold your tongue? Or can you speak your mind with force and clarity and charity? If you are an undergraduate planning your future on what terms are you planning it? In the same spirit and on the same values as a person would who is not a Christian? Or not?

Now I do not for a minute expect anyone to have completely gotten rid of all worldly motives. They lie submerged in the depths of our unconscious life (even if not higher up), and they break out when we least expect it. All I want to say at the moment is this—all discussion of God's guidance is sheer idle chatter if we are consciously harboring worldly motives. If I make up my mind on a certain cause, simply because I like the look of it, and think it will be profitable and pleasing, and then ask God to rubber stamp my decision, then it is no good me pretending that I want guidance, or that I am at all likely to get it. All that is negative. It has to be said, but perhaps it doesn't get us very far. Let me try to find something positive about—

Christian Common Sense

Go back to the situation of 1 Corinthians, the point where Paul has no word of Christ, and no flash of inspiration to guide him. I remind you of that because I have something to say here. There are times when all the guidance we need is contained in a plain word of Christ. This happens less often than one might think for the simple reason that we live in 20th century England and not 1st century Palestine and the circumstances of our lives are different from those within which Jesus spoke. Sometimes to rely naively on a word of Jesus is to be misled. For example, the saying about non-resistance to evil does not justify pacifism. I say that, who am not a pacifist, but I know that many pacifists would say so too, and would find the grounds for their conviction elsewhere.

Again, I believe that sometimes some people have received overwhelming and supernatural guidance. St. Paul saw a vision of a man of Macedonia who summoned him, "Come over into Macedonia and help us." I have no doubt that happened to St. Paul. I have no doubt that sort of thing has happened to others. I am quite sure that it has never happened to me and I believe it does not happen to the majority of Christians. What then? This is where Christian common sense must operate as the means by which we receive God's guidance. And the question we have to tackle is, how can we acquire and train a Christian conscience, and a Christian common sense?

Early in the second century Ignatius wrote "he who has truly mastered Christ's spoken word is able to hear his silence too." That is what we must seek, and of course Ignatius has already pointed the way:

(1) Scripture, first and all the time. It is no good thinking you can move on to Christ's silences until you have understood his spoken word, and that means living in the Bible. How much of the hesitation and uncertainty of the Church today is due to our sheer unfamiliarity with the Bible? When I go back to my old college in Cambridge, I can look on a walk called Ridley's Walk, because when Ridley the martyr was master he used to walk up and down there, learning the New Testament by heart. And it is not my opinion but his own statement that that knowledge, though some of it slipped from him when he left academic life, not merely kept him faithful but pointed out the way for him. Scripture then first and always.

(2) Prayer, which I dare to put second only because in these days the Bible needs so much emphasis. There are many kinds of prayer and the kind I am thinking of is hard to put into words. It is not asking for things, though that is a proper part of prayer, whatever philosophical problems it may raise. Nor is it waiting with a carefully evacuated mind. It is thinking God's thoughts after him and with him. Of course, not one of us can do it properly. We are not God and we never shall be. But we can try to stop looking at our circumstances from our own point of view, and look at them from God's. Up to a point it can be done. I remember as a child being left in the Hampton Court maze. I couldn't find my way out. But up in a tower in the middle of the maze stood an official who could see the whole, and guided me out. I couldn't climb up his tower, but by following his instructions I could in some measure see with his eyes.

This leads to (3) Learning to think as a Christian. It is not the duty of every Church member to learn theology. It is his duty to learn to think as a Christian. There is a difference and I can illustrate it thus—if you come up to university to read history, you do not come to learn a lot more dates to add to 1066 and whatever else you learned at school. You come here to learn, to think to study, and to evaluate evidence, to reconstruct the past as a historian does. Of course, in the process you do learn more dates, but that is not the essential point. In the same way, it is your job to learn to think as Christians do, to let your thinking be molded to the pattern of the grace of God in Christ Jesus. You may learn some theology in the process; well and good. But that is not the essential point.

(4) All this Bible study, praying, learning is to be done not only alone but in fellowship, in the company of Christ's people. The common corporate experience of the people of God is one of the greatest factors in the education of our Christian common sense. It is something to which the total experience of the Church in all ages and all places contributes, but it is focused upon the congregation or smaller group in which our Christian existence is nourished. If you want to receive God's guidance, always seek and never despise the advice of your Christian friends. In the end, you must settle matters between God and your conscience alone; but don't fail to learn from your fellows.

(5) Anyone who wishes to be guided by God must be prepared to develop the habit of unselfish thought and unselfish practice; I would almost dare to say a habit of Christlikeness, certainly a habit of Christian discipline. It is no good expecting on some great occasion to expect some divine leading as will make possibly a supremely Christian act, if in all the smaller circumstances of life, we are constantly pampering ourselves and choosing the easier way. I do not say that the hard way should be chosen simply because it is hard. But I do say that we shall find ourselves taking the easier way without prompting and that the hard way, which is at least sometimes right, is the way that requires practice.

One word more in conclusion. Paul gives his opinion as one who is faithful to Christ. And how magnificently faithful he was! But it never occurs to him that this was any credit to him. He was faithful simply by God's mercy. The moment we begin to think our Bible study, our prayers, our self-discipline are a credit to us, we immediately place ourselves outside the structure of the Christian faith. We never cease to depend entirely on the mercy of God. And the more clearly we recognize that, the more likely we shall be to walk humbly with our God, and receive whatever guidance he has for us.

"Christian Hope and Its Foundation"— 2 Corinthians 1:20-22

[Preached once at Onny on 10/23/38][1]

One of the greatest forces in human life, one of the greatest forces which is able to influence a world in which a person lives is hope. If we had no hope for our future, and for the future of the world there would be little point in carrying on an existence which would be, after all, only a losing battle all the way. In one way or another, hope is the spring of the great enterprises of human beings. Scientists would not continue their investigations, but for the hope of fresh discoveries of truth, the hope of making the world a better place for people to live in. We should cease to make laws and enforce them if we did not hope that through them society might be improved. If we had no hope of peace in the world, we might well throw up all our attempts at negotiations and all our efforts to prevent war. Have you seen people who have lost hope? People for whom life has delivered such a cruel blow, or hearts and homes have been left empty by crushing poverty, by pain, by the loss of a loved one? You can afford to lose a lot if you have not lost before.

And there is no greater or truer hope, none more certain, none more capable of transforming life than the hope which is in Christ, the hope of the Christian Church. Imagine a handful of people left alone by their leader in a world which if it was not hostile, was at least indifferent. That world they set out to convert, unafraid, undeterred by the difficulties and danger. No wonder that one early Christian wrote about a "lively hope"! Of course, it wasn't only a hope of what they should be able to do by themselves. It was

---

1   Editor's Note: The handwriting is not clear enough to be sure of the name of the location where this sermon was preached but it appears to be Onny. This is the very earliest of the sermons in this collection, preached when CKB was 21.

a hope, a confidence that God's work was before them and that God would look after it; and he would look after them too. In life or in death they were in God's hand and they hoped in Him and they were not put to shame. It was this very hope that was able to triumph over torture and death, which attracted many people to Christianity in the days of the persecutions. They watched these Christians, humble folk often, of no position thrown to the beasts and these wretched artisans and slave girls went to their deaths not only unafraid but with shouts of praise for their victory.

Many a time had Paul and Silas, in the stocks or in prison been singing hymns and praising God and the prisoners had listened. They always do. Shut up in the prison house, away from the light of hope they have come with wonder upon this lively hope. You may read their tombstones—"eat, drink, and be merry for tomorrow we die." Not only that, but ever since the hope and confidence of Christian people have had great converting power. "Our people die well" said John Wesley, and it was not an idle remark. God has made his promises for our good both now and forever, and we know he will not fail.

Has Christian Hope a Foundation?

We know! But how? There are two sides to the question. You may speak of the glorious hope of the Christian martyr but there will always be some who will call it deluded obstinacy. The Church is a society of hope, it lives not only for the present but for a future which it holds will be more glorious than the present. "I reckon that the sufferings of this present time are not worthy to be compared to the glory that shall be revealed to us." But how do we know all this? How do we know it is true? You and I and all of our Christian brothers and sisters trust in the promises of God and that he will not let us down. But what right have we for thinking that?

There is today a great quest on the part of many people for reality. It is expressed in things both good and bad. It is expressed in a dislike for formality and convention. It is expressed also in materialism, a disbelief in the existence of anything that cannot be seen or handled or heard. What have we to say to that? Is our belief just an "unsubstantiated projection," a hope beautiful and cheering but devoid of reality—a delusion? Or have we solid ground under our feet?

The Tension of the Present and Future

When we ask this question, and seek for an answer we find ourselves in a state of great tension because we must freely acknowledge, as Paul does, that it is in hope that we are saved. Yet, it is a hope that is firmly grounded in the past and the present. That is the only ground for any hope. You trust your friend because in times past he has proved himself a true friend, and in the present you are conscious of confidence in him. It is something not dissimilar when we say—

> His love in time past
> forbids me to think
> he'll leave me at last
> in trouble to sink;
> while each Ebenezer
> I have in review
> confirms his good pleasure
> to help me quite through. (John Newton)

This is still hope, but it is hope based upon a very serious reality. We do not suppose God will be good in the future as a bare hope; we know he has been good—"before now the Lord has helped us." We believe in the reality of another world after this because we have already known its power. "The men of grace have found glory begun below." "Shall I doubt his tender mercy, who through life has been my guide?"

There is something now as well as then, something present as well as hoped for, and the measure of our hope will be the extent to which we have taken God's present gifts. Paul is able to speak of the Church as having nothing and yet possessing all things. Indeed, it is at the very moment when we have nothing but our hope, when we cling steadfastly to that and forget ourselves and our own merits and our own possessions that all the love and mercy of God are poured out upon us as a present blessing. In the Bible, it is the barren who bear children. It is those who "we killed all the day long, who are accounted as lambs for the slaughter" who are more than conquerors, because we cannot be separated from the love of God. That at least is ours now, we don't have to wait for that. But because we have that love of God now we can well afford to wait for God's time. We can be content to hope.

It seems to run in a circle. Our hope is not baseless, for it is based in a past experience and upon our present confidence. Yet we only know God's present blessings and his constant love when we can relinquish all but faith and hope. "Nothing in my hand I bring, simply to the Cross I cling." It is when we know that our hands are empty, when we know what we can bring that God's mercy overflows on us. There are two things on which the Church's hope is founded, two things that give us the right to hope. The first is—

God's Yes

Come back to the text. The Corinthians had been accusing Paul of fickleness, he was the sort of person who always said yes and no. You never knew what he meant. Naturally and rightly, Paul denied the charge. He was not a fickle-minded person. But in any case, whatever the apostle was like, the Christ he preached was no Yes and No Man. "Say what you will of me, but you'll not say that of Christ. He is God's own everlasting Yes." Whatever God has promised, whatever good things he has in store for us, to all of them Jesus Christ not only says but is Yes. He is God's Yes, God's Affirmation, God's fulfillment.

If you want to know God's will for you, look at Christ. Do not look anywhere else. Do not think of the sternness, the severity, the inexorable nature of God. Put all your trust in Christ, look at him, look and live. Look at him and see God's love streaming forth to you and to me, God's salvation made near, made real, made available to you and me. See the Father welcoming his Son, see him sending forth his servants to gather in the sick, the lame, the blind, to his feast, compelling them to come into the house of his love, so that it may be filled. Hear him say "Father forgive them" or "come unto me all ye who labor and are heavy laden and I will give you rest." Great human beings had wondered and trusted and hoped in these things, and Jesus is God's Yes. It is true God does forgive, God does reinstate you as his child. "And can it be that I should gain an interest in my Savior's blood"! Yes! Jesus is God's Yes to that. He is God's fulfillment. Whatever God had promised to humankind, is fulfilled in Jesus. The new day of God's rule trembles at the point of dawn.

> Blessings abound where'er He reigns;
> The pris'ner leaps, unloosed his chains,
> The weary find eternal rest,
> And all the sons of want are blest. (I. Watts)

And blessings do abound, the prisoner is set free, the weary are refreshed, and you and I in all our sin and need may come to Savior who is full of compassion and find that in Him God will say Yes to all the needs of our hearts.

The Earnest of the Spirit

But you will say "wait a minute, things are not quite as good as that. We have not really reached the Golden Age just yet. It sounds all very well but we can still pick holes in what you say. You say that God's purpose has been fulfilled in the world? Well what about that which is on the minds of all of us? What about war? There is a war in Spain, there is a war in China. We were nearly at war and we are not out of the woods yet. And what about unemployment. The unemployed person must get a great thrill out of hearing that God's will is being done. And slums and poverty and rot and disease and death and the rest? And what about ourselves? We are not perfect and we know it. We know what it is to do things we ought not."

All this leads to the second thing on which our hope is founded and that is what Paul calls the earnest of the Spirit. That means this. When a person did not want to pay for an article at once he paid first an earnest. It was a sort of pledge that he would pay the rest. It was an installment though it is a good thing to notice that it was often a large proportion of the total price. So what Paul is saying is this—

"I know that we do not yet experience all that God has in his plan for us. We must still hope, never forget that. God has bigger things for you than you have yet known. But God has given the first installment, God has given a pledge of what is yet to come. You have more than a mere hope. A part, a large part of your hope is already realized. God has given you the Spirit." Now that is for us both a blessing and a responsibility. The Spirit means a power which is always available for us, and also opportunities which we ought not to miss. It is through the Spirit that these things which Paul says constitute the Kingdom of God may be obtained—righteousness, peace and joy. And these can begin now.

If you are conscious of sin in your life, if you know that you have habits and ways that bring pain to your friends and make you ashamed, a bad temper, a biting tongue, then know this—that God will give you the power to conquer habit and dethrone sin. It's no good saying you've tried and failed.

Everyone fails who tries by himself. Ask God for power, the power of the Spirit. Indeed, you need not ask for it, it is his gift. Will you not take it?

God in his Holy Spirit will give you peace. Do you not need it? Do we not all need that? We are so busy, so tired; life is hard and worrying. We have anxieties of all sorts. And the peace that passes all understanding is his to give. And he will give it and it will guard your heart. No, you are wrong if you think this means an escape from care. If you want a joy that is thorough-going that does not disappear when life goes wrong, but is rich and over-flowing, take it from God.

The Resources of the Church

All these things are for the people called the Church of Christ. And how often we lose heart and get discouraged. We think that there is little left but hope, and some people have so little of that, that they have to talk about good old days! If only the Church of God would understand what resources it has. If we could but open our hearts to take in the Holy Spirit and all his gifts, what could we not be? There would be faith and hope and love; a hope confident and well grounded, but more than that. Such a present experience of the power of God that would set us singing and set our hearts on fire with the love of God a fire, that in the mercy of God might spread to others wherever we went.

"Things Not Seen"—2 Corinthians 4:18 and John 14:8, 9

[Preached fifteen times between 5/4/80 at Wesley House, Cambridge, to 5/22/05 at Sherburn]

2 Cor. 4 will do to start with. There is enough there, indeed Paul himself might well have said a good deal more than enough. For what was on show, what was to be seen, in Corinth was not particularly attractive. These chapters perhaps reflect one of the more favorable moments in the history of Corinthian Christianity. I am not sure of it, and in any case Paul could see through the rather rosy account that Titus had brought. He knew what had happened and had a pretty good idea of what was still to come. And he didn't like it. I have heard ministers complain of their circuits, congregations, parishes. Sometimes the complaints have been justified; sometimes there is more justification for complaint the other way. But I have never known a circuit like Corinth. When the members were not fighting Paul, they were fighting each other. They produced immorality that pagans themselves would have been ashamed of. And they were proud of being such progressive Christians. They made a shamble of Holy Communion. When Paul refused to take their money, they said he didn't love them. When he organized a collection, they accused him of appropriating the funds!

That was not all. Exactly what threat hung over him we do not know, but he had had the sentence of death within himself and he recalls it here. "Our outer self is decaying." And gradually it comes home to the strongest and toughest of us that that is true. If we are cheerful and courageous enough, we may be able to call it, as Paul does, our light affliction and almost shrug it off. But even the youngest of us know something of the pressure of duty and responsibility.

Well then, what do we do now? Shut our eyes to it all? Pretend that it isn't there, like Nelson when he was signaled to withdraw? He clapped his glass to his sightless eye, and said "I'm damned if I see it." No one would blame Paul if he did. There is something to be said for it, sometimes. A friend of mine at one time used to read Aristophanes after Sunday evening church. Myself, I should regard that as a somewhat extreme course. It is hardly looking at the things that are not seen.

No, it is clear beyond doubt that whatever Paul may have done, he was not pretending that Corinth did not exist; as he wrote these words he was writing to Corinth wrestling with its problems. And he was not contrasting this world with a Platonic ideal eternal world. What he says is that the things which are seen are temporary. They do not last. He is setting out to see things in this true perspective.

This is something that anyone, any minister, has to learn. It doesn't mean that what goes on in Corinth, or whatever your circuit may be, is unimportant. It means that you can only get Corinth right if you see it—*sub species aeternam, sub species invisibilis*. You may look at this from both sides. The real peril in Corinth was the unseen peril. It is a matter of distinguishing the disease from the symptoms. We know the symptoms. I have just mentioned some of them and doubtless many of you are prepared to write them up in great detail in answer to Tripos questions. What Paul is doing through this letter allusively, disjointedly, perhaps is to get behind the things which it was all too easy to see, to that which lay behind them all, like self-centered existence which, sometimes, under a splendid show of religion, displaces God from his throne.

We need to be aware of this in ourselves. The most religious, most virtuous minister may cherish in his heart that love of self, which though it may never lead him into violence and immorality, will rob his ministry of all its power. He and his people will wonder what it is that robs their work of its power and effectiveness; and he and they will never guess, unless they learn to look at what is not seen.

We need to be aware of this in our people. It is the peril of the false prophet that he treats the sin of God's people lightly. And the minister will not be very helpful as an adviser, as a spiritual guide, if he cannot see a bit more clearly the hidden pressures, the unseen forces that corrupt and destroy people's lives. It is not enough to see what lies on the surface. We must learn also to look at the things not seen.

We have looked at this matter from the negative side. There is a positive side. I have said that in the Corinthian letters we see Paul getting behind disunity, incest, litigiousness, and so on to the unseen causes of them. How is one to counter those causes? One possibility was to use visible or at least audible means. Call it wisdom, argumentative skill, helped out with the phenomena of inspiration and ecstasy. There is room for wisdom, there is room for inspiration, but it is not the wisdom of the world that Paul chose to use. "I resolved to know nothing among you except Christ and him crucified." Judged by ordinary standards, there was nothing to see, nothing but weakness and folly. But this was where reality lay.

True for Paul, true for his successors. How easy to throw your weight around! Paul knew the temptation and so do we. I have never recalled it in public before but my father told me once of a man in one of his churches who saw fit to act as a minister, inhibiting the work of the whole church. My father told me how he had said, but said only to himself "if I chose, I could by my superior power of logic and argument speak and crush you." But he didn't say it; he didn't do it. It wouldn't have lasted. It would have been seen and temporary. Instead, in agony and in patience a quiet power cleansed the church. We need to learn it, in our churches and in ourselves.

It is time to move on. I have been giving St. Paul, not to mention you, a great deal of advice and it would be no more than just that you and St. Paul should ask for something more. How do we acquire this true proportion between the things seen and temporal, and the things unseen and eternal? Above all how can we achieve the paradox of looking at things that are not seen? Suppose we take the supreme invisibility. If we can deal with that, we can deal with all the rest by a process of *ad maiore ad minus*. By the supreme invisibility I mean of course God. That is not a truth I invented or discovered. The New Testament says it—"No one has ever seen God."

Yet people long to do so. Philip is expressing the desire of all religious humanity (and a great deal of it is at bottom religious) when he says "Show me the Father, that is all we want." For we know deep within us, the truth of Paul's words. Things seen do not last, things unseen last forever and God is eternity itself. There is no rest for us until we rest in Him. "Show me the Father, that is enough." Give us that and we can let the world go by. You know Jesus' answer "he who has seen me, has seen the Father." "Th' invisible appears in sight / And God is seen by mortal eye" (Charles Wesley).

This is not the time to begin a discussion on Christology, and I have no intention of doing so. How a person can be both God and a human being I am content to leave to the Fathers of Chalcedon and to anyone else who is willing to have a shot at it. What I am saying is simply this—all the invisible that matters is to be seen in the visible Jesus. That is what God has given us in Him. Let the Christology be, I am thinking in practical terms. It was this Christ who said to Paul "my grace is sufficient for you, my power is made perfect in your weakness." It was dying that Paul carried about with him and his life too. Insight, understanding, endurance and unfailing love. This is their source.

"The Congregation's Responsibilities"—2 Corinthians 13:5ff.

[Preached three times from 9/5/70 at Elvet to 9/21/80 at Billingham]

These epistles to the Corinthians, and especially this second one, are mainly about the relationship between the minister and the people, between the Corinthians and their apostle, Paul. That is why I have gone to them now, to see what they have to teach us at this point in the service, where, as we welcome our three new ministers, it is written in the book that someone "shall briefly remind the congregation of their responsibility." I notice that no one has to remind the ministers of theirs. I suppose it is assumed that all ministers have good memories and need no reminding. I'm sure that must be true of our new ministers, though I know it isn't true about me; perhaps it is a good thing that we shall find in the end that the two things are tied up together.

But that anticipates the end, and we must proceed in order. You might well have thought the text complicated and obscure; perhaps it is. But the situation is clear enough. The Corinthians, possibly the first but by no means the last congregation to have a good opinion of itself, were putting their minister to the test, trying him and examining him to see just how good an apostle he was. And you have no need to pretend you don't do it. I was born into this; I moved to my first new circuit at the age of four, and long before the sermon testers were trying me out in the pulpit, I knew what it was on the first Sunday of the connectional year to walk to morning service and sit with my mother in the minister's pew while everyone was sizing up the minister's family. Minister's families need a lot of grace, and I hope you will be very gracious to them. But to come back to Corinth, in many ways Paul didn't come up to the Corinthians's standards and here (see vs. 3) they are even questioning whether Christ spoke in him.

What this means of course is that their standards of judgment were wrong. So are ours too sometimes, even if we do not lay too much weight on the hat that the minister's wife is wearing, or possibly isn't wearing, tomorrow morning. This will come out later. Here, in our text, we find Paul replying to his critics. "You want to try me out, you want proof that Christ speaks in me? You'd do better to test yourselves. Try yourselves to see if you are in the faith, if Christ is in you."

Now this is not simply a "same to you" argument, though I should not blame Paul if it were. I'm sure that many a minister has felt like saying "Alright, if you know so much, have a shot at the job yourself, and see how you get on." Paul is going much deeper than that, and saying something positive. You are concerned, aren't you, that Christ is in you? You are aware of your own faith? What does that show? Of whose ministry is that the result? Paul is not patting himself on the back, he had no need to do so. He is pointing out that the validity of his own ministry and the validity of the Corinthians faith belong together. They can't be played off against each other. Christ in them, means Christ's word in him.

What this points to is that the life of the Church is a joint undertaking, and the goal of it is a full Christian life all around. The goal of it is not the greater glory of the minister, as Paul says in this letter. "Since we preach Christ as the one and only Lord, we cannot lord it over your faith, we can only be slaves, your slaves for Christ's sake." Equally, it is not the glory of the congregation at the expense of the minister, again in this same letter Paul speaks of the authority God has given him "for building you up." This is only one goal, that the church as a whole should reach the full maturity of Christ. And to that end as the passage I am quoting says (Eph. 4.12-13) we are all ministers. There are some special ministers—apostles, prophets, evangelists, pastors, teachers, but all are ministers with a common goal.

Will you see this in practical terms? Stuart Rhodes, Cecil Smith, Nelson Charles have come here to be your ministers. Who will keep the Christian ideal shining before them? Who will point them to God's Word? Who will demonstrate to them the power of prayer? Who would give them friendship when they were lonely? Who will comfort them when they are sorrowing? Who will cheer them when they are depressed? The answer is that if you don't, nobody will, and they will go their way friendless, cheerless, comfortless. You are their ministers. Let us take this further, keeping Paul and his

Corinthians in the back of our minds, but not forgetting that we are a Methodist circuit in 1970. There are two things to say about your responsibility to your minister:

(1) Let them be what they are. I know that a Methodist minister is expected to be and do everything, from stoking up the church's boiler onwards, and most of us are prepared to have a shot at most things. But don't forget what they really are, men and women of God and servants of his Word. You must let them be this, not least by not requiring them to spend all their time doing something else. It has not, if you will allow me to say this, been always fully understood throughout this circuit that normally a minister needs every morning in his own study. Of course, if there are emergencies he will do whatever is needed, but normally he will be there. He is not wasting his time nor is he trying to turn himself into a second-rate academic. He needs that time and place for prayer, for study of God's Word, for reflection on life and death and all the shifting patterns of human society, so that when he comes to the pulpit, he may come to you from the secret place of the Most High, with the word of truth by which people live.

You owe your minister help in his visiting. When he visits you, remember he has come as a man or woman of God. I see no reason why a minister of God should not begin by talking about the latest football scores, but he doesn't want to finish there. Don't make it hard for him to help you in the Christian life. And see that he knows of cases of special need. His routine visiting will take him a long way, but he hasn't second sight, and if some perfectly healthy member of the congregation is suddenly whisked off to the hospital he will not know unless someone tells him.

There are tasks you can take off your minister's shoulders. You probably can't preach as he does, but you may be better at accounts. Remember, he isn't slacking, but he does want time to do his own job. Let your ministers be what they are. The second thing is like the first—

(2) Be what you are, and you are also a man or woman of God. This is your deepest responsibility. You are not expected to preach but you are expected to be a Christian, and you will not be the sort of Christian you ought to be, if you neglect your own prayers and Bible reading. This is not time for generalities. I'm going to say three specific things—A. Will you please go to Church regularly? There are few things which will so build up your life, few things that will so encourage your minister. Probably you will do this, will you also encourage your fellow ministers to do it? And don't be content with once on Sunday, we need you twice. A generation ago we

used to talk about instructing the saints in the morning, and converting the sinners in the evening. There is a changing pattern of social life today, and church arrangements will reflect it. But both jobs need to be done; the saints have to be on hand both times, to be instructed, and to help and encourage the sinners. B. Love one another. Of course, this is part of what being a Christian means, but it is desperately easy for Christians and Church members to fail here. There are few things that can so weaken a church, discourage a minister and hamstring his best work. You cannot live in the Church as long as I have done without knowing places where feuds between Church members have sapped the Church's vitality and reduced its influence to zero—or less. If there is anything of that kind in this circuit then get rid of it. If you are not those responsible for it, find those who are and put it right. But above all take this not just negatively but positively; cultivate fellowship with one another, and let your love for one another flow out into a universal compassion and concern that cares for all the sorrowing and needy you can reach. And C. Seek the lost. I have said most of what needs to be said about this already. By caring for them, by bringing them into the Church's fellowship and worship, by seeing that the minister knows about them, in these and countless other ways you can fulfill the church's mission in continuing the work of the Son of Man who came to seek and to save that which was lost. Finally, hear Paul's word once more. "Try yourselves, test yourselves. Be a little less anxious to try out how good your minister is at speaking the Word of Christ, and ask if Christ is in your own heart. Then together we shall go forward in his name."

"Conversion of St. Paul"—
Galatians 2:19-20

[Preached five times from 1/23/44 at Bondgate, Darlington, to 4/7/57 at Bishop Auckland]

January 25th is the date in the Church's calendar assigned to the conversion of St. Paul. Of course, the actual date of that event is unknown, but it is a good festival to keep, for the event itself is of fundamental importance not only to the Church itself, but also to the whole of Western civilization. No sensible person speculates on how different things might have been if certain events had not taken place, and it is most foolish of all to try and limit God in the ways in which he does his work. But as events have fallen out, the conversion of St. Paul is a keystone in the arch of history. But for him, Christianity might never have been more than a Jewish sect. But for him, European civilization might still have been pagan, or perhaps we ought to say a good deal more pagan than it is. But something happened to this Jew, this sturdy little man with bowed legs and a hooked nose (so an ancient document describes him) and what happened not only changed his life, it changed history.

What was it that happened? It would take more than one sermon, it would take more than a whole course of lectures in theology, to answer that question. But we must make some attempt at it tonight, by our exposition of the text, which is a summary of what Christ meant to Paul. "This," says Bengel of Gal. 2:19 "is the point and marrow of Christianity" and he was right. We have fortunately gotten past that stage of timidity of thought when people thought they could bypass Paul and find a simpler faith in the Gospels. We know now that Jesus and Paul were talking about precisely the same things; that for us St. Paul is the way into Christianity, that there is no Christianity without dogma, and that anything that is not dogmatic is not Christianity. The first thing to say about this conversion, this Christianity is that it is all based on—

Jesus Dead and Risen

That is very important; it is not based on any experience, opinion or fad of St. Paul's, but on this particular real person. This appears clearly enough from the thrice iterated narrative of the conversion in Acts. There is a lot of fancy psychological nonsense talked and written about Paul's conversion. We are told that he was a dissatisfied seeker after righteousness in the Law. On the contrary, he was like most of us, a good deal too satisfied with himself. He was far more satisfied with himself before his conversion than he was afterwards; that is the right way around.

More of this later; however, for the present let us observe that the story in Acts tells us not a tale of frustration and the integration of personality, but of a meeting between Saul, busily bent upon the persecution of the Church, and Jesus. Paul is conscious of the presence of a divine person—"Who art thou Lord?" "I am Jesus whom you are persecuting." That simple encounter was, of course, far more upsetting than any ordinary psychological process could be. Saul had known all about Jesus, all the external facts. His opinion about Jesus was as clear as that of the Christians. Jesus had been a messianic agitator and now, thank God, he was dead. Quite suddenly, Saul found that it was impossible to doubt he was the Son of God and that though he had really been killed, he was alive.

If that was true, and Paul could not doubt it, it changed the whole color and shape of life. It did turn the world upside down. It changed the center of gravity of time and made it move to a different beat. Everyone, including St. Paul, was hoping that God would send his Messiah, that people, through tribulation maybe, would enter into his promised Kingdom. They all hoped and believed that that was something that was to happen. But the new faith in Jesus upset all the calculations. Here was the Messiah already and a very different Messiah from the figure of popular hope. In fact, he had taken upon himself all the afflictions there was to bear and had overcome it in his resurrection. Therefore, he had opened the Kingdom of Heaven to all believers.

Without waiting for the last day, human beings might taste in advance the powers of the age to come. Present and future are side by side. That is why Christian people are such funny mixtures. It has been my lot to correct a good many Greek exercises in my time. Some of them have been exceedingly bad. I have even found a verb, or an attempt at one, like this. It had a future ending, a present stem, and in front of it an augment, the sign in Greek of past tense. What tense was that? A mixture of past, present and future. We are like that. We are all solecisms. But the future is there because of Christ crucified and risen.

For Paul, the whole thing began and came to rest there. "I made up my mind" he said to the Corinthians, "that I would recognize nothing but Christ and him crucified." When he sums up the Gospel he heard and passed on he says "Christ died for our sins, according to the Scriptures; he was buried, the third day he rose from the dead according to the Scriptures." Of course, that is not what most people think Christianity is. I should very much like to do some mass observation on the subject. What do you think Christianity is? There would be some strange answers. Going to Church, being good, I don't think for a moment many of the answers would get close to the truth. An Anglican minister went into a school for the first time and asked among other things, "What do you think my work as a clergyman is?" He picked out an intelligent looking boy and got the answer "to be nice to everybody, sir." Believe me, perhaps more often than we have the courage to act on it, it is sometimes a Christian minister's duty to be damned nasty.

I was very glad to hear Mr. Colin Robertson say last Thursday that the message of the Commando Campaign is the Incarnation of God. That is the only Christian message, that the acts of Jesus are the acts of God, that through his death and resurrection you come immediately into the presence of the eternal God. All that it has been necessary to say, but we must go further with the themes of death and life and ask in what sense—

St. Paul (or Any Christian) Is Dead

First of all, it is a sense intimately united with the death of Christ. I have been crucified with Christ. This is not an escape into the mystical world of unbeing; it is tethered to the most real and most beastly of all realities. Nor is this death decrepitude. Some of the relics of old, unreformed Cambridge lingered quite a long time in the persons of the old life time fellows. There was one old man, a fellow of Kings, who lived all day in his rooms, but every evening about five he would totter down the staircase and onto the lawn in the shadow of the great Chapel. With his stick, he would prod viciously at the worms in the dirt and exclaim "There, ye ain't got me yet, damn ye!" It is not a matter of having one foot in the grave and living only half a life. I know this is a paradox, and not easy to grasp but it must be said; it is a matter of being wholly dead, and wholly alive at the same time.

"I died to Law," says St. Paul. Law is a way of life, supremely it is a religious way of life. It recognizes that a person is under obligation to his Maker. So far, so good. Paul always believed that. It was the essence of his religion. Because of his keeping of the Law (and he tells us he was blameless in it) he had a standing before God. What was it that shook him there? It was Christ, the fact that Christ was killed and that his righteousness was vindicated by the resurrection. It was the law, his religion that put Christ to death, and on its own premises, the law had done rightly. But since Christ was proved to be in the right by God's raising him from the dead, the law in condemning him, had in fact condemned itself. It was obvious that the way of the law was a wrong way, and therefore it was simply no good being blameless by the Law's standard. Blameless men (according to the law) killed Jesus; Saul, a blameless man according to the law, was persecuting the Church. This was abominable! His very goodness was foul! The sweet fruit of holiness turned to maggots in his mouth. Not his sin but his goodness condemned him.

You will never understand Paul and you will never understand the Gospel if you can't understand that. You will never know what God can do until you know there is nothing that you can do. And when I say nothing, I mean nothing. In the old Wesley hymns there is a section entitled "Praying for Repentance." More than one hymn begins with the line "O that I could repent . . ." but I can't, I can't, I can't take even that first step without God. There is the same thought in Mr. Wet Eyes says in Bunyan's *Holy War,* "I see dirt in my own tears, and filthiness in the bottom of my prayers."

All this means that a Christian person recognizes that Christ is the only way to God, who is life. It does not mean that a Christian is a wild, lawless, impulsive creature, how can he be when he belongs to Christ? But he knows now that all his painful striving to whatever law he has set himself is gone, and now he is free; like Christ he has entered into a death struggle with the law. The law has got him down, killed him, as it killed Christ. But out of that old dead self, rises with Christ a new person. Therefore, we must ask thirdly, in what sense—

St. Paul or Any Christian Is Alive

We must begin our answer in the same place—it is with Christ. More, it is Christ living in us. And who shall say what that means? It is too great a task for me. "Christ in you the hope of glory." "This is an outpost of heaven." But note these things. It is a life of faith. Christ is not plainly and evidently there to the senses. You will not sit in a corner like Jack Horner and say "What a good boy am I! I must be a Christian." You will have to cling to Christ by faith. You will have to trust him when you find yourself utterly untrustworthy. You will have to rest entirely upon his love, who gave himself for you. That is the only security, in a life in utter dependence upon God. We are all too often like Tobias in Bridie's play [*Tobias and the Angel*]. The angel Raphael does everything for Tobias, but then we find him saying "I killed the fish, I frightened the robber, I climbed the wall. How brave I am!"

A life of faith. Faith which works miracles. 'Perhaps it was some miracle he did' says Nicodemus in Andrew Young's play entitled *Nicodemus* (1937). And John replies—

> It was indeed; more miracles than one
> I was not blind, and yet he gave me my sight
> I was not deaf, and yet he gave me hearing
> Nor was I dead, and yet he raised me to life.

Christ lives in me! How much faith and how much miracle is in your life? The life which rests on Christ's love is as endless as Christ's love. In one of the best of his war sonnets, Rupert Brooke speaks of safety, the hid security of eternal things.

> Safe shall be my going,
> Secretly armed against all death's endeavors
> Safe where all safety's lost; safe where men fall.

Such preeminently is Christian life, because it is the life of him who loved me and gave himself up for me. That last word—me! How Luther takes it up. "Read with great vehemency these words—*me* and *for me*, and so inwardly practice with yourself, that you, with a sure faith may conceive and print this *me* in your heart, and apply it unto yourself . . ."

This is your privilege, your responsibility. Christ loves you. This is his offer, not only to St. Paul but to you. You don't need to be a saint, you only need to be a sinner, to be able to go home tonight and in the silence with God say quietly and soberly: "I through law, died to law, so that I might live to God. I have been crucified with Christ; I live no longer, but Christ lives in me, and the life I now live I live by faith in the Son of God who loved me and gave himself for me."

"Living by Faith"—Galatians 2:20

[Preached seven times between 3/28/75 at Bondgate, Darlington, to 3/28/99 at Byers Green]

Usually these Good Friday mornings we have begun with some sort of portrayal of the Crucifixion, sometimes a simple narrative representation based on the story in the Gospels, sometimes a theological reflection on what it all means, most often based on the same passage in the Epistles. I suppose that in point of fact, things will not turn out very differently today. Yet I am approaching the whole matter from a different angle. I will tell you why. A week or two ago I was asked to speak in a college chapel in a series of meetings all listed under the heading of the Christian Response. It was an odd list. The Christian response to hunger and poverty was clear enough, but I was puzzled by the title Newcastle. I have driven into Newcastle at such hours when the driver's response has been anything but Christian. *Newcastle* however proved to be the title to a film. Last on the list stood the Response to Calvary. As soon as I saw it, I thought, that is the theme for Good Friday 1975. We have looked at the reverse of it enough. We have surveyed the wondrous Cross, but what is our response? Can we examine it, study it? For this is the most important response of all.

I would hate even to appear to minimize the importance of a fully adequate Christian response to such things as world poverty, world hunger, but unless there is a fully adequate response to Calvary, there will be no Christian response to anything else. I sometimes think that is the most serious deficiency in our church life today. We are ready to begin anywhere but at the beginning. We run from one good cause to another, and they are good and I want to support them, but we do not ask either why we should or how we can be good. And the Cross is the beginning. I have quoted to you before, the first time was many years ago, "I saw how when Christian came up with the cross on his back, the burden loosed from his shoulders and fell off his

241

back, and began to tremble and so continued to do so until he came to the mouth of the sepulchre, where it fell in, and I saw it no more." "Then" continues Bunyan, "was Christian glad and lightsome."

Most times it is easy to get rid of the Cross. We can be like the boy turning over the pages in a picture book, and turning on quickly when we come to the grim pictures of the Cross are reached. The world grows more and more skilled at hiding death in general, perhaps also at hiding the death of Jesus. But today for an hour you cannot hide, you cannot run away, and you shall not forget what we are here for. You may not even say, "But we live on the other side of Easter and we see things in a new way." For this is true, but what Easter means is not that we have a new uncrucified Christ, it means that the crucified Christ is always with us. What then is the response? What do we make of this strange man on the cross?

The Beginning of the Response

The beginning is given in a *valid description* of the event itself. The Son of God loved me and gave himself up for me. This saying interprets the event by using appropriate language and putting it in the right context. Years ago, one of my teachers showed me language and context will interpret actions. We may say X lifted his foot and propelled an inflated piece of leather through white painted wooden posts. This could be a completely accurate account of what happened. It is no less accurate but misses out the context if we say X scored a goal. It is still accurate but involves more context if we say X won the cup for Darlington.

In the same way, behind what Paul says is the plain historical fact that Jesus died on a Cross. This he does not need to narrate, he knows his readers know it. We know it, but when we look at the event what do we see. There are two words of action, he loved, and he gave himself up, and these interpret each other. What does love mean? It is curious how it can mean not merely different but opposite things. Hot always means hot, even though what seems hot to me may seem cool to someone else, but we both share the same idea. Not so with love. Often we use this of what we want to get, what we like to have. "I love cookies" we say, which means I want to have them. "I love that woman" which means I want to have her as my wife. "I love music" and that means I want to listen to it and to make it.

But this love here is a different love. We know this sort of love though we do not speak of it quite so easily. He loved, and he gave. We can say that woman loves her child, she would do anything for it. This is what the love of Jesus means—he loved, he gave himself. He loved, not in the sense of he wanted to possess. What a terrible sort of love that can be, the more terrible because people can think it Christian. One has seen a fiend devour another, a husband a wife, parents a child, always with the classic "I love him so much, I can't let him out of my sight." "I would do anything for my children" can mean "I would pay any price to bag them up body and soul so that I have them in my grip forever." But the love of Christ is self-giving love. He loved me; and the definition of that love is he gave himself for me.

There is as I have said no narrative in this text to substantiate the proposition, but it could easily be supplied. It is written on page after page of the Gospels. Jesus gives without regard to the cost to himself. Take a familiar story—the house so crowded that four men come carrying a stretcher can't get inside. So instead they climb on the roof, make a hole, and lower their paralyzed friend down. How easy for Jesus to simply do the thing they wanted, not simply because healing is a good thing or because it was asked, but because by doing it he could have increased his reputation with the people at large. "How wonderful Jesus is!" people would have said. But he could see something else was needed more than healing, and he gave it. "Lad, your sins are forgiven." And since he was no fool, he must have known what the response would be. "Blasphemy! We'll get him for this." And of course, in the end they did, and all this self-giving, this self-giving up came to a climax at the Cross. The whole story is of one who gives himself up, gives himself away. There were so many ways out, even after he had rejected the back gate of the garden of Gethsemane.

What is love, in the Christian sense? It is a clumsy phrase, but I can't do much better than "non-self-centered existence." It is life which, as Jesus put it, you have denied yourself. Note what that does not mean. We often, not least in the observance of Lent, take it in the sense of denying yourself something—cigarettes, sugar in tea, and so on. But Jesus does not say, "if you mean to be a disciple you must deny yourself something," he says "you must deny yourself." And if you don't know what that means, then the story of Peter will tell you. He denied Jesus, saying "I just don't know the man, he means nothing to mean." What Peter and we Christians have to learn, is to say that of ourselves. Peter—"I don't just mean the man, he means nothing to me; I'm simply not considering his interests."

What you see in the Cross is that kind of love; Jesus says, at the cost of life itself. Never mind me; it's only the rest I'm concerned about. It is there in the story-telling only John tells about the arrest—"I am Jesus" he said, "that you are looking for. Let these others go." Before we leave this half of the verse, there is one other thing to note. Who did this for whom? The Son of God who loved me, and gave himself for me. What this means is we see here God's attitude towards the world, God's meaning for the world. This is the truth that lies behind all human life. This is what God is like—pure self-giving love. But it is not only God's meaning for the world; it is God's meaning for me. He loved me and gave himself for me. I suppose the most famous words Luther ever said were "Here I stand. I can do no other. God help me. Amen." But the most famous he ever wrote were surely his comments on this verse in Galatians: "Read with great vehemency the word *me* and *for me*." This is not only God and the world, this is God and the individuals. God and you. This is his direct and personal approach to each member of the race. It therefore calls for an individual response, and now at length, though we have been talking about it all the time, we must come to it directly.

The Response

A response, if it is to be meaningful, must always be made in terms of the question or challenge given. If you bowl a crooked ball to me, I do not lift my leg and bang it into the back of the net, I crack it through the opponents for four (or, it bowls me, but that is not the sort of possibility one dwells on in advance). To shift our ground, if you ask me what happened in 1066, I do not reply in terms of the square on the hypotenuse. I must reply in terms of the question, I must reply in terms of the approach.

What then is the response to the love that was given on Calvary? Plainly, it is to live by faith. But what does it mean to live by faith? It would be possible here to talk in a circle and to say that what it means is to respond to Calvary. That in fact would not be bad, anything but a vicious circle, for we know now what Calvary is, and knowing what Calvary is we begin to know what faith is. Faith is not a creed, it is accepting and reproducing the love, the self-giving of the Cross.

Firstly, it means accepting it. This is the first element of the *response*, that is, a recognition that the initiative was with God. That is something that Christians have always been slow to learn. Go back to the beginning of the Galatian paragraph and you will find one of the most unseemly incidents in the whole New Testament. Paul and Peter find themselves in the mixed Jewish and Gentile Church in Antioch. And all the Christians, whatever their background, ate together at the table that was not theirs but the Lord's. Then a message comes from James—you must not do this in defiance of the age old Law of Judaism. Only if men will take the first step in obedience to the Law can they be admitted. And Peter says "Oh well, yes I suppose that's right" and he backed out. And Paul said "You hypocrite! How can you? Does anything matter so much as that we are all Christians? As that the Son of God loved us and gave himself for us? This puts us all on the same level as pardoned sinners who can do nothing but respond to God's first step." Peter had always been the same. It was Peter who, when the Lord approached with the towel and basin, said "Thou shall never wash my feet."

We can only respond, we can only accept the forgiveness we could never deserve. But in this is our cleansing and our freedom.

O Love, Thou bottomless abyss,
My sins are swallowed up in Thee!
Covered is my unrighteousness,
Nor spot of guilt remains on me,
While Jesus' blood, through earth and skies,
Mercy, free, boundless mercy, cries. (J. A. Rothe, trans. by John Wesley)

The love of God sets us free, because it cuts the chords that bound us to the old self-centered life. You cannot simply say "I think it is wrong to be self-centered, henceforth I will turn myself inside out." Nature abhors a vacuum and so does the self. Cast out one demon and if nothing powerful takes its place, it will return with seven more demons worse than itself. The only way not to be self-centered, is to be God-centered. The only way to be free is to accept the rule of God.

This is where we move on to the second level of the response. Not only accepting but reproducing the love of God. This is the point where we come back to all the responses which perhaps I dismissed too quickly at the beginning of the sermon. Response to poverty, response to hunger and so on. Those who have accepted and begun to reproduce self-giving love will not need to be whipped up to minister to the poor and the hungry. Again, you only need go back a dozen verses in Galatians to hear the appropriate response "which very thing I was eager to do." But today I make no apology for saying, begin at the beginning. The Son of God loved *you* and gave himself for *you*. What will *you* make of that?

"God Sent Forth His Son"—
Galatians 4:4

Editor's Note: C. K. Barrett planned and drew up a series of three short addresses on Galatians 4:4-6. They were for some form of alternative service, and there are no dates or locations attached to them. Further, we simply have a detailed outline for each one, and in none of the sermon notebooks are these expanded into full manuscript sermons. Nevertheless, the outlines are illuminating as they show how C. K. Barrett intended to preach a series of addresses, however short or long, on this passage in Galatians.

"When the fullness of time came, God sent forth his Son."

Point (1): "The scandal of particularity." There is no difficulty in understanding this philosophical objection. Yet even if we share this attitude there are two things to be noted: (a) Christ is part of our world, a fact to be taken into account, and (b) the New Testament always presents him with the provocative question—What think ye of the Christ? Work out the picture from Paul's point of view.

Point (2) The timing. The fullness of time from (a) a political point of view—Pax Romana, roads, language but (b) note too the world of religion, the decay of the older religions (much like our own time), oriental cults both noble and disgusting, and Emperor worship. But there is another factor, Judaism and the Old Testament. The theme of incompleteness, the desire for fulfillment. Where is the place of understanding? This leads to

Point (3) Direct consideration of facts about Jesus himself—God's Son, born of woman, born under the Law. This is either revelation or rubbish, but it is not dull.

Point (4) What is the crucial thing about Jesus? Miracles? Note the beginning of Mark, use of signs. There is a drive toward understanding, but it is never thought that the meaning is self-evident. "Sins are forgiven thee."

Johannine discourses. His teaching was not law, it was both old and new, but in an eschatological setting—the Kingdom of God. But even the teaching of Jesus points to a particular place of understanding.

Point (5) What is crucial is the Cross. The Son of Man and the mercy of God. Here we see what it is to be born of woman, born under the Law. The problem of forgiveness, justice, and love. "Maybe he can forgive what you've done to me, and maybe he can forgive what I have done to you, but I don't see how he is going to forgive himself."

"That He Might Redeem"— Galatians 4:5

"That he might redeem those who were under the Law."

Point (1): At the end of last night we had come to the Cross, and seen a hardly resolved tension between the justice and mercy of God manifested in a world of sin. We see that the problem lies in forgiveness. "Shall not the judge of all the earth do right?" Is it morally right to forgive Judas? This, and the opposite extreme—legalism, non-moral.

Point (2): So we turn to Paul's speech to the Galatians. "Redeem ... under the Law," and before we go further two things are to be noted: (a) something had happened to the Galatians; (b) the ministry of Jesus. He makes clear the duty of human beings, love etc. and releases them for it. E.g. the paralytic woman. His forgiveness does not mean any relaxing of the necessity of obedience. We see then that Jesus is redeeming from the Law by fulfilling it. Now let us see what that means.

Point (3): Law implies justice. There can be no decent life without justice. And since the justice of this world is deficient, there must be divine justice.— Stoppard Brooke. Yet here the fulfillment is a paradox. OT equivalent of salvation. Putting someone in the right, vindication of those who through sin have gotten into trouble. And as Paul says, he justifies the ungodly. Explain the meaning of justification.

Point (4): And law means religion. Wrong sort of fulfillment suggests that Jud. is + when in fact it is -. Again, the time fulfillment is a paradox. For the misuse of the Law is to use it for ascent. The meaning of this in modern and universal terms (Mr. Wilford). The love that redeems is always understanding love (*The Man Who Was Thursday*).

Point (5): Now how is this redemption? First of all, let us look at humanity and the world. The fact of evil. BLM on irresponsibility. And guilt. We know we are not facing up rightly (not bothering about sin). And death. The

New Testament has two chief ways of the regarding the death of Christ: (a) victory. Luther quoted in "I was in prison." "Let the devil be as angry as he pleases, he may as well give up the idea that he can snatch us out of God's hand."; (b) sacrifice. Beyond comprehension. But sacrifice is a thing shared which creates a relationship between the worshipper and God. Studdert-Kennedy quote "When Jesus came to Birmingham . . ." Something fine and true there. We do encounter him, and he is able to bring us to God.

"No More as a Slave but a Son"— Galatians 4:6 and 5:22

"No more a servant but a son . . . he sent the Spirit of his Son . . . the fruit of the Spirit is . . ."

Point (1): Paul moves at last from the past and future terms (which are determining) to the present. This is the most perplexing thing of all, not the easiest. Consider the Galatians. Who and what are they? What makes them Christians? I must talk of Christianity restoring people's liberty. This shows a misunderstanding of Paul and Luther. The Galatians bring themselves under the slavery of religion and in so doing escape from the service of Christ.

Point (2): Note that Paul necessarily begins with God's Son. Jesus' certainty of his sonship, not only as a boy but in Gethsemane—Abba. We do not always have this confidence. It is very comforting to remember that Paul teaches that our sonship lies in him, and not in ourselves. It depends: (a) not on our feeling but upon the reality created by the work of Christ (see above); (b) not on our goodness but on the obedience of Christ. We are not the means of our own salvation.

Point (3): Sonship and slavery. That is Paul's contrast. Purchased our freedom. This means that our freedom is in Christ and in service to Him. This, if we could understand it, is the secret and mystery of Christian freedom and bondage, when to serve as a slave is to reign as a king. The way of service leads to liberty. Poem. We must see that this does not mean any release from doing God's will. See the Gospels again.

Point (4): Sonship and the Spirit. It is the Spirit who creates the relationship to God, and the Spirit who produces fruit. This is realized eschatology, and note common views of the Spirit. This leads to—

Point (5) The Spirit and the Cross. For Paul, all spirituality is governed by the concrete scene of death and disaster. He can never forget it. Mysticism and speculation are checked by it, this act of passion where God nailed to the cross the bond against us and made us free.

Conclusion

We have seen then how everything centers here. Our sin, God's righteousness, God's love, our life. Event and interpretation. History and the present challenge. If you see the Cross then you will say … "demands myself, my soul, my all." Grunewald. At least I can point like Grunewald's John the Baptist.

"Freedom and the Flesh"—
Galatians 5:13

[Preached three times from 7/29/01 at Bishop Auckland to 9/19/04 at Sacriston]

St. Paul was a man to take risks. How would you like, for example to escape from the great walled city of Damascus as he did? See him let down from a high window, swinging at the end of a fraying rope. Above was heaven knows what sort of incompetent Christian neophyte hanging on, he hoped, to the rope, and letting it down bit by bit. And in all probability, waiting for him below, a crowd of accessories. Paul thought they would be Arabs, Luke thought they would be Jews. Perhaps some of each, briefly united by their hatred of common Christian enemy. It was a risk alright, but he had to take it. How else could the Gospel continue?

He grew used to it. Everyone who talks about Paul should be able to recite this text—

> Are they ministers of Christ? I am talking like a madman—I am a better one: with far greater labors, far more imprisonments, with countless floggings, and often near death. Five times I have received from the Jews the forty lashes minus one. Three times I was beaten with rods. Once I received a stoning. Three times I was shipwrecked; for a night and a day I was adrift at sea; on frequent journeys, in danger from rivers, danger from bandits, danger from my own people, danger from Gentiles, danger in the city, danger in the wilderness, danger at sea, danger from false brothers and sisters; in toil and hardship, through many a sleepless night, hungry and thirsty, often without food, cold and naked. And, besides other things, I am under daily pressure because of my anxiety for all the churches. Who is weak, and I am not weak? Who is made to stumble, and I am not indignant? (2 Cor. 11:23-29 [NRSV])

How often did he take risks, risks to himself for the sake of the Gospel? But it is a different kind of risk that he takes in Galatians 5. You might say he is risking the Gospel. "You were called for freedom" he says and emphasizes it. Freedom is the Gospel. He has already said it in near enough the same words (5:1). And to whom is he writing? To people who perhaps twelve months before, perhaps six, had been straight heathen, capable of any sort of behavior. What a risk he was taking! You were called for freedom. Christ did not come to make you a present of a book of rules. He didn't come that you might get yourself entangled in the last book of rules there ever was—the Jewish Law. He came to set you free, free to come to God exactly as you are.

You may perhaps remember that about a year ago I preached a sermon here for which I borrowed the text my friend Ernst Kasemann used just before he was apprehended and thrown into jail by the Nazis. One of the best books he wrote (but any one of you could read it, it does not require any technical theology) is called in its English translation *Jesus Means Freedom*. And so he does. Here was a man himself who was free, free of the Law. He never wanted to be free of the great basic precepts of the Law. The first commandment is "thou shalt love the Lord thy God with all thy heart and with all thy soul and with all thy mind and with all thy strength" and of course he did. The second is like it; "Thou shalt love thy neighbor as thyself." And, of course, he did. He served them all his life and he served them with his death. But all the little pettifogging regulations? What mattered was applying the basic law with common sense. Do you think that what goes into your mouth at meal time can defile you? It may make you sick, but that is a different matter. What defiles you is what comes out of your heart, and mouth—foul language, lies, wicked speech, bragging, falsehoods. These will defile you, and so he taught.

And so he acted. No work on the Sabbath day, a day for everyone including doctors. They might work to save life, if life was in danger, but not otherwise. "Nonsense," said Jesus, "you don't treat your cattle that way, you take them out to grass and water." "And here," said Jesus, "are people bound by their bodily infirmities. What better way is there of celebrating God's infirmities than setting them free from their bondage, free from their paralysis, free from their leprosy, free from their blindness." This was the service of God, but more than that, free from the moral bondage too. Here is the rich, the disgracefully rich Zacchaeus, who had climbed a tree because that was the only way to see Jesus. And when Jesus brings him down and shows him compassion and sympathy, yes sympathy, that no one else has shown, what does he say? "Behold Lord, the half of my goods I am giving to the poor; and if I have taken anything to which I was not entitled, I'm giving it back four times over." The man is free, not bound up in his own money bags. "Go in peace," Jesus will characteristically say, "and sin no more." He was setting people free.

Paul was saying all this to the Galatians, but he was saying it in a different idiom. For one thing, he was speaking to different people, not to people who were caught up and entangled in all the details of a fine moral law, but to people who were bound in the age-old habits of traditional pagan religion and a loose moral life. For another thing, surprising though it may seem, I doubt whether Paul knew as many of the stories of Jesus as we know who were brought up as children on the Gospels. He did not begin, as I did a few minutes ago, with stories from the ministry of Jesus. He went straight to the end of it. "The Son of God loved me and gave himself for me. I do not make void the grace of God, for if righteousness comes through the Law, Christ died for nothing." If I can make myself right with God by observing all the details of the Law, good as the Law is, then the Son of God might happily have enjoyed life in heaven and never have come down to die on the Cross for me. Paul was right of course. The Cross, by any showing, is the climax of the whole story. Deal with that and by logical implication all the other details of the story are covered too. But people had come to Galatia and were teaching the Galatian Christians "Christ alone will do you no good. You become members of God's people by circumcision and by going on to keep the Law in its fullness." Paul says "No, that way will destroy the Gospel."

Does it sound like a theological quibble? It was splitting the Church in two. Previously, the whole Church, Jewish and Gentile Christians had shared the Pauline custom of regularly sharing a fellowship meal together. Paul, I suppose, started it. Peter joined in, Barnabas joined in. All were together, all joined in, for all were united by their common faith in Christ. What they had been in the past was neither here nor there. How could it compare with the common faith in the one crucified and risen Savior? There came a message from Jerusalem which set off one of the saddest stories in the New Testament. Jews must not eat with Gentiles unless the Gentiles are prepared to keep the Jewish Law. So the Jewish Christians, including even Peter and Barnabas walked out. Not even to preserve the unity of the Church would Paul agree. You were called for freedom, give up your freedom and you lose the Gospel. So the Galatians were free! What a risk. Free to go back to their old Gentile life? Paul has—

One Safeguard

And this will take some thinking about. "For freedom Christ set you free, but don't use your freedom for an opportunity for the flesh." And what does that mean? We all think we know and often enough we get it wrong. Sins in the flesh, well we see them in other people, and suppose that at least we have nothing to worry about. Crude, gross, ugly things they are, and we have been brought up to avoid them—gluttony and drunkenness, fornication and adultery, sloth and idleness, perhaps we come a bit nearer to these, but we work for our living, we have to, most of us, or we shouldn't live.

Some of the Bible translations don't help us. We had better avoid the word "flesh" say the translators or we will misunderstand. So, they talk about our "lower nature" or our "unspiritual side." And this is misleading too. It implies that if I have a lower nature I must also have a higher nature too and all that I need to do is pick the right one. Flesh is not a bit of me, the bad bit. It is me, my mind set on myself, me with all my instincts of self-preservation, of self-propagation. What that means is made clear by the balancing clause, in which Paul brings out the practical side of the Christian calling. "Don't use your freedom as an opportunity for the flesh, but in love serve one another." Flesh is self-centered life, and love is self-giving life. You are not set free to feather your own nest, you are set free in order to give, to spend yourself in loving service to others. Luther had a wonderful phrase which I may well have quoted in the pulpit before now. He spoke about the heart turned in upon itself. That is what we are like by nature. The knee is nearer the shin, said the Roman Emperor Claudius. What comes nearest to me is what matters most to me. Let the other suffer so long as I am all right.

But it was not for that, that Christ set you free said Paul here to the Galatians. Not that you ought to do the works of the flesh, and what a mixed lot they are—"fornication (first because it is so obvious), uncleanness, coarseness, enmity, contention, jealousy, anger, divisions, party spirit, envy, drunkenness, revelry." But that you might bear the fruit of the Spirit—love, joy, peace, patience, kindness, goodness, faithfulness, meekness, self-discipline. I have already begun to infringe upon what was to be the third point in this sermon. Having seen something of what this meant in Paul's Galatia, of freedom from the Law, freedom to come to God just as they were,

What Is There in It for Us?

For this is a place where we have to be careful, not least when we are enjoying singing "And can it be, my chains fell off, my heart was free"—Really? I remember my father telling me of a mission he shared in, in Hull and of a visit to a meeting at Hull Mission. It was a class of men, all of whom were converts from the lowest kind of life. "As they sang 'And can it be' you could nearly hear the chains clanking on the floor as they fell." Well how many ex-drunken blackguards are in this congregation? I think none. So what do we mean when we sing it? You may begin by remembering that the hymn was written by Charles Wesley, and he was a good boy if ever there was one. What did it mean to him? He was of course thinking of the story told in Acts 12, of Peter, imprisoned by Herod, and about to be brought out for execution. But an angel opened the prison door, struck off his bonds, and led him out through the city street. "I rose, went forth and followed thee"—one better than an angel. Charles knew, though not so well as his brother, what it was to be threatened by mob violence, by death itself. And he had followed the Lord out to bear witness in the city street.

It begins to make a picture. Freed from cowardice, the cowardice that inhibits our testimony. Freed from the bondage of inhibition that holds us back. Freed from the isolation that prevents us from joining in the work of our fellow Christians. But above all, and the key to everything else, freed from flesh, from self, free from concern for our own well-being that forgets the love we owe to the rest of humankind. "For freedom did Christ make you free; live in the freedom he has created for you."

"Glorying in the Cross"—Galatians 6:14

[Preached thirty-three times from 3/26/44 at Bondgate, Darlington, to 3/12/95 at New Hunwick]

We have now come to the end of our series of sermons for Lent. I have spoken of the crosses of Moses, Job, the Servant, and Jeremiah.[1] I can truthfully say though each time I began with an Old Testament character and an Old Testament text, I finished not far away from that "green hill" outside a city wall. Each time a finger has been pointed from there to the Cross of Christ. Christ crucified, to the best of my ability has been placarded before your eyes. Now I am prepared to sum up as well as I can, using these words of Paul: "Forbid it Lord that I should boast, save in the death of Christ my God."

The epistle is ended, and Paul is throwing out a number of compact aphorisms and writing them down with his own hand. "Tertius, give me the papyrus." And then Paul takes "a final flame" as Erasmus said. Nevertheless, behind what he says is a profound thought and a piercing insight. Let us see what is implied first by—

We Ought Not to Glory in Anything Else

Paul was at this time dealing with people who thought they had a special glorying of their own, a religious privilege which marked them off from other people. Paul had himself plenty of which he could boast, but he would not. He was a Jew as much as these other folk, and he had been a good deal keener about it than them. He had advantages of birth and education that were denied to them. He had been a free Roman citizen. He had been trained at the theological schools in Jerusalem and he had some

---

1   Editor's Note: This entire series can be found in Ben Witherington III, ed., appendix to *Luminescence: The Sermons of C. K. and Fred Barrett,* vol. 2 (Eugene, OR: Cascade, 2017).

sort of acquaintance with Greek literature. But no, he would glory in none of these things.

Paul's opponents are by no means the last persons who have wanted something to boast about. It is the most natural thing in the world to want something to be proud of, something to glory in. You can see this quite clearly the whole string of compensations which modern life has to provide for people. In modern life, because that is what we know best and also because much modern medicine today means the giving to people of drugs and stimulants for which they clamor, I say you can see it in the artificial compensations of modern life. That is because of course the average person has nothing very much to boast about in himself. Most of us are not noteworthy for beauty or for brains or for strength or for commercial or administrative power. Therefore, because a man is not a good footballer he goes to see Darlington play and glories in his team's successes (that's what I mean by compensation). Because he is not beautiful himself he buys good or striking clothes that he may be proud of. When a person has no brains (by a strange sort of inversion) he is proud of his ignorance. Or perhaps he is proud of his school, or a school friend of whom he is proud. What lies behind all these compensations is this: we want to glory in ourselves, and if we can't do it directly we will find some way around it by compensation. If I can't glory in my own football success, then I will glory in my team, and it is *my* team. Of course, if it stopped there, it wouldn't be so bad. But it goes further. A good deal of boasting in your country comes down to the same thing; one's country becomes a great "I" and one gets a personal gratification out of it.

I am afraid this can happen even in regard to our Church. What can seem more innocent than to be proud of your Church? And yet again and again it has seemed to me that this was only a cloak for pride in oneself or an expression of it. God, like one's country, can become another "I." I'm not going to make rash universal statements, but I am sure that a lot of our boasting is really boasting in ourselves. And it is the sure straightway to a disaster. We may even be proud of our wisdom, and that leads us straightway to Job. Life always has an extra trick up its sleeve, something that we cannot understand, and all our cleverness comes down to the ash heap. Or we may be proud of our goodness, and that leads us the way of Moses. In the end, we find out our impatience. We find our goodness powerless before the absolute claim of God. We cannot deserve nor can we achieve forgiveness, for ourselves or for others; we cannot attain to our proper status before God. What is more, and this is Paul's chief argument, if all this will do, then Christ died for nothing. Let us see this next.

We Ought to Glory in the Cross

I have forgotten now the name of the Roman princess who set out hunting for relics of the Cross of Christ, with this test to prove the genuineness of any piece of wood that claimed to be a fragment of the Cross. A dead person touched by the genuine relic would come back to life. As it stands that is of course a debased superstition; yet it will serve as a parable of the truth. The Cross of Christ does bring life, it does touch dead souls and give them new vitality. I don't think there can be any questioning of that, and it can be illustrated times without number. You will remember the Roman centurion who, when he saw how Jesus expired, was moved to confession "truly this man was Son of God." You will remember the Ethiopian eunuch who was reading about the Servant of God in Isaiah 53, when Philip joined him and preached Christ crucified, and there and then a new life was born. One instance after another your own mind can give you. You will remember Bunyan's Christian who when he came up with the Cross, lost his burden. But always remember that the great thing about Bunyan was not that he was a very great man, but that he had the experience ascribed to Pilgrim. What is important is the way he got it. As he walked along a street in Bedford, he heard a few old women talking in the sunlight on their doorsteps, and they were talking about this, and they were ordinary simple folk. Similarly, Charles Wesley thinking about the Cross could write

> Nay but I yield, I yield
> I can hold out no more,
> I sink by dying love compelled
> And own thee Conqueror.

Only Charles could write that, but think of the persons who sang it and meant it. It is no different today. Do you know the words that Tyrell wrote to von Hugel: "How gladly would I be out of it all, yet that strange man on the Cross drives me back again and again." I could tell you of others for whom the only remedy for sin and the only medicine for sorrow is in Christ crucified.

There is pragmatic reason enough for glorying in the Cross, and surely you must see why. All our other boasts belong to our own circle, if we do not glory in ourselves, we glory in our possessions, or our associations and so we get wrapped up in ourselves. All our life spins around in a closed circle around self, turning about its own axis, like a miniature solar system. We are the sun and everything revolves around us. Nothing we can think of can change that for us, any more than any internal explosion within a central gravitational system can radically alter the relations of the parts. Only something from outside can do that. Even a God of our own imagining will not do it. But here is a factor, a God whom we could never have imagined, a God of infinite power who stoops to our level and lavishes upon us a love unto death. There are no words to express what this means, it is too wonderful for us.

> What language shall I borrow,
> To praise the heavenly Friend,
> For this thy dying sorrow,
> Thy pity without end? (Bernard of Clairveaux)

If the King or the Prime Minister went out of his way, at great personal cost, to do you a favor, it would be something to glory in, would it not? How much more when God dies for you! "My sinful self my only shame / my glory all the Cross." Let us finally ask what this means,

What It Means to Glory in the Cross

I am going to be as simple and practical as I can. First, to glory in the Cross means to believe in it, to have faith in it. I can hear you object at once! But you said you were going to be practical and here you are talking not about doing but about believing. That is so unpractical. Well I don't agree with you. I will complete a quotation I began just now.

> Lord make me thine forever,
> Nor let me faithless prove,
> O let me never, never
> Abuse such dying love.

Faith in the Cross means that and more. It means acceptance of what Christ did, and being faithful to it. And that is the perfectly practical point I have already spoken of. There is a poem of Studdert-Kennedy which I should like to quote to you in full, but it is rather strong meat and some of you might be shocked. He describes vividly some of the ugly passions that can and do live in a person's mind then concludes—

Dear God! That loose lascivious force
That leers in my own soul,
Canst thou not smack it with thy Cross
And make me clean and whole?

Yes he can, and again and again when nothing else would purge a person's life of its foulness, the Cross of Christ has done it.

Secondly, we glory in the Cross by proclaiming. That is not easy. It is much easier to talk about anything else but that. That is why, God forgive us, even Christian preachers talk about it so little. One of the earliest pieces of epigraphy bearing on Christianity is a caricature, a man kneeling before a crucified figure, and the sneer, "Anaximines worshipping his God." I know it is hard but that is no excuse for not doing it. You can see what I mean when I put it in the reverse direction. Baring-Gould, criticized for his "Onward Christian Soldiers" on the ground that the Cross came in too often, offered to alter it. He came back with the version

Onward Christian soldiers
Marching as before,
With the Cross of Jesus,
Stuck behind the door.

Is it necessary to say more? He loved us to that measure, and can we be too timid to confess it?

Third and last, we glory in the Cross by revealing its spirit in our own lives. I will give you another illustration, a modern version of the parable of the Good Samaritan. A man named Allen was staying at a Mission Hospital where there was no doctor. A man came in with a fractured skull demanding immediate attention. There was a government doctor two miles away but he refused to come. So Allen got in the car and drove 75 miles over bad roads. Yes the doctor would come and over the 75 miles she came. She dealt with the fractured skull and went the 75 miles back. She was a German. Which doctor showed the spirit of the Cross?

The cross He bore is life and health,
Though shame and death to Him,
His people's hope, His people's wealth,
Their everlasting theme. (Thomas Kelly)

"The Difference that Christ Makes"— Ephesians 2:12-13

[Preached ten times from 6/17/45 at Bondgate, Darlington, to 12/9/79 at Twindon]

The difficulty with this passage is knowing where to stop. I do not mean so much with the sermon as with the text. One has often heard preachers who didn't know when to stop preaching, perhaps you have classed me among them. But this morning my difficulty arises at once, because in a very characteristic way this epistle keeps piling fact upon fact and once its eloquence has gotten under way, it is hard to check it. But check it we must if we are to get anywhere. And there is quite enough here. We learn first—

What It Means Not to Be a Christian

I will not apologize for dealing with this negative point. It has been all too little thought of in recent years. No New Testament writer can think with equanimity of people who are away from Christ. Hear them—"save yourselves from this crooked generation." "I have great sorrow and unending pain in my heart, for I could wish myself anathema from Christ for my kinsmen's sake." "The Word of the cross to them that are perishing is foolishness." "How shall we escape if we neglect so great a salvation?" "Without [outside the heavenly city] are the dogs and the sorcerers and the fornicators and the murderers and the idolaters and everyone that loves and makes a lie."

But all this is nothing compared to the attitude of Jesus himself. "When he saw the multitudes he was moved with compassion for they were distressed and scattered as sheep not having a shepherd." "O Jerusalem, Jerusalem which kills the prophets and stones those that are sent to you! How often would I have gathered your children together even as a hen gathers her own brood under her wings, and you would not!"

We shall not have recovered a real New Testament Christianity until we have recovered this horror at the mere possibility that some people should be living without Christ, still more that some should be dying without Christ. With that horror will return the evangelistic love which has to a great extent been jettisoned by the church of these days. If only more of us in Darlington would cry out in our hearts and really mean it, as we see the crowds hustling up and down the High Row. "O to save them! To persist for their saving!" Methodism would be returning to her first love of her first works. But we shall not get there merely by a scattering of exclamation marks through my sermon notebooks. We must do some thinking together and still more we must examine God's Word.

The next verse or two shows what the writer is thinking of. He speaks of a "middle wall of segregation." In May of 1871, a Frenchman M. Clermont Ganneau making archaeological investigations in Jerusalem picked up a stone. It was part of a wall in the old Temple area and it bore an inscription. This you may translate roughly as follows—"No one of another nation to enter within the fence and enclosure around the Temple. And whoever is caught will have himself to blame that his death ensues." Nothing could be plainer. We knew, of course, before this discovery was made, that the wall was there. But it is rather a thrill to spell out for yourself the letters, even in the photograph of the stone, which is all that I have seen. It makes the situation very vivid.

Here on one side of the wall is the inner part of the Temple with all that meant—the right to approach God, a share in his love. On the other side stands the Gentile, the outsider, the one who has no share in it at all. These are the folk who are described in our text as without God. It doesn't mean simply that they don't believe in him, it means that there is a great gulf between them. There is no contact. Further, they are aliens, outside the covenant, outside the promise. You who know the Old Testament know what is involved there. These folks stand outside the stream of divine activity. It moves by and leaves them untouched. They have no part in his purpose and that means no hope, no hope of a worthwhile life here, or hereafter. For if life cannot be redeemed here, there is no hope for its continuance hereafter.

I came across a note the other day sent by a mother to a school mistress, excusing the absence of her daughter. It ran "Miss _____ : Please will you excuse Mary from being away last Wednesday as her Aunty got buried and also had a cold in her glands and still has a cold. Kindly Oblige, Mrs _____." One is sorry for Aunty still suffering from her cold, but you see the point no doubt. If life after death is to take with it the colds and other ills of this life, there isn't much point in having it. The only hope that is worthwhile is a hope of real redemption. What it means not to be a Christian. How do these folk live? And how can we who know something different let them go on living and dying like this? But let us do some more thinking.

What Difference Does Christ Make?

That of course is a question people are always asking, and if we cannot answer it with some sort of conviction I suggest that we should shut up shop at once. I don't know why we so often seem to advertise the church in a manner none of you would ever use for your business. "Trade isn't very good in these days, and we are not really sure we have got anything in the shop that you really want. But it would be very encouraging if you would come in and look around the counters." That isn't very impressive really. We shall not win the world by asking for its sympathy. We shall only win it if we can say "You poor, lonely lost men and women, come and share in this mighty thing that Christ is doing with us."

Well, what is he doing? You have the answer to that question and I cannot impose one on you . Least of all can I exhaust all that might be said. But I am going to throw in a few ideas with two hopes in mind: (1) that they may help to make your own thinking a little more systematic and help sort out your ideas; and (2) that they may suggest some lines of development in your own Christian life. First then, Christ deals with that wall. "You" says our text, "who were once far away, are now brought near." The wall is down. It does not exist. How has Christ done that? Through the blood of Christ, as our text tells us, that it has happened. He has done it by substituting a new basis of nearness and farness.

The old Jewish rabbinic tractate Pirke Aboth, fundamental for much of Jewish religion as one of these fundamental rules says "Make a fence for the Law, guard it, hedge the essential commands with others for their greater security." But it was possible to be on the wrong side of the fence. The coming of Jesus meant that there was a different way to God, or rather God is coming out from inside the wall. This breaks up all our petty ideas of near and far. It is like moving your coordinates in geometry, all your measurements alter. Better, it is like a child outside a great walled garden and then the door opens as father comes out. God has come out to wandering, lonely persons. He is near them, he is near all people. A medieval writer said once, "the devils are as near to God as the angels, only the devils have turned their back on Him." God has come near to us, it cost him the Cross to do it, but he has done it. He has broken down the wall.

Secondly, he has admitted us into a fellowship. He breaks down the wall between people. He is building up a new redeemed society where true fellowship is possible, because the causes of friction are being taken away. You have to think your way back to the old world if you are going to get the richness of this picture. Our text, speaking negatively, says that those who are without Christ are aliens from the commonwealth of Israel. They were, that is, stateless people. There are a few such people now and you run into their problems now and again. There were many more 2,000 years ago. Some were slaves, some were criminals, some were adventurers. But they had no rights, no homes, no privileges. They stood outside organized society. No one would befriend them, no one would protect them. It made all the difference to be part of a state, to have its backing at home or abroad, to belong to a real community.

Christ brings us into the most wonderful community that was ever made. You have heard me criticize the Church. I have never been afraid to tell Church people their faults, though I believe in washing the dirty linen at home. But faults and all, there is nothing like the Church of God, that sacred and wonderful mystery. Christ gives us a home, he gives us his promises, he gives us brothers and sisters, he gives us the backing of the rule of God. He admits us into the fellowship of his Kingdom. He offers to us the possibility of a daily walk with God. He offers it to everybody as a regular normal thing. No other religion can make that claim, much less substantiate it. For most of them communion with God is the rare zenith peak of life, a moment to be prepared for over decades of training, and then remembered for the rest of life. The greatest of the Neo-Platonists had experienced it, two or three times only. But Christ offers a daily gift of fellowship with God even to the very beginner in the Christian life.

Brother Lawrence, in one of his letters wrote: "In a conversation . . . with a person of piety, he told me that the spiritual life was a life of grace, which begins with servile fear, which is increased by hope of eternal life, and which is consummated by pure love. That each of these states had its different stages, by which one arrives at last at the blessed consummation. I have not followed all these methods. . . . At my entrance into religion I took a resolution to give myself up to God. . . ." And so, Brother Lawrence began at once upon the practice of the presence of God. So can you. You do not have to come out of the world, but in your daily task if it be an honest and useful one, you can do all things for God's sake, and live with him.

I cannot tell you how I long for a deeper richer experience in myself and in the Church. That and nothing else will solve our problems. It will take us back to where we began this morning. It will make us see how exceeding abundantly above all we ask or think God can do for us; in doing that it will make us realize what the folk outside are missing. It will quicken our zeal and love for them as nothing else can do; it will give us a vital fellowship into which we can bring them.

"The Meaning of Love"—
Ephesians 3; John 15

[Preached once at a wedding in Durham 8/16/86]

It might well seem that there is no aspect of marriage that is not more than already adequately covered by the joint resources of a theologian and an economist, a fact that underlines an observation printed in the *Times* a few days before an occasion similar to this one, though it received a good deal more publicity. "Sermons at weddings" the writer said, "are very difficult and perhaps undesirable." It is therefore a good thing that the passages of Scripture you have just heard prompt me to remind you, require me to remind you, that there is something you do not know, something indeed that none of us knows, the love of Christ which surpasses knowledge. It is also true that the same verse invites you to know what you cannot know, to know the love of Christ which surpasses knowledge. Of course, we all understand how to interpret this. The writer has hit on one of those splendid memorable epigrams, that every university lecturer hopes he will be able to coin now and then, the lucky ones manage to produce them once or twice in a lifetime. We understand, I say, what he means—here is something you will never know to the full, never get to the bottom of, but something you must begin to grasp now, and must, as life goes on, come to know better and better.

You can hardly avoid talking about love at a wedding, not only, Susan and John, the love you have for each other, but our love for you both, which brings us here to rejoice with you and to join our prayers with yours. That last is understandable enough, and so are other things. That does not mean they are unimportant or that we can ignore them, far from it. There is a physical attraction between man and woman, male and female. There is a psychological compatibility between a particular man and a particular woman. And these grow into the sentiment of love. Nothing here to surpass anyone's knowledge; and we all know too how little a bond these things can produce, how easily physical attraction may either wane or grow into rank profligacy; how easily psychological compatibility may turn, through irritation, to loathing or hate. There is nothing here to surpass our knowledge and we need, those who marry today and whose memory takes them back many years, a deeper love to sanctify these.

What is this love of Christ which surpasses knowledge? For an answer to the question we turn back from the Epistle to the Gospel. Here is the highest form of love, the love of Jesus for his disciples. It is a hard, but inspiring love. "As the Father has loved me, so have I loved you." But the Father's love had sent him down from the bliss of immortality to live a human life and die a terrifying human death. This was the Father's love for his Son, and this was and is, the Son's love for his disciples. From this the next step follows—"if you keep my commandments, you shall abide in my love." Love does not mean (you will discover if in God's goodness you become parents) I don't mind what you do; love minds infinitely. Not that it loves only the good, still less the goody-goody. But, says Jesus you abide in my love, you dwell in the circle of shared affection, if you do what I say, if you play your part in the purpose I represent.

Why am I saying all this today, which you two know so well? For two reasons. First, because it is the truth about God and his love and this is what we live by. God's love is for sinners, not for plaster saints but for people like us. Because it starts there we know it will persist through all circumstances. Life will not always be exactly what it is today. The sun does not always shine. Unless you are something more, though I really think I mean something less, than human, there will be difficulties, problems, sorrows, disappointments. These, like the joys of life, are the things God uses as they are incorporated into his purposes for the good of the world. The privilege of obeying his commandments is the greatest that we have for it means sharing in his work. And this, in different ways, we know that you two will do.

And secondly I am telling you this because what is true of God's love is to be reflected in your own. There is nothing wrong with sentiment; we can allow you a good deal of it today. But beyond all that, love means the iron determination that Jesus showed as he did the Father's work. It means the steady resolution always to consider the other's interest before you consider your own. Such disciplined unselfish love will sound forbidding only to the superficial. It is, in fact, the way to happiness. "These things" said Jesus of obedience and self-denying love, "these things have I spoken unto you, that my joy may be in you, and your joy may be fulfilled." May this joy, the joy you have in each other, a joy fulfilled and sanctified in your common discipleship to Jesus Christ be yours today and through all the years to come.

"I Believe in Jesus the Redeemer"— Philippians 2:6-11

[Preached three times from 7/23/44 at Bondgate, Darlington, to 6/8/52 at Bishop Auckland]

Set beside our text these words of the Apostle's Creed:

I believe in Jesus Christ, his only Son, our Lord,
who was conceived by the Holy Spirit
and born of the virgin Mary.
He suffered under Pontius Pilate,
was crucified, died, and was buried;
he descended to hell.
The third day he rose again from the dead.
He ascended to heaven
and is seated at the right hand of God the Father almighty.
From there he will come to judge the living and the dead.

We come now to the central and distinctively Christian articles of the Creed.[1]

I have a word of Introduction to say, and it is one that could without any difficulty grow into a whole sermon. Perhaps someday it will. The point is this—we are making here highly dogmatic assertions about Jesus. I know many people who feel they cannot accept these assertions because to do so would fetter themselves, and prevent them from entering into the fullness of the inheritance of the world's thought. This is especially true, I think, of the best young people today, who are strenuously seeking a unified view of life and history.

---

1   Editor's Note: This sermon was originally part of a series, then later a stand-alone sermon. The series was on the articles of the Creed, beginning with a sermon on "I Believe" followed by "God as Creator," then this sermon.

This fear is not justified. I am not retreating one inch from the position of Christian orthodoxy. What I say is that it is only from the position of Christian orthodoxy that world thought and world history can be understood. I well remember once lamenting to a very great Cambridge theologian that I had not read Classics before I turned to theology. "No!" he said very vehemently. "You are doing right as you are, first learning theology, and then going to the Classics. It is the only way you can understand them. If you go from the New Testament to Plato, you will understand them both. But if you go from Plato to the New Testament you will probably understand neither." As far as it can be done in a short time, I want to show how the faith in Christ does this. We shall take the most fundamental points.

Jesus Christ Is God

If you had not been accustomed to hearing that statement week after week, you would be staggered by it. Jesus Christ is God. *Apparently*, it is a sophistry about a human being or a blasphemy against God. People are so used to it that it is often dismissed as a pious commonplace. But it is not a commonplace at all of any sort. To say that the eternal, unknowable, unchangeable God came on earth as a human being may be incredible nonsense, but it is certainly neither ordinary nor negligible. Yet neither is it a remote piece of fancy, out of touch with everyday life. You have probably heard of Richard Hooker, one of the greatest English theologians who lived 300–400 years ago. In the great fifth book of his Ecclesiastical Polity he prefixes to his discussion of the practical Church questions of his day, a detailed discussion of the person of our Lord. In this he was following St. Paul, for in this very passage Paul is really concerned to encourage unity and kindness among the Christians of Philippi.

I want to emphasize that because it is a fact often forgotten. As I write this sermon this morning I am interrupted. I must go out to take a funeral. What does it matter there that Christ is God? I look out my study window and see the children playing in the garden of the Nursery School. Does it matter to them that I am writing these tremendous theological statements? And far away there are men flying, sailing, riding in their tanks to battle, storming over the countryside in a hail of bombshells. Does it matter that Christ is God? I feel that I must face these questions very frankly, because I know well that many people outside the Church think our faith simply irrelevant to their world. And I think that there are at least some of you who can feel the power of a warm piety, but do not see where the

Bible and the formulated Christian faith comes into it. A great part of the answer will come in our next two points about the deeds of Christ but there is something to be said here too.

Jesus is God manifest. You remember what we talked about last Sunday. God the Creator must be creative love, we said. Hence we believe in his love, his providence now. But how do you know? Can you just look at creation and say "Yes of course God made it, and his purpose in making it was love"? I don't see how you honestly can. Of course, the creation is a signal instance of God's goodness and mercy, but do people just look at it and think of that. I'm afraid not.

The simple fact is we know God through Jesus Christ. In him the pattern of God's purposes rises to the very surface of life and can be grasped by faith. Then, when that has been seen, we are in a position to look elsewhere and try, if you have sharp enough eyes, to pick up the same pattern. If there is a red thread of purpose running through life, as through a mountaineer's rope, there is one place where that thread comes to light—that is Jesus Christ. The thread runs throughout the rope, but only at one place can you see it. Or, I may put it this way, at school we had an open-air swimming bath. It was surrounded by trees which made a very pleasant scene, but unfortunately meant that the water often became cloudy. The result was this. If you walked straight up to the deep end of the bath and looked in you saw a certain murkiness, a "trail of green gloom." If you then walked down to the shallow end the shadows thinned out and you could see a pattern on the tiles at the bottom. Then if you walked back along the edge, keeping your eye on the bottom (and avoiding the danger of falling in) you could still pick out the pattern as you advanced to deeper water, and if things were not too thick you could see it where you could not see it before—at the deep end. Having once picked out the pattern where it was clear, you could still see it where before you could not.

In my sermon, last week on God as Creator, I said that our creation implied a purpose in life, but I said little about that purpose. That was because from the mere fact of creation, it is possible to see that there is a purpose to life, but impossible to see what the purpose is. It is only in Jesus Christ, God manifest, that we see what our high calling is. It is in him that we see what it means truly to be in the image of God. He is our vocation. In order to develop this, it will be necessary to pass on to the other points which come into view here.

He Humbled Himself

So says St. Paul, poetically. He was found in fashion as a man. He became obedient unto death, even the death of the cross. So also says the Creed in direct terms. He suffered under Pontius Pilate, he was crucified, dead, and buried. Here is the most astounding statement of all, and such it has always been. In the very early days of Christianity, the educated heathen were sneering—"If God had come into the world he certainly would have cut a better figure than your crucified Jesus." And so nearer to our time, Nietzsche, for example, pointing out how odd it was that when God went to reveal himself, he should have had to learn Greek for the purpose, and that he hadn't learned it better when he was at it. And, of course, Nazi philosophy despises effeminacy and weakness, and the defeat of the poor Jew.

What does this mean? That when God came into our world, it was to a life of suffering, and to death? If I had an hour, I could hardly begin to answer the question. One does not like to speak at all, only do so, as Augustine said, that one may not be quite silent. The first and last and middle word of the Cross, is the love of God. Never mind the philosophical and theological reasons, if there be any, why it was necessary for God incarnate to suffer. It seems that it was necessary (if the word can be properly used). And knowing the necessity, God went straight into it, walked into it with his eyes open. And he did it for us. So Luther "he has redeemed me, a lost and damned man, and has won and delivered me from all sins, from death, and from the power of the Devil, not with gold and silver, but with his holy and precious blood, and with his innocent passion and death, so that I might be his own, and might live under him in his Kingdom, and serve him in everlasting righteousness and innocence and blessedness." What can one say?

> What language shall I borrow
> To praise Thee, heavenly friend,
> For this my dying sorrow,
> Thy pity without end?
> Lord make me Thine forever,
> Nor let me faithless prove
> Oh let me never, never
> Abuse such dying love. (Bernard of Clairveaux)

Yes, for just mark this inspiration that I may not be charged with being abstract. Paul had begun the chapter by saying "have this mind in yourself that was also in Christ Jesus." "Dying love" love unto death is the standard for our love. Isn't the solution of all our Church problems here? And see the contradiction human beings have made for themselves. Our true existence is in the image of God—and see how we contradict ourselves. Our true humanity is the manhood of Christ, and our actual humanity is that of Pilate, of Caiaphas, of Judas, of Peter. Each of us is a battlefield on which the battle is fought, the battle of Christ and ordinary sinful human nature. But the story does not end in the confused melee of the battle. For we must come to the full close—

He Is Exalted

He was raised from the dead, he ascended into heaven; he sits at God's right hand, he shall come to be our judge. You see the force of this do you not? The government of the world is in the hands of Jesus of Nazareth. The plan itself was not broken by the Cross, that catastrophe only broke open, as it were, the outer case that the plan of God might be clearly seen. The love of Calvary is at the heart of the universe. And the distinction of good and evil is in the hand of Jesus. He is the judge. His goodness is eternal goodness and all that contradicts him is evil and sin. The standard of right and wrong is not expediency but his holy love.

Now finally and in sum: is all this relevant to our world or is it not? All the clever brains trying to understand life—the little children, the soldiers, the mourning and the dying. Where do they all come in? The disciples of Jesus went out of the upper room knowing where they all came in.

"They had seen the strong hands of God twist the crown of thorns into a crown of glory and in hands as strong as that they knew themselves safe. They had misunderstood practically everything Christ had ever said to them, but no matter: the thing made sense at last, and the meaning was far beyond anything they had dreamed. They had expected a walk-over and beheld a victory; they had expected an earthly Messiah and they beheld the soul of Charity. It has been said to them of old time, 'No man shall look upon my face and live' but for them a means had been found. They had seen the face of the living God turned upon them; and it was the face of a suffering and rejoicing man." (Dorothy Sayers).[2]

---

2   Editor's Note: This lengthy quote is taken from the conclusion of Dorothy Sayer's 1938 reflection on the Creed entitled "The Greatest Drama Ever Staged." If one reads through the whole reflection, one can see how much it has influenced this particular sermon of CKB. It can be found online at http://thestarsplitter.blogspot.com/2014/04/the-greatest-drama-ever-staged-and.html.

"St. Paul's Conversion"—Philippians 3:7

[Preached ten times from 1/30/55 at Elvet to 1/22/95 at Newfield]

I wish to say two things before I begin with the text: (1) this is the first of a series of sermons which will be followed after the service by a discussion. No doubt something has been said to you on that score already but I must add something on my own account. I have not lived in universities for the last 18 out of 20 years without learning how to discuss all things in heaven and on earth. Yet there is a difference between a sermon, on the one hand, and a lecture or essay on the other. A sermon is not simply a public address on a religious subject; it is not simply an exposition of a passage of Scripture. It is these things, yet if really it is a sermon and not a lecture, it is something else too. It is a means by which God himself speaks to us. This is not an event the preacher can command or arrange. It is independent of his learning, his eloquence, his enthusiasm. But it does happen, and it is the only raison d'etre of preaching.

Now this sermon will contain biblical exegesis, historical reconstruction, psychological analysis and likely much else. All this can be discussed until the small hours, if you wish; but if, as may be, you hear God's voice in your conscience, you do not discuss, you obey. Of course, there is still room for a different kind of discussion, that you may know exactly how to do, but make sure it's that kind of discussion; (2) This is a purely personal and practical point. I am asked to remember that January 25th is the feast of the conversion of St. Paul and to preach on conversion. Just twelve months ago I preached here at Elvet, noted the date, and preached what was practically a sermon on conversion. I bring attention to this at the outset because it seems impossible to me to preach two entirely different sermons on the same theme. Accordingly, if I repeat myself the fault is not entirely mine!

I need not, I think, stay to point out that this third chapter of Philippians is one the very few passages in his epistles in which Paul gives any account of the beginning of his Christian life, and of what lay before it. He never founded his theology in his conversion experience, vital as it was. Christianity is not the creation of Paul's religious experience. And correspondingly it is to be hoped that we shall not try to substitute some conversion experience of ours for the factual, historical foundation of the Christian faith. Indeed, conversion is not merely an experience, in the usual sense. Let us develop that in the first point. In the first place, then—

Paul's Conversion Was the Conversion of a Religious Person

To some of you that may sound like a contradiction in terms, but it is by no means so, as a few minutes reflection will show. Just over a fortnight ago I read, as you may have read, the *Manchester Guardian*'s obituary of the Italian field-marshal, Graziani. The whole story was admirably sketched, not least the marshal's record in Abyssinia—the walls stripped, that whole villages might die of thirst, the Ethiopian soldiers dropped from airplanes like bombs upon their own villages, to teach the inhabitants a lesson. There was his favorite proverb—"a forgiven enemy is worse than a thousand foes." The last sentence of the obituary was "He was fervently religious." One may guess that the world would be a happier place if he had been less religious and more Christian. It is often true that religious people most need conversion, and fair also to add that when it happens to them—the results are tremendous, greater even than when the drunken-wife beater becomes a new man.

Let us work back through history. John Wesley was a religious man. At the time of his conversion he had been a don in orders, leader of the Holy Club (dare one say, President of S.C.M. or Meth Soc?) and for some years a missionary. None was more fervently religious than he. But quite evidently, this "religion" was not conversion. Clearly you can have religion and have it badly and not be converted.

You may go back 200 years to Luther and find the same state of things. Luther was living a religious life in the technical sense, he was a monk. If monasticism could have worked, he would have made it work. But religion failed to give him peace, and real conversion when it came made him leave much of what he had called religion, and as he said it made him who was a monk marry a nun!

Wesley, Luther, but pre-eminently Paul was a man of religion. He tells us so in this chapter. In the best, finest, most earnest religion the world had known, he had been blameless. But this was not conversion. A strict life, a high code of ethics, a water-tight theology, none of these things made him a Christian. At this point I wish to draw two plain and practical inferences. They aren't the end of the sermon but they are worth keeping in mind.

The first is for the religious and that means probably most of us who have been brought up in Christian households, attended Sunday School and Church, been at Christian schools and so on. All these things are of course good, but they are dangerous for it is easy to confuse the practice of religion with Christianity itself. Paul was a Pharisee, and the Pharisees were good people—so good that if Christ himself were to disagree with them, they were quite unable to doubt that he was wrong and they were right. The more religious you are by nature, the more rigorously you should examine yourself. It was to the Corinthians, the most religious of all his flocks to whom Paul wrote "try yourselves to see whether you are in the faith."

The second is for the irreligious, the secular-minded. I know people of this kind, some with relief, some with wistfulness, that the Christian faith is not for them. They are not naturally good, or naturally religious. That is neither here nor there. You may miss some of the things that the religious person has, but you are no stranger to the faith. We will see in a minute that the religious person has to begin by questioning his religion, perhaps you can simply short-circuit that first step. What is this first step? It is clear Paul's conversion meant—

A Re-Evaluation of Values

"What things were gains to me," he says, "these things I have counted as loss for Christ." The metaphor is commercial and perfectly clear. His assets were henceforth to be reckoned as liabilities. The blue ink on his balance sheet was turned to red. What his assets were, we know quite well because he tells us in the first verses of this chapter: (1) Race. He was of the stock of Israel, of the tribe of Benjamin, a Hebrew of Hebrews. He belonged to the chosen people who thanked God daily that they were not like other people; (2) Religion. As touching the Law he was a Pharisee. Race alone was not enough. Within the race, he belonged to the right caste. He did everything God required of him.

No one could ever confuse him with the lower breeds without the Law; (3) Enthusiasm. As touching zeal, he persecuted the Church. No negative piety was enough for him. He knew the way to take with dissenters and it was the shortest way. He would persecute the Christians out of existence, cost what it might, and they would disturb the peace of Judaism no more; (4) Morals. As touching the righteousness which is in the Law, and this was no mean standard, he was blameless.

Now the moment of conversion meant for Paul that all these things, which he had not merely accepted but welcomed, which actually constituted his life, were queried and challenged. All the old securities were gone. He could no longer rely upon his race, his religion, or his personal achievements. That is not something peculiar to Paul, it is part of the pattern of Christian life according to the New Testament, and if we want to know what the Christian life means, and what conversion is, this is where we must begin, and we can begin in Paul's own terms.

I trust that it is unnecessary to begin with race. I hope there is no one here who thinks that his race gives him a position of advantage with God. Don't misunderstand. I am not denying my own people. There are few better places to live in than England and for all our faults, few people with cleaner hands than ours. But you surely do not suppose you are dearer to God than the Fiji Islanders. More, you, all of you, fight racial prejudice wherever you meet it.

But let us move on. Religion and our own personal achievements—zeal, knowledge, skill, influence, position. If you really are confronted by God, all of these things, your very existence, are questioned. All the easy assumptions on which common life is based are challenged. And I have no time to analyze this fully but I can at least give you a line as a basis on which to work.

Our thought is usually anthropocentric, centered on ourselves. In modern terms this means either the Cartesian *cogito*, or the Kantian "I ought." In each case the subject of the verb is "I," the human "I." But suppose God is real, and God is all we are not. That he is what lies beyond the line of life and death—why then our thinking is questioned, and it must be done again. Or consider human religion and morality. Here the simplest hint is in the Sermon on the Mount. Good straight, human-centered religion and morality say "thou shalt not kill; thou shalt not commit adultery, thou shalt not forswear thyself. An eye for an eye and a tooth for a tooth. Thou shalt love thy neighbor and thou shalt hate thy enemy." Step by step Jesus follows this list, questioning the basic assumptions of the religion and the morality of his day. Take God seriously, and how is anger better than murder, lust than adultery? An eye for an eye is common sense, no says Jesus, turn the other cheek; love your neighbors and hate your enemies is common sense. No says Jesus love your enemies.

Make no mistake, conversion is not comfortable. Conversion is not just a matter of shouting glory hallelujah in an ecstasy of religious bliss. I have heard people say how some staggering blow, such as a great sorrow or a desperate illness, or being sent to a concentration camp, has as it were stripped them naked, and made them question even their own existence. Conversion if it is real, means all that. What are your gains, what are your losses? When do you draw the line between credit and debit in life? But we have not finished yet. Long before Christ, Socrates said that an unexamined life isn't worth living[1] and we must go further than negative analysis and criticism. In conversion, for Paul—

Christ Was Central

I have counted my gains losses not because I thought it would make a pleasant change but for Christ. The fundamental thing that happened in Paul's conversion is that he met Christ, met him personally, so that henceforth it was impossible for him to doubt that Christ was alive, and was the Lord of this and every world. This was all that mattered. Paul therefore scrapped all his other assets or gains, and reckoned Christ his only asset. It was like the parable of the pearl of great price. The merchant sold all his other pearls so that he might acquire the only one that really mattered. So when Paul disposed of his assets—race, religion, achievements, he did not put in their place a giant question mark. He put Christ there. Not my faith, but his faithfulness; not my righteousness but his, not my love but his.

So, positively, conversion means (as the Methodist fathers put it) venturing on Christ. It means trusting him and obeying him. It means you accept your values from him, that you are no longer the center of your own existence, you have given that place to him. I can end this sermon I think only in the way I ended my sermon a year ago, with the impudent and ill-mannered question—Have you been converted? That does not mean—Have you undergone some prescribed experience? Have you signed on some dotted

---

1   Editor's Note: Actually, CKB has Plato rather than Socrates here in the sermon, but it was Socrates who first enunciated this principle.

line? It does not even mean—Are you a religious person? Or are you very virtuous?

This is what the question does mean. Have you ever questioned the assumptions on which your life is based? Are you satisfied with the comfortable, conventional axioms of ordinary thought and practice? Are you yourself the center of your own life? Or has the tremendous fact of the living God shaken you out of complacency? And are you prepared for Christ to rule in the central place in your life?

"Our Citizenship Is in Heaven"— Philippians 3:20

[Preached eight times from 6/3/45 at Bondgate, Darlington, to 10/15/85 at Hawkhurst]

The context of these words is very plain spoken. Paul is dealing with people whose conduct is so dreadful it moves him to tears. They have no god higher than their own belly, their own sensual appetites. They are enemies of the Cross of Christ. Their minds are fixed solely on the transient, quickly passing fantasies of this world. Inevitably, their only end can be destruction. They have nothing in themselves, in their quite worldly sensual make-up to withstand the ravages of time.

But it is not so with you! exclaims Paul. That isn't the way with you. For our citizenship, for Christians, is not earthly, sensual at all; it belongs to heaven. This verse is one of the hardest in the New Testament to translate. Not that its meaning is obscure; but that it is so prolific. Citizenship—city, this is written of course in Greek and to a Greek there were few words that meant as much as "city." Social and political life had its center in the city. It meant home. All the things dearest to a person. It is difficult to express all this in a few words, but what the text means is that for us Christians all that is in heaven; that is the sphere of our strongest loyalty, our deepest love, and here we are a little colony of folk living abroad. Not an independent dominion but a colony.

Under Authority

Now let me tell you what it is that has sent me to this text. I am thinking about worship. I am concerned with the question of course we have come to Church for. I have been intending to refer to this subject since our last

Friendship Tours, getting on a few months ago. Some of you will remember that in a number of discussions we talked about the sort of thing we do in our services and considered whether some things might be changed or added to make the services more helpful. I found the discussions very helpful, and I hope that in time we shall see many practical results. But after the last discussion I took the liberty of having the last word, and pointed out that though of course we are at liberty to plan our own services, yet we do not come to Church simply to do what we want to do. We come to find ourselves *under authority.* I know one person at least to whom that was a new thought, in many years of church going it had never occurred to him. It may be so with others. I want to bring it out now.

Our citizenship and our central authority is in heaven. We are living away from home. We come here to renew our contact, to remember our obedience. It was the rule, and no doubt still is, in monasteries that every day the monks should assemble and hear a part of the rule under which they lived, e.g. the rule of St. Benedict for the Benedictines and so on. We come to do something like that, not only to recognize formally an authority, but to recapture the spirit of this community, this venture on which we are engaged, the spirit which it is so easy to lose in the bustle and business of everyday life. I want to develop this in a few ways.

The Church Is Our Home

It is the place to which we belong. It is not a superfluity on top of life. It is not a luxury. It is not like one of those voluntary questions you meet in some examination papers; you can pass the examination without answering them, but you must have a shot at them if you want to get a distinction. Many people think it takes all our time to live a good life; the worship of the church is an extra for the superlatively good people, like going to a luxury hotel in Scarborough. No, that is not so. The church is the home of us all, because heaven is the home of us all.

I wonder if that is how we feel about the church. Where do you feel most at home? I am asking myself that question, and I find it a rather disturbing one. Take these other folk Paul is talking about. Jolly, friendly people they are, fond of a good meal and a good drink, not very particular about some of the things they do. I'm afraid I find it easy, too easy to feel at home there. And feeling at home is a thing that reveals your character, to yourself at least, as much as anything can do. Thank God, and it is no credit to me personally so I can speak openly about it, that I have been so brought up so as to feel at home with the underdogs of life. Some people are so stuck up that they can only feel at home in a fine drawing room, they give themselves away. Give me a humble cottage every time. I'm not sure what that shows. A little while ago, I was in a Darlington home, and someone said to me, "I can talk to you, you're not like the others, you're not gentleman like."

But I'm more concerned with the other side of the question. It's a bad phrase maybe, but you can only expect a heavenly minded man to be at home, really at home in the church. That is why there is a very definite limit to the popularizing of services. A service at which some people would feel at home would not be a real service at all. You may know the little rhyme that has more than humor in it—

Although at first Hell might seem to be worst
Yet time its affliction might soften
But if you are bored by praising the Lord
You'd be more bored by praising him often.

Never forget in all the ordinary intercourse of life where you belong. Some of us have names, names that are a constant check on our actions. If we were in some company, the incompatibility would appear at once. Do you remember what Tom Brown's father says to him? "You tell the truth, keep a brave and kind heart, and never listen to or say anything you wouldn't have your mother or sister hear, and you'll never feel ashamed to come home, or we to see you." There's a lot in that. The fellowship of the Church itself, and still more the heavenly fellowship of which this is a colony should mean something like that to you.

John Henry Newman said once, "our one chance against sin is that we be shocked by it." There's a lot in that. If it's an even choice to you "I'll do this or that" scales weighing; well, sin can offer a very attractive way. But do you face the evil possibility with a shudder? "Good God no, I couldn't." Then the scale is tipped and will be tipped decisively. This service reminds you where you belong. But it does that in a way so concrete that it must have a special designation.

It Is God's Gift

The bread which comes down from heaven, as Jesus puts it. My thought on this line has been colored by what seems to me a most striking illustration of it. You may have seen the film *A Song to Remember*. I saw it during my holiday but I believe that it has been shown in Darlington. It is a rather romanticized version of the life of Chopin. I take the story as it stands in the film. Chopin was a Polish boy, brought up in Poland a hundred years ago when that unhappy country was oppressed as it is now, only with the difference that the tyrants were Russians not Germans. There was then an "underground movement" to which Chopin belonged. But the chance came for him to go to Paris, the chance to win fame as a pianist and composer. It was settled that he must go. If only he could make his name, people would say "a people who can produce this music must be free." So, he went to Paris for a cause. He had to be smuggled out of Poland by night, crossing the river in the mist in a little boat. Before he sets off, he says goodbye to a girl partisan. She stops, picks up a handful of earth and puts it in his hand. He looks surprised, "It's Polish earth and never forget it." Well, he gets to Paris and after reviews he does come right to the front with a bang. But the "cause" is forgotten, for he has found attractive and daring Georg Sand, the French woman writer who took a man's name. In spite of illness, life is very pleasant, very gay. But things are bad in Poland; money would be useful, money could buy leaders out of prison. Will Fredric, they ask, risk his health and play concerts to raise money for Poland? No. And then they send him—a little bag. A little blue velvet bag. He opens it, strange—it's dust. No, it's earth. Polish earth. And with that the man leaves his gay life and plays and plays and plays for Poland, kills himself with playing at age 39.

Something is given to you here like that. Given to you in words, given to you in the sacrament that brings our Gospel to a blazing focus in the same concrete form as Polish earth. A word, a piece of bread, a glass of wine. And do they not, these memorials of the Christ, who died for you and who suffers for you, do they not call to you in all your sin and suffering, call to us all as day by day we prostitute our lives and our gifts to the world? You do not belong there; that is not your home. "You are mine; you are the children of God, and never forget it."

"Saints in Caesar's Household"— Philippians 4:22

[Preached five times from 11/8/44 at Bondgate, Darlington, to 11/5/61 at Hetton]

I have so many things to say to you today, so many subjects to talk about, that I could very happily go on talking to you for 90 minutes, or two hours. How happily you would go on listening to me for that period is another question and I don't propose to try it on. But I do want to maintain at least the things that are on my mind, that you may know what I am thinking of. First of all, this is Woman's Own Anniversary for this Church, something that will help you in the life you have to live. I know it can be a rather dark little world, and it needs the Gospel badly to put some light and seriousness in it, and something that will convey to you our admiration for the work you are doing, and encourage you to continue with it.

Again, in the Church's year, this is the festival of All Saints, one of the most significant and moving dates in the calendar. Why Bondgate should identify WO Anniversary with All Saints Day I don't know—if I thought I knew a year ago, I am under no illusion now. But seriously, I love this festival of All Saints, and I want to make much of it. You see, I know so many saints both here and in the other world, and there are few thoughts that inspire me more than the thought that we are one with them—

> One army of the living God,
> to his command we bow;
> part of his host have crossed the flood,
> and part are crossing now. (Charles Wesley)

And then of course, I want to say something to follow up the Christian Commando Campaign. I want us Church people to see quite clearly our responsibilities. I want us to be built up with such a warm vital fellowship that the whole of Darlington may feel at home with us. It has been my privilege in the last fortnight to make many new friends. If they come, and I hope many of them will, at 74 West Crescent, I think they will feel at home. I want them to feel equally at home if they visit our Church. Finally, I want to allow for the possibility that some of them are here now and I want to say something in the atmosphere of this beautiful place, which may do something to make the Christian message clearer, and the Christian life more attractive than they could be in a factory. All that is a tall order, and it took me some time to find a text for the sermon, but I am sure this is a good one.

I am not sure where Paul was when he wrote this letter. The Bible itself does not tell us. I think that he was at Rome, others think he was at Ephesus. In any case, he was in prison. But in spite of his imprisonment, the faith was spreading, and he can send to Philippi greetings from many Christians (of course, "saints" means Christians, this was before the stupid and mischievous separation of the two titles). Some of the saints were of Caesar's household. One has heard preachers whose enthusiasm was greater than their knowledge of Roman history, speak of the great courage and faithfulness necessary if one was to be a saint in so iniquitous a place as the household of the Emperor Nero. That really is a misunderstanding, a false emphasis. Caesar's household is the Civil Service. No doubt it was and is difficult to be a saint in the Civil Service, but the importance of our text is not that it speaks about saints in especially difficult and dangerous places, but about saints doing an ordinary job. It is that idea that I want to develop in a few points, and apply to the things I have in mind.

The Need for the Saints

I have spoken to you of this before, but I make no apology for doing so again. It would probably do more good than harm if I were to speak of it from this pulpit every Sunday, provided that you will remember that "saints" means not people of pre-eminent piety, but Christians who are wholly given to Christ, Christians who mean business. There is no doubt of this, that in the past the Church has been made by its saints (in the proper New Testament sense). I am not the man to underestimate the contribution of a Paul, an Augustine, a Luther, a Wesley. No doubt they were essential to the life of the Church. But they would have got nowhere without the backing of the simple unnamed saints. They were the great missionaries as well as the backbone of the Church.

Who first carried the word of the Cross across the borders of Judaism and spoke to the Greeks? The Acts of the Apostles cannot tell you; this vital step was taken not by famous persons but by simple ordinary Christians. Who first brought Christianity to Rome? We don't know. Again and again it has been the work of ordinary Christians that has built up the Church, and the power of Christ to transform the lives of ordinary people has been the supreme attraction to Christianity.

You have heard of Sam Chadwick, one of the best-known Methodist ministers, who year after year preached every Sunday to 2,000 people in Leeds—for a long time in the Coliseum Theater. He had one piece of advice for filling empty chapels. It was "get a Lazarus." He was referring to the story in the Gospel of the raising of Lazarus from the dead by Jesus after which it was said "they came not for Jesus' sake only, but also that they might see Lazarus, whom he had raised from the dead." And Sam meant, "find someone notoriously evil and get him made notoriously good—then people will come not to hear the preacher but to see the saint." It was a method he had tried. It was when he was at Stacksteads in Lancashire that he cried out "Oh that Christ would raise some well-known sinner from the dead." It is a matter of history that the thing happened there. But it is always true.

If the Gospel of Christ has not the power to make bad persons good, we can shut up shop at once. We have nothing else to do. If it can be seen and known in this town that Christ can take lives that are evil and make them pure; lives that are pointless and make them powerful; lives that are hopeless and sorrowful and make them glad with a peace that passes all understanding—then Darlington is going to sit up and take notice. These things have indeed been happening. We have got our fingers on them, and we must not let them go. If we are to have a grip on the town we must keep a grip on ourselves. Christ needs not flabby, sentimental well-wishers, but saints.

What is a saint? Perhaps that is a hard question. I will ask an easier one. What is a member of the Methodist Church? Most of you are members and you ought to know. I wonder if you do. You can read the answer on the back of a December class ticket. There are two points: a desire to be saved from your sins through the Lord Jesus Christ, and secondly the test of sincerity—a person must give evidence of this desire in life and conduct. Simple enough but it is all that matters. It is people like that we need. People who are clinging to Jesus Christ as their stay in all the storms of life, trusting him as the one who is able to deliver from evil, and who accordingly are living after the Christian standard. If one learns anything out of Commando Campaigns, and other evangelistic work, it is this—The most effective addresses are not necessarily the most logical and interesting. A person does not necessarily come to Christ because his intellectual problems are resolved. It is a strong direct reliance on Christ and the power of sheer goodness and love that win people for God. What we need, what we need in this Church is people with that faith and that life. They are the strength of the Church and the finest witness to the world. One might have developed this theme in many ways, but I must be content with two. Think of both—

The Saints in the Church and in the World

What I am really concerned about here is the obligation of the Church in fellowship, in evangelism, in service, which for us must now be expressed in the follow up to the Commando Campaign. I want to say with the utmost solemnity that if we do not take our full share of responsibility we are accountable to the Almighty. A few weeks ago, there was in our service here a young man whom I (with many of you) was proud to shake by the hand. He was just back from Arnheim. You know what that name means. It is a name not merely written on the pages of British history, but written on the hearts of English people. There is no need to remind you of what happened. Of the 8,000 men of the Airborne First Division who were landed on the far side of the river at Arnheim, and who there carried out their task. They did what they had to do, and waited and waited for the relief and reinforcements that never came. The main body of our troops never made contact with them. It was not their fault, there were reasons for that. But the fact remains, and remains one of the outstanding tragedies of the present war.

It is quite possible for the Darlington Christian Commando Campaign to become a tragedy like that. It was fine to share in the enthusiasm and thrill of a meeting like last Wednesday night; but mere thrill gets no one anywhere, and if we now settle down as if nothing had happened it will be better that nothing should ever have happened. Let me make clear what I am asking for. There is the saint's responsibility in the Church. I have met during the Campaign itself (I am giving away no names at all, there is no possibility of that) a person who had attended Bondgate but found there no real friendship, no fellowship—and had therefore left. That is not the communion of saints. I cannot make everyone welcome here. A dozen folk can ruin the atmosphere the rest of us try to create. What are you doing?

And how often are heard the criticism—"the folks who go to Church are no better than those who don't." I know all there is to be said to invalidate that, but are you no better than others? If not, what did Jesus die for? I think too of the saints in the world. In one factory, a man said "The Christian will get a hot time after this." That was not meant unkindly; he meant that the Christians would be bombarded with questions. That you ought to expect and ask for. You ought to rejoice in it. I want to have in every factory a holy fifth column as a friend of mine calls it carrying the war into every country. All this is of course a personal issue. How is it between us and our Lord? Are we saints? Or are we playing at being Christians?

"Turning from Idols to God"— 1 Thessalonians 1:9-10

[Preached seventeen times from 10/24/43 at Bondgate, Darlington, to 10/19/80 at Carrville]

Unfortunately, I don't have anything like enough time to give a full exposition of this great text. I wish I could do so; but I can't. I can only take certain things out of it. It gives us an account of what I understand to happen when anyone becomes a Christian, and I want to think about that. It is Paul's own description of what happened when he first preached in Thessalonike, and what happened there is of momentous importance. This little mission went about from one town to another in Europe, and what took place when he preached has stamped the whole of the history of the West for the last 19 centuries. We may regret or celebrate the fact, but what we cannot do is deny that it is a fact. I don't know whether European history will go on bearing the imprint of the Christian faith. It may be that we are indeed faced with what Spengler called the Decline of the West. But up to this point, all the best things in the history of Western Civilization are bound up with the faith. That is, in the long run, what happened to the Thessalonians and others like them, when St. Paul preached. What was that? For that is the thing I am concerned about, and concerned to offer you. You may get modern language but you will get no modernizing from me in the sense of essential variation in the Christian message. First, it means turning from—

The Idols

Please be under no illusions here. You are not to think of the Thessalonians as ignorant savages, worshipping wood and stone. They were not. It is true that in their worship they did use images, so today do millions of Christians;

misguided Christians, but still Christians. The Thessalonians, Paul's congregations in general, were quite as well educated as you are, and in many ways, more civilized than many people in Darlington in 1943. It is only in the application of science to life that we are ahead of them. We are not wiser, or gentler, or purer than they were.

Certainly then, when Paul says "idols" he is not thinking of images as such. You can get from these verses an admirable definition of what he does mean, and one which fits many things in our world. He says "you turned from idols to God who is living and true." And going by contraries, you can say that an idol is something that is not living or is not true, or both. There are many idols today that answer that description. Let me clarify them. In many ways, the most venomous are the things that are living but not true. They are virulent and dangerous. Perhaps the most obvious are the false political ideologies (forgive the word) of today. That Nazism is not true, that it is false way of understanding and going about life, we should, I suppose, all agree, though we might not all see it in the same way. The worst thing about it is that it is precisely an idol, that is, it sets itself up in the place of God. Blood, soil, race, *Soldatentum* become pagan gods, and they are worshipped with bloody sacrifices. Nazism is root and branch a false thing; but that it is a living thing who can deny? We have all felt its living power, in one way or another. I have stood in Berlin in Unter der Linden, and seen them marching, soldiers in field green and boys in brown shirts, in thousands until my eyes were tired of looking at them. There is a thing that is living but false; and it is an idol. People worship it and it grasps them, holds them in its power.

One of the most dreadful pieces of writing I have come across is at the end of Philip Gibb's book *The Cross of Peace*. One of the characters is a German. He has worked for peace. He can see (in 1933) the coming of Nazi power and he dreads it. Yet, he feels, and this is wonderfully brought out, that it is getting hold of him too, the infection has fastened upon him, the poison is coursing through his veins. False, but living is the deadly thing.

It would be wrong to suppose that there was room for nothing else in this class. I have seen films and plays. I have read books that have just the same properties. They are living because they are cleverly written and produced. They get hold of you. But they are wrong, false. There is twisted, perverted thinking behind them. I'm not thinking simply of crime films and books; there is nothing wrong there. I rarely read novels but when I have time for one, I'd rather read a good murder than anything else. I'm thinking of books and films that are not so much wrong and wrong-headed, which breathe a bad atmosphere, which breed a false, because cheap and nasty, outlook on life. So much for one category of idols. We take next things that are true but not living.

I am not very worried about these in connection with most of you. Probably I am more tempted than anyone else to worship these idols. For me the idol commonly takes the form of pure and scientific scholarship. Most folk may find it hard to understand but I do take real delight in setting the precise meaning of a Greek particle or a Hebrew root, or in determining just what Alexander the Great did in 350 B.C. Now undoubtedly when I have found out things of this sort I have found something true, which therefore has its own proper value, but if it be left to itself it is something that is not living; what is more it is something that dries up the source of life and breeds dry rot.

For other people the same idol takes different forms. For some it means a dwindling existence among the complicated machines of modern engineering. The machines work, every bearing is true, but there is no life in them. Or for some it may be the exact handling of financial matters. Every column is exactly balanced, every penny is accounted for, and so far, you have truth, but you have not life. Or perhaps you are concerned with the neat arrangement of your home, and every detail is polished and in its proper place; but your vision becomes limited until it becomes bounded by the sink on one side and the gas oven on the other. Here are things that are true, but not living, hence they can be idols, idols to which life is sacrificed and from which no compensating vigor pulses.

But we must consider one final logical class—things that are neither living nor true. I am going to mention just one thing, but it is one which in different ways affects the whole world today. I will give it, with apologies, the name of secularism. By secularism I mean the understanding of the world, of our life in it, in terms of itself. Perhaps that definition sounds like explaining the obscure by the more obscure. If that is so, I am sorry, and I must simply try to illustrate what I mean. I will not use philosophical names, but I mean doing and thinking the thing that seems useful and pleasant at the time, without any consideration of any external and absolute standard of right and wrong, or of anything else.

Let it suffice to point to this sort of thing first—the big scale in the international politics that led up to 1938 and 1939. On one side, there was the insatiable pride and lust of conquest, which was concerned always to rob and plunder and exalt itself, and which was restrained by no absolute "Thou shalt not!" On the other (for we must not excuse ourselves), was a weak temporizing timidity, which would take no stand against what it mildly condemned because it was spurred on by no absolute "Thou shalt!"

But we dare not stop there. "Things are coming to a pretty pass when we allow religion to interfere with a man's private life."[1] There too, many people live without the absolute "Thou shalt" and "Thou shalt not." They live entirely in this world, and no external force or consideration is allowed to disturb them. Now that is false, it is not true. I shall have more to say on that on the positive side later. But it is not living either. It leads to no virile creative life. I can tell you where it leads on the world scale—it leads to Munich. And equally on the smaller scale of personal life which in some ways is so much more important, it leads to Munich, to compromise, to temporizing, to shilly-shallying. It pumps no red blood into our veins. The tumult and the shouting dies, and we fall asleep on our knees before our idols. "There are your gods, O Israel!" St. Paul says you turned from idols to a—

God Who Is Living and True

To become a Christian means that decisive turning. I hope that the criticism I have given has been such as to make you dissatisfied with sham gods, to make you want something better than them. But what? To what are we to turn? St. Paul says to God, God thought of in terms of Jesus. This God, he says, is what the idols are not—living and true.

First, he is true. That means much in Paul's thought, more than I have time to discuss. For the present I am content to take it to mean that God is real, and that belief in God offers a view of life that is real and true and makes sense. That God is real, I am not disposed to offer much by way of proof. The important thing is the fact of Jesus. Jesus did live, and his life has to be explained in some way. There is only one explanation that really explains him, without explaining away the facts and that takes account of God. You simply cannot make sense of Jesus if you do not believe in God. Further, you cannot make sense of him if you do not believe he came from God and went to God; that he himself was God.

Moreover, the faith in God which rests upon the fact of Jesus is verified by the fact that it does lead to a true understanding of life. I cannot say this

---

1   Editor's Note: This quote shows up several times in the corpus of the sermons by CKB. It was originally made by a British Lord and member of Parliament.

convincingly in two minutes but I could in 2 hours. The only really convincing explanation of the world must assume that it was made by God, but that raises difficulties. What about the evil in the world? So, the only God that satisfies the conditions is the God whose Son was incarnate and by taking upon himself human nature and suffering and dying makes atonement for human beings and so redeems them from the bondage of corruption.

God is true, and God is living. That is to say, he is not only reality, he is creative reality. God is not merely an explanation, he does the explaining. God is not merely a solution, he is the solver. God is not merely the truth, he is the life. Again, for Paul this is no mere abstract assertion. It all depends in a perfectly definite way on Jesus, Jesus who lived and died, whom God raised from the dead, who delivers us from the wrath which is coming. I believe in the wrath of God.

I am not instructed in the New Testament to embrace any attractively sentimental religion. I believe in the wrath of God and everyday I thank my Lord Jesus Christ he delivers me from it. He delivers us from the wrath of God because he breaks the power of the idols, and redeems us from our sin. That is what I mean by the creative reality of God.

> He breaks the power of canceled sin,
> He sets the prisoner free,
> His blood can make the foulest clean,
> His blood availed for me. (Charles Wesley)

That is the testimony of generations of Christians, people of every sort. Do you doubt that? How shall we clarify them to convince you? Tinker, John Bunyan's tailor John Wooliman; soldier, Cromwell to Montgomery; sailor, Drake to Nelson; rich man, Richard Whittington; poor man, Hadrian IV; beggarman the first Franciscans who came to Canterbury and Francis Thomson; and thieves the converted penitents with whom Charles Wesley rode to Tyburn. All these people know that what I say is true, that God is real and that he is a living God, that he is not merely actual but creative, that in Christ he has come into the world to accomplish the most amazing act of liberation that can be conceived, an act into which you and I, one after another, if we will, together may enter.

The whole point is this—are you going to continue in service to idols, to values and to morals which destroy life or pervert it, or if that be possible, do both at once? Or will you take the only alternative and serve God who is living and true and so find in him the only true realization of your life? That is what Paul invited people to do 1900 years ago. That is what I do now. For in the last resort that is what Christianity means. It is not good works, it is not piety. It means serving God, not the devil, whether the devil be dreamed up with a tail or horns, or as an angel of light; whether he wear a brown shirt or an academic gown. Which will you serve—truth or falsehood? Life or death? May God move you to choose life.

"The Glory of God"—1 Timothy 1:11

[Preached fifty-one times from sometime in 1938 at S.H.M. to 6/26/94 at Trimdon Grange][1]

About ten years ago the Anglican Church wished to introduce in its services a new Prayer book. Since that Church is a state church, it was necessary that the purposed change be discussed in Parliament. The course of the debate does not concern us, but it was wound up by a communist M.P. saying that it didn't really matter anyway, because nowadays the working man was much more interested in the rent book than the prayer book. It is not everyone who is witty enough to say that sort of thing, but isn't it what many people are thinking?

Rent books we can all understand, and if you choose to ignore them it is not very long before there is trouble and someone wants to know what you are doing. But often enough a prayer book or a hymn book or a Bible seems a long way from reality and you can let them alone and have nothing to do with religion and nothing seems to happen, or at least you don't notice it. What is this Christianity and has it any claim to be classed with the rent book and the payroll in importance? Is it as important as politics? Does God and what he does matter as much as Hitler and what Hitler does?

In the face of this sort of problem it is tempting to speak of Christianity as some sort of social program, as a practical alternative to Communism and Fascism, that is to make Christianity into just another human scheme, the best of all because true, but still engineered and work out by us. Now this has to be put aside. It is quite wrong and quite fatal. It is certainly not the religion of which the New Testament speaks. It is indeed true that Christianity

---

1   Editor's Note: Surprisingly, it is this sermon that is the most preached sermon in this particular collection of CKB's sermons. In Witherington, *Luminescence: The Sermons of C. K. and Fred Barrett*, vol. 1, it is the less surprising Parable of the Prodigal Son that is preached over forty times during his ministry.

has the most important of social results and that the world will never attain to unity and peace and justice except through the redeeming and reconciling work of the Christian Church. But Christianity did not arise and cannot continue in the hope that human beings will be able to make themselves better by achieving. Christianity is certainly not a scheme whereby human beings plan to obtain honor and glory for themselves. In fact, the theme of Christianity is the glory of God. That is why I have taken this text. The beginning and end of religion is the glory of God—"our strength thy peace, our rule thy blood, our end, the glory of God." Christianity is based upon the glorious work of God in his saving activity in Christ. God's glory irradiates the Church and the lives of individual men and women who are following Jesus, and we look for the life and the glory of the world to come. This may sound rather abstract, and inferior to the social program of which we hear spoken; but that it is not will appear when we consider three points in detail.

God Has Manifested His Glory—In Christ

There can be little need to say much about the various aspects of the glory of Christ. It leaps to the eye from the printed page of the Gospels. There is a glory of sheer moral excellence. You cannot fail to be struck by the unselfishness of Jesus, by his immediate pity for the sick and the suffering. And you notice how bold he was in challenging all the conventions and factions of his age. He knew who it was who needed a physician and he went to them. Society was split in one very sharp and deep cleavage in Palestine in the time of Jesus. There were the religious, the Pharisees; people who kept every detail of their religious ceremonial law, and who with the greatest care segregated themselves from the rest—from the folk who were too careless and slack to take their religion seriously. There was a gulf between them like that between heaven and hell. It was just unthinkable that any religious teacher should have anything to do with the outcasts.

But Jesus, and he seldom seems more glorious to me than in this, broke away from all the standards of respectable society and went to those who needed him most, just because they needed him, though he knew full well that in doing so he was bringing down upon his head the wrath of a powerful aristocracy. But there is more than this. If you read your Bible carefully, you will find that God's glory does not mean the majesty of an enthronement far from every human ill and inglorious need. This glory means the saving presence of God with his people. It means his redemptive activity in the world. The fiery cloudy pillar is the symbol of God's glory and it appeared at the deliverance of God's people from bondage, to protect them from their enemies, to guide them into the promised land.

And especially in this sense, the glory of God was seen in the face of Jesus Christ. The life, death, and resurrection of Jesus were the means by which God chose for his glory to rest upon humankind, the means by which they should be saved from all evil. It is rather surprising that the New Testament often connects the death of Jesus with glory. "The hour is come that the Son of Man should be glorified." It seems hard to find the glory of God in the most ignominious death a person could die. Yet it is here that the true glory of God is revealed. It is on the basis of this and this alone that the Christian Church exists, God's saved people, the people through whom he means to save the world. The whole structure of Christianity rests on the fact that God manifested his glory in Jesus, that by him God was revealed and that in Him God was at work redeeming and reconciling human beings to himself.

God Is Manifesting His Glory—in the Church

It is not enough that we should be able to look back to a time, less fully known due to scanty records, and say that *then* God's presence could be known and seen in the world. The glory of God which was revealed in Christ is still being revealed. It was part of the work of Jesus to call into being a new community, a fellowship of men and women who should bear his witness into all the world. They thought of themselves as people carrying good news, and the news was about God's glorious work in Christ, but it was not just a report. You know the difference between two sorts of newspaper reporters. One can take some great event and write it up so dully that you are bored; another will deal with the same event and so enter into its spirit that through his writing you are caught up into the original enthusiasm of the occasion, you are fighting the battle or hearing the speech, or playing the football match.

Now there was something about the glorious event of Christ that inevitably spread to those who spoke about it. It was not just news, it was good news. There was a power in it to be glad about. There is the glory of moral conversion, the transformation of human character, the work of God in a human life as real as the work of God in the Cross of Christ. Throughout the history of the Church we see people's lives strengthened, the crooked made straight, we see people lifted out of infamy and sin, made new and pure and good; vice conquered, bad habits dethroned. That is the glory in the work of God. And there is the glory of the "lighted mind." People who had lived in fear and despair are brought out of their prison and made to live in the mountains of God.

There is glory, but there can be no glorying. That is excluded. All that we may be and do is not ours but Christ's. But because it is Christ's, the glory of God is in it. You may speak of the martyrs of the early days of Christianity, glorious in their courage and faithfulness. It is easy to deny that, easy to say it is just fanaticism. Look at them a little closer. There is one memorable scene. There are two women, one of them had become a mother but a day or two before. And they are walking out into the arena to face wild beasts. Fanaticism you say? But who are they? One is a Roman matron of the highest class, the other a mere slave girl, an almost unbridgeable social gulf. Fanaticism might have perhaps made either face death alone, but that which joined their hands was no less than the love of Christ and the glory of God.

There came a time when almost universally the Church was seeking its own glory, and ignoring God's. And God raised up Martin Luther. He did not come from the highest ranks of human society. "I am a peasant, and the son of a peasant" he said. "My mother carried on her back the wood that gave us heat. My father's toil [as a miner] nourished me and made me what I am." But it was given to him to insist that glory belonged to God alone, and because of that, the glory of God was shed about him in power, so that by the force of his simple personality, he was able to defy the gathered powers of evil. Christianity is based on the glorious work of God, but there is a sense in which it is not finished. It is ongoing. It lights up the lives of men and women. It inspires them with joy and power; and with a burning desire to pass on what they have found.

God Will Manifest His Glory in the Future

God has shown in glory in the past and manifested his glory in Christ. He is still showing the same saving power in the life of his Church. And the future belongs to him too. What do we expect as the end and goal of human life? Must the old round of failure and sin go on forever? Is the best we can hope for just a Utopia, a perfect human society which would be only human glory? Especially if we now experience the glory of God, have we any hope if we expect any less in the future? Our only hope lies in the resources of

God's mercy and goodness. Yet so often we run away from these and try to find peace of mind and conscience in lower securities. We are afraid of God's mercy because it means his judgment too.

One of the greatest persons who lived before Christ was Socrates, the Greek philosopher, wisest of men, best of friends. He felt it to be his mission to make people think; to put questions to them that would show them the shallowness and falseness of their lives. But in the end the people determined to put him to death, and in sorrow he pointed out that they were killing their best friend. They wanted to run away from the searching questions which were for their own good. And the only way they could escape from Socrates was by killing him. And so, we try to escape from the searching questioning of the God who seeks our good. It is what people always do—they crucify their king.

Charles Wesley spent more time in prison than most respectable people do. He was especially often in the cell of the condemned criminals at the Newgate jail. "I went to Newgate and preached to the 10 malefactors who were under the sentence of death. . . . I promised them all pardon, in the name of Jesus Christ, if they would then, as at the last hour, repent and believe the Gospel. . . . At night I was locked in with Bray in one of the cells. We wrestled in mighty prayer. All the criminals were present, all delightfully cheerful. . . . We sang 'Behold the Savior of mankind, nailed to the shameful tree! / How vast the love that him inclined to bleed and die for thee!' (Samuel Wesley). It was one of the most triumphant hours I have ever known. . . . I never saw such calm triumph. . . . We sang. . . .

> A guilty, weak, and helpless worm,
> Into Thy hands I fall;
> Be Thou my strength and righteousness,
> My Savior, and my all. (Isaac Watts)

I could do nothing but rejoice . . . that hour under the gallows was the most blessed hour of my life." To stand under a gallows means judgment, but to face the judgment is to find the mercy of God in it.

"The Spirit of Power, Love and Discipline"—2 Timothy 1:7

[Preached nineteen times from 9/3/44 at Bondgate, Darlington, to 2/10/80 at Gilesgate]

In a very brief introduction I want to say two unconnected things. First, as a preliminary note, the word *fearlessness* is a poor translation and the *fear* of the Authorized Version is a shockingly bad one. Fear can be, at the right time, a very useful feeling; certainly there is nothing to be ashamed of in being afraid. The boldest persons are often afraid, only they don't show their fear. The word really means cowardice, a fear, about which Bengel says, the causes are in the mind rather than outside it.

Next, I want to very clearly associate the text, and the whole of this service, with the present occasion, the beginning of the Methodist year. Again, we are facing a winter's work. To a great extent the programs are made. We know, roughly at least, what the framework of the events will be; all that is important. But what matters quite as much as what we do is the spirit in which we do it. This is a statement notoriously true in Methodism as a whole. We have in Methodism a system of church government as near perfect as may be; far better than any episcopal system ever devised. The crucial point in Methodism now is not mechanism; we may add a few more standing orders now and again, but really they are neither here nor there. The crucial point is the way in which we work the machine. That is true with us too. We have the machinery, what of the spirit in which we work? How are we facing this new year of grace? I shall speak first of—

The Spirit of Cowardice

It is not God who has given it to us; our text and no less our conscience assures us of that. But I cannot but feel that many of us have caught the miserable germ somewhere. Years ago now, Professor Gilbert Murray coined a phrase to describe the Hellenistic Age which came after the great classic period of Greek thinking and writing. He spoke of the "failure of nerve." People lacked the fearless freedom of intellect their ancestors had had; philosophy became superstition.

I detect something like a failure of nerve in modern life. It is expressed in all sorts of ways. I shall not go into them. The most notable is the rank growth of dictatorships. One of their fundamental causes is a failure of nerve. It is perfectly true that democracy is a dangerous, slow, and costly business. Only the fit can stand it. It is much easier to shelve your responsibilities and let your dictator do everything for you. This is a very important truth for the modern world to take in, but that is not my primary concern as a preacher. What is infinitely more important is that this same failure of nerve seems to have penetrated the Church also. There is a spirit of cowardice even there. I would illustrate this over quite a wide field. Let me first give you some illustrations you will not expect.

I see an indication of nerve failure in the great stress laid these days on Christian unity. I don't want to be misunderstood here. Of course, I believe in the unity of Christians, at least among the Protestant Churches, and I can honestly say I don't feel a spark of malice against Christians of any sort. What I don't like is the notion that we must all get together to save our skins. "Let us all hang together or we shall all hang separately." We must be united for the world will never believe a divided Church. As if a united Christian front were a refugee to fly to when the Gospel has failed! If we believed our own faith, we should be content with that and not want to be added up with Anglicans, Baptists, Congregationalists and all the rest of the ecclesiastical ABC and made into a mere average.

I see an indication of nerve failure with regard to the Gospel in those Methodists, especially in those Methodist ministers, who have left our church for Anglicanism or Romanism. Methodist orders, Methodist sacraments are not good enough for you! We have no apostolic ministry because we have no problematic succession of bishops to trust in. It is because people are afraid that they run to Canterbury or Rome.

But let us come nearer to home. Is there a failure of nerve, a spirit of cowardice in our own church? If I may speak for myself, I think the answer is yes. It was most aptly put by a member of our own congregation not long ago. He pointed out to me that when the older Methodists talked to one another, the first thing they spoke of was their faith, their religion; with us it is the last thing we come to. As a statement of fact, I find that in general it is exactly true with the addition of this proviso, religion is the last subject we come to, if we come to it at all. I wonder why that is. I have tried to answer it for myself. Part of the answer unquestionably is a proper reticence about the deep things of life. I have tried to persuade myself that that is a complete cause; I wish it were, but I cannot stand before you with a good conscience and say that it is.

I know the spirit of cowardice if you don't. Why should it be true that the things I was ordained to preach should be the hardest things to say? How is it I can never make an appeal to people to make a decision for Christ without almost wishing that the pulpit floor would open and swallow me up? Why, when I have stood in a crowd in the Market Place answering all sorts of questions without any hesitation should I be scared stiff about approaching an individual person to speak to him about Christ?

Forgive me that I have spoken at such length about myself. I have done it very deliberately. I would rather make myself Aunt Sallie than anyone else. I can only leave it now to ask yourselves how far we are afraid of ourselves as Christians, how far we seek refuge in all the paraphernalia of the Gospel and avoid the real thing. Well I shall not press this further now, there is no time to do so, but that person whose conscience does not convict him of cowardice, cowardice about accepting Christ's offer, obeying his commands and doing his service, is at liberty for the rest of this service to close his ears. I am going on now to the positive thing—

The Real Christian Spirit

The spirit of power and love and discipline is what God gives. I want you to notice first the rather conscious allocation of words that meets us here— power, love, discipline. The average 20th century person would not expect to see them side by side. We hear and see much of power these days, but we don't often connect it with love. We know power mechanism which doesn't suggest anything affectionate. We know power politics, which has as little to do with love as chalk with cheese. The word *love* is familiar enough but we don't often connect it with discipline. Love's present meaning is either undisciplined lust covered with a veneer of romanticism, or else weak sentimental attachment, neither of these involving discipline.

Yet here are these three words brought together in an attempt, inadequate of course as all such attempts are, to describe Christian life. God has given us a spirit of power, love, and discipline. Let us try to understand these fundamental Christian qualities over against the spirit of cowardice. The spirit of power does not mean, I take it, the capacity to do whatever you please. It is God's empowering for his own service, always with the motive of love. The electric train has power, while it is on the rails. The Christian has power while he is on the lines of God's will.

I hesitated a long time over the illustration of this point, not because I could find no example but because I did not know which one to choose. I am going back to the early days of Methodism, but I am not going to talk about John Wesley and the early preachers. They were not responsible for the phenomenal growth of Methodism. I speak of the ordinary, simple Methodist people, thousands of whom could neither read nor write. For power and love, take one story which belongs to a town I know well. It is of Honest Munchin, a miner. His conversion meant some persecution from the men he worked with. But when they mocked and swore, he would go off to a quiet corner and pray for them. Once when he did so, his mates followed him with lumps of coal in their hands. They came near to him and heard him praying aloud for them, each one by name. They were so abashed they were slinking away when suddenly there was a roar, and a crash. The roof of the pit had fallen in, and they were cut off without their tools. Hearing their cries Munchin called to them "What cheer comrades, what cheer?" and then bade them get on their knees and pray. They did so, and one at least found peace then and there. Munchin got up and said "Mates we've prayed to God to help us, and now we must work as well as pray." And so they set to work, toiled with bleeding hands and torn nails until they collapsed. Just in time came the sound of a pick; they were rescued. They were too exhausted to walk, and one by one they were carried out. As they waited their turn Honest Munchin led them in a prayer of thanksgiving.

I do not give that as an instance of courage and coolness. I give it as an instance of Christian power and love. That is the sort of life our Gospel means. That is what I have the high privilege to offer to you Sunday by Sunday. It means adequate power for every emergency and for every commonplace of life; it means love that the tidal wave of hatred cannot quench. I try to picture what life like this would mean today. I try to picture an individual with this love and power in his heart, never ruffled by criticism, never overcome by enmity, continuing in a persevering affection, never at the mercy of circumstances, always revealing the life, and life to spare Jesus offers. I try to picture a church like that; a church undeterred by the waves of dissension, undivided by the cleavage of criticism.

And the whole governed by the spirit of discipline; no emotion for emotion's sake, no uncontrolled power, a people that know just where they are going and who are trained and disciplined to that end. Are we more like a mighty army, or an undisciplined rabble? And I try to think what a people like that could do, but there is no end to the picture! Let us ask lastly—

To Whom and on What Conditions Is This Spirit Given?

I know the answer and I shall not mince my words. They are given on the basis of the work of Christ. They are his gift, his free gift. They are given to those who want them. But let us see this clearly. There are many people who do not want them. That is what the spirit of cowardice means for many people. They do not want the fullness of Christian life. That is not surprising. You remember the young man, Timothy, to whom our text is addressed? You can imagine his circumstances. Born in a good home, provided, apparently, with a good education, with everything to make life agreeable. He is startled out of all that. The new life of power and love and discipline is only to be had at a cost; at the cost of hardness, the witnessing of a confession before hostile listeners, those very things we are afraid of now. I can understand people being afraid of Christian life. I can understand a Church preferring a quiet, peaceable existence, a life of happy fellowship among the members.

That's why I want to use at the beginning of this year one of the great old evangelical phrases, which is why I am appealing to you to "venture on Christ" to take him at his word, to cast yourself at his feet. I am not telling you there is any easy way to it. If there is, I don't know it. I wonder what it felt like to drive into Paris with the liberating army; I wonder what it will feel like to drive into Berlin. I would give a good deal to be in it. But I can't. It would mean nothing to me if I was suddenly taken out to France and on to Paris now. The real victory is only for those who made the venture of D-Day, those who have endured hardness as good soldiers.

So it is for us. The spirit of love, power, and discipline; the spirit of victorious life is for those who make the venture of faith in Christ, who sink their natural cowardice in his love. Oh that we could join ourselves together in solemn covenant as the army of the Lord to do his will and to speak his words and to live his life.

"The Prophets"—1 Peter 1:10-12

[Preached eight times from 3/10/57 at Easington Lane to 12/6/97 at Trimdon Station]

The writing prophets cover at least three hundred years, the prophets as a whole 500. Imagine a survey of English (religious) literature from 1457 to 1957. Yet there is a striking unity in the prophetic movement which does make it possible to summarize it. The prophets did predict, but they did much more.

They Denounced Sin

It was always easy to denounce sin in others; they denounced it in their own people—Amos 1–2 cf. Micah 3:8. The courage and the power of the prophets in doing this is notable: Elijah with Ahab in regard to Naboth (1 Kings 21); Nathan with David in regard to Uriah (2 Sam. 12), Isaiah with the sinful nation (Isa. 1:2-5). They denounce sin not simply as anti-social (though note Amos's insistence on social righteousness), but as a revolt against God. And they are not deceived by religious practice, which may simply cloak sin (1 Sam. 15:22; Isa. 1:11-17; Amos 4:4). This leads to—

They Declared the Truth about God

Note how Amos declares God's righteousness (Am. 5:18-25; 9:1-4,7). Hosea declares his love, in part through the story of Hosea's marriage and Israel depicted as God's child (11:1-9). God cannot refrain from loving him. Isaiah declares God's holiness especially in Isa. 6 but also "the Holy One of Israel" (12:6; 17:7 etc.). Jeremiah holds personal converse with God (espec. 12:1-6). Ezekiel has extraordinary visions of the glory of God (espec. Ezek. 1). Of course, we cannot really share out the attributes of God among the prophets in this way; each of them know the *whole* God. Yet even prophets have practical understanding, and one sees one thing more than another. There is a moral in this.

They Interpreted God's Will

They were not content to talk like a theological textbook. Because God was what he was, certain claims followed. Thus, we can go over some of the above points. The righteous God required righteousness (Amos 5). The holy God required holiness (Isa. 6). And the prophets worked this out in terms of their own age. Isaiah confronts Jerusalem and promises safety if people will be quiet and trust God (Isa. 7:1-9, 36-37, especially 37:10-12, 21-23, 29, 36-38). But in a later generation this leads to complacency, and Jeremiah pronounces doom, counsels desertion to the enemy (32:28-30; 37:1-2,12-15; 38:1-2). Later still after the exile, it is the task of the prophets to encourage the rebuilding of Jerusalem and the Temple (Hag. 1:1-9; 2:1-9). All this comes within the framework of the unfailing demand for social righteousness.

They Bore Witness to Christ

The whole Bible is a book about Jesus Christ, who is *the* Word of God. This does not mean that it is an Old Moses' Almanac, nor need we suppose that the prophets always knew how these words would be fulfilled. It is probable that there were some initial disappointments. This may well have been true about Isaiah 53 (in a small way a preacher sometimes finds this). See also Jer. 31:31ff. The root fact is that the prophets are always talking about the same God who sent his Son into the world. The more clearly they see him, the closer they are to Jesus. Like an ante-natal photo of a child in the womb, it is useful but not to be compared with the child!

We should begin with Christ; he helps us understand the prophets more than they help us understand him. Yet the thing to emphasize is the unity of Scriptures which are all about the Redeemer God.

"Of the Sanctification" 1 Peter 2:9-10

[Preached thirty-four times from 7/26/44 at Eppleby to 9/27/98 at Bearpark]

Luther very aptly heads the last section of his creed "of the sanctification." Already we have thought about the creation, or rather about God as Creator, and about the redemption or rather about God as the Redeemer, now we thinking about the sanctification, about God who sanctifies, and the sanctified people whom he makes. These are the words in the creed in question: "I believe in the Holy Spirit, the holy catholic church, the communion of saints, the forgiveness of sins, the resurrection of the body, and the life everlasting." Without any further introduction, I want to say several very important things about ourselves.

The Church Is Holy

That is to say you and I are saints. Most people I know find that rather shocking. That is probably my fault because I tell you more often that you are sinners than that you are saints. But of course, both statements are true. It has been said, rightly I think, that the trouble with the Church in these days is that we are too proper to call ourselves sinners, and too diffident to call ourselves saints and the result is we are merely respectable.

Of course, you are saints, that is to say holy men and women, for the Church is holy. But now that I have used that word I must be very careful to say what it means. Holiness is a very ancient notion. It lies at the root of all religion, whether Christianity or of the most debased degrading superstition. It denotes that which marks off a special person or a special thing for supernatural purposes. In very early thought (and among primitive people today), this holiness is thought of pretty much as we think of an electric charge or an infectious disease. In the last week or two, I've been visiting at the Isolation Hospital. Before I go into the ward, I have to dress myself in a white coat, and when I come out, I wash my hands. That is precisely what primitive people do when they visit their shrine. They put on special clothes and they wash. The idea is that they don't want to take away with them the holiness of the shrine they visited, exactly as I don't want to take away with me the disease I have been in contact with. I may put in a word incidentally here. If, as I rather suspect, our habit of wearing Sunday clothes is a relic of this old notion of infectious holiness, I regret it. Perhaps the greatest weakness to which Christians have been subject throughout church history has been that of leaving their holiness behind when they leave the Church.

But I hope I've made clear to you the meaning of holiness. It means being devoted to God, being connected with and used by the supernatural. It is a religious, not an ethical notion. That is true of Christian holiness too. It does not mean being a perfectly good person. It does mean that whatever sort of person you are, you belong to Christ. Of course, that has its consequences. A holy person connected to a Syrian fertility goddess would quite naturally be a temple prostitute. A holy person consecrated to Jesus Christ will also live a corresponding life. But that comes second. You are not a saint because you live a good life; but because you are a saint you inevitably live a good life. But for them—

The Church Is a Holy Nation

That is, it is not merely an aggregate of holy individuals. It is, if one may use assonance, holy as a whole. It is not a handful of holy individuals that gives the Church its characteristic quality of holiness; the fact that we are members of Christ's Church conveys on us all the privileges and responsibilities of the holy priesthood. It is our privilege and responsibility to stand before God and pray for ourselves and the world. I think we have lost to some extent the notion of the separateness of the Church. That is of course a good thing, in so far as it means that Christians are not so peculiar a people in the wrong sense of the word. There have been times when Christians thought it a real personal duty to cut themselves off from the life of the world and to make themselves as odd as they could and some of them succeeded to a remarkable degree. Most of us have got beyond that now. We have lost most of our standoffishness and priggishness.

In fact, it may be that we have gone too far. The Christians are described in our text as a holy nation; the phrase was soon picked up by Christians and non-Christians alike. We soon find the description of the Church as the third race. They were not Jews, they were not pagans. They must be some third thing that has not been previously met with. Is that so today? God knows we want no pride or Pharisaism. But can you today draw a line between the Church and the world? In many ways, it is much more difficult to do so today because Christian moral principles have been worked into (even if they are now being worked out of) the common life of the community. In a society, for example, where lying and stealing are common, the Christians stands out as he cannot do in a society where lying and stealing are condemned by the common standards.

I am not thinking of such trivial and false distinction as are all too often drawn—the Christian does not drink, the Christian does not go to the cinema on Sunday, and such like. What I am thinking of is such a phrase as that of Glover's: the early Christians out lived, out thought, and out died their pagan contemporaries. In virtue of our special relation with God we ought to stand out in that way. Do we? We must now speak of the ground of this holiness of the Church.

The Church Is Holy by the Mercy of God

Once you were not a people at all, now you are God's people. Once you were outside the scope of his mercy, now you have taken within it. The phrases go back to the book of Hosea, and the symbolic names given by the prophet to his children. The pity God has for his people is that which is described by Hosea. It is his free love, given without reference to merit, given in fact to people who have thoroughly deserved God's hatred. Again, we are dealing with God's creative love. He loves those who are nothing and nobody and by his love makes them into a people for himself.

This, says the New Testament, is true about us too. We don't become holy and we don't become God's people by our own achievements but simply through God's mercy. This will reinforce what I was saying a little while ago. With this in mind you will find it impossible to be proud and to set yourself up on a pedestal against the outsider. Everything you are is simply by God's grace. It is a humbling fact. We know that from ordinary experience.

In the last week, I have received from a certain great scholar a vast amount of work which he has done for me. Quite freely he has put at my service what must have been many hours of work from one of the finest brains in the country; and he has done it simply out of kindness. It certainly is a humbling thing, even though it makes one very happy and grateful.

And it is not just a few hours work God has put in for us. It is 20, 30, 40 even 80 years' work and that in one life on this earth. How much before and after is simply out of our knowledge. And not just pleasant intellectual exercise, but the agony of Gethsemane and Calvary. That is the measure, if it can be measured, of his pity and mercy for us. He has taken the wreckage of humanity and given us the dignity of a royal priesthood. He has made us a holy nation. Further—

The Church Is Holy Through the Holy Spirit

This is part of what Luther says on this section of the creed: "I believe that I cannot of my own understanding or strength believe in or come to Jesus Christ my Lord, but that the Holy Spirit has called me by the Gospel, and illuminated me with his gifts, and sanctified and preserved me in the true faith, just as he calls, gathers together, illuminates, sanctifies and preserves in Jesus Christ all of Christendom throughout the earth in the one true faith." What? Can we not even believe, have faith, of our own accord? No, this too is a gift from God worked in our hearts by the Holy Spirit.

If you want a philosophical discussion of how this works out with our freedom (or does not work out with it) I'm afraid you must wait for another time. It cannot be done now. But I am sure that there is an analogy to the process in all sound education. No good teacher today, or indeed at any time is ever content with the "knocking in" type of education. I believe that has its uses. There are some things that go in best that way, Latin grammar for instance. But there are things more important than Latin grammar (even I will admit that), and they have to go in a different way. And all good teachers will proceed like this. The pupils must be led to discover great truths for themselves. You cannot simply tell them, "this is what Shakespeare or Plato or whoever it is, means." If people do not discover that for themselves, it will never mean anything to them. Yet the teacher does not simply leave them alone, all the time he is guiding them, influencing their own progress, working through the process of their own mind. So, God works through the processes of our own minds and life, directing us to the real holiness, sanctification, of which I have spoken. The Church is holy by his mercy and through the Holy Spirit. There is one thing more to say—

The Church Is Holy for a Purpose

And you may sound forth the glories of God. God has called you out of darkness and into light. God has made you who were nothing into a people, his people, a holy people a royal priesthood. God has done all this; now you must tell the world. Your position is one of responsibility as well as privilege. It is a commonplace that every advantage we have lays a duty on us. So it is here. If God has done this for you, can you refrain from praise? Can you accept his goodness without a word of thanks? Of course, you will not. I forgot who said "If the Lord will save me, he shall never hear the end of it."

And if God is like this, if he is the God of glorious goodness, the God who creates out of nothing, can you refrain from telling others about him? Will you not rather point them to their Savior? All this belongs to your holiness which is not something I am urging you to strive for, but which you already possess. Because of what by the mercy of God you are, the Church needs, God needs, the world needs a holy people. In *The Green Pastures,* there is a scene in which God consults Abraham, Isaac, and Jacob about a new leader for his people. Isaac asks, "Does you want the brainiest or the holiest, Lord?" God answers, "I want de holiest, I'll make him brainy."

I'm sure that is true, and true now. You know I am not the man to belittle brain power and hard thinking. But the people we need today are holy people, people devoted heart and soul to the Lord Jesus Christ.

"The Victory of the Saints"— Revelation 7:9-10

[Preached six times between 11/7/43 at Bondgate, Darlington, to 11/4/51 at Stockton]

There are many very good reasons for observing the Festival of All Saints. One is that it is our own festival, for we must not be led astray by "catholics" (so-called) and made to forget that we are saints. So the New Testament would call us. Today we are to remember and to investigate what we ourselves are and what are "our friends above who have obtained the prize."

Again, we should do well to recognize that we have here realized before our eyes, the very thing which the world is striving now to attain, and seems quite unable to grasp. Here is the truly international community. Here are men and women gathered out of every nation and speaking every language. They all admit their separate national loyalties, but they are united in a common allegiance. They speak all the different languages people use, but they sing together a common hymn of praise.

What then are we dealing with in this prophetic vision and what is its meaning for us? Unfortunately, there is no time now to go into a detailed interpretation of these verses in this historical setting. John is thinking of those who in spite of and through suffering bear witness to their faith. Naturally, for him that thought took form in the shape of the actual martyrs of his day, and they were not a few. But in saying that, no one could number the host in question, he quite deliberately removes all the particular limitations and sets his thought free for Christendom of all ages to use and to profit from. What then are the themes with which we are dealing in this picture? And what do they mean for us? First, the keynote of the whole scene is—

Victory

The whole thing in these days might be inscribed with a large capital V, and the song of the saints sing to a now well-known rhythm. To this fact, the small details of the picture point. The palms carried by the saints are the symbols of triumph. The white robes which they wear signify something else as well, but they here signify the dress of rejoicing and gladness. And of course, the great song begins at once with the word *Salvation* which means deliverance, rescue from the enemy and hence victory over them. Such is the theme which John is emphasizing with every stroke of his pen—victory. And that is odd as it is a plain contradiction of the facts. Judged by every ordinary standard, these were beaten people. They had failed and suffered for their failure. They had been rash enough, living in the Roman Empire, to suggest an authority higher than that of Rome. They had been unwise enough, when put to the test to rely upon that authority. And manifestly, it had failed them. The Roman magistrates had condemned them, the Roman soldiers had led them out to death and nothing had happened. The sky had not opened to bring them relief, the persecutors had not been struck down by a lightning bolt, they had lived on in ease and comfort. The case was manifestly a case of defeat. But John, true to the Christian tradition of turning things upside down, says it was victory, and will think of it in no other terms.

If John wasn't simply talking nonsense, there must be more in Christianity than meets the eye. Plainly, it involves more than a superficial reading of the surface facts of life. That is why Christian preachers are always being accused of talking in paradoxes, in apparent contradictions. Listen to the greatest of them all, St. Paul: "as deceivers and yet true; as unknown and yet well-known; as dying and yet behold we live; as chastened and yet not killed; as sorrowful yet always rejoicing; as poor, yet making many rich; as having nothing and yet possessing everything." And John is simply adding "defeated, and yet victorious."

This may sound perilously close to being nonsense, but it is part of the essentials of Christianity. Faith, in the nature of the case, means always prying beneath the surface of life and seeing its real meaning, and the real meaning of life is not always the most obvious one. There is abundant justification for this in history. The whole story of Christianity is one of dying in order to live. That is true of the movement as a whole. The little mustard seed of the primitive Church was pressed down into the ground, it was oppressed and persecuted, trodden down and officially suppressed. The Roman verdict was "you are not allowed to exist." But the little weed (as the Romans thought of it) sprung up again from under the iron shod heel. And the Church has now outlived four Roman empires. The same thing is true in modern times. Persecution has driven the Roman Church back into the fundamentals of its own Protestant Christianity and in prisons and concentration camps the seed is growing again. It would not do to speak too hurriedly, but it may be that the same is happening in Russia, that the old Church has laid in the ground, and that out of the ground a new and living faith is springing; at all events, many reports suggest this is true.

I had no difficulty in finding a saint, and a woman saint at that, to illustrate the same thing. There is one who will spring to your minds at once—Joan of Arc. Nothing could be more completely like failure than the closing scenes of her life. A moment of triumph, then, captive on a petty raid, a wearying and humiliating imprisonment, a long trial with quaint twisted justice about it, and at the end, death in the flames. The end? No, not quite. "The last of her?" says the Earl of Warwick in Shaw's play. "The last of her? Ha! I wonder." No, and the vindication of Joan was not her beatification nor her canonization by Rome, but the birth out of her suffering and death of a new France. The death of the saint was her victory. So, I might go on with the tale in an historical manner. But that will not do. We do not learn our faith from history. John ascribes this—

Peculiar Christian Victory to God

The unnumbered host sings "salvation to our God who sits upon the throne, and unto the Lamb." God and Christ are the source of the victory. That means to say that John is pressing back this strange paradoxical sort of victory into an origin in God himself. And sure enough we find it there; it is part of the Christian doctrine of God. It is written in this book of Revelation in a burning unforgettable metaphor. Jesus is the Lamb of God, and the Lamb is in the midst of the throne. He has all the glory of the undying eternal God. No honor is too high for him. Before him every created being falls on its face to worship him. There is a daring picture, you look closer, and you find that the Lamb is standing, as though it has been slain. The Christ whose name is above every name, whose Kingdom is an everlasting kingdom, who is most high in the glory of God the Father—he is a gibbeted outcast!

Do you see what this means? It means first that Christian victory, the victory which is promised to all Christians, which is offered to us all, comes from God. It is not to be found in ourselves, it comes from no other resource, no one else can offer it, but God does offer it. He puts it into our hands. It is therefore utterly secure, there is nothing that can shake it, nothing can take it away from us. All the security of the throne in heaven is behind it. Why are government savings certificates and bonds the safest possible place to have your money? Because they can only be lost if the whole country is broken up, in which case any other sort of security would vanish too. As long as the country stands, all is well. In the same way, the victory which comes from God is the securest thing that can be. It can only fail if the whole government of the universe fails. The voice that rolls the stars along speaks all the promises. Everything else may fail, but what comes from God can no more fail than God himself.

But this ascription of victory and salvation to God means another thing too. This victory is no soft option. It cannot be an easy thing. You cannot have it laid on like water or electricity. Some people talk in such a way as to suggest that you can. "Listen in to God" (or some other disrespectful phrase) "and life will work smoothly." Frankly, I do not believe it. I know fightings without and fears within just as Paul did. And surely you see why. Salvation belongs to—to the Lamb, the Lamb who was slain! God himself, the source of all victory, came once into our world and lived as a human being. And he died as a human being too. "Dying, and behold we live!" That is the way of God's victory. There is no other way except the way of the Cross. Every victory God gives has the Cross stamped on it. The mark is always there.

That's why the word to us always is "in this sign conquer." I wonder what Constantine really made of it when he saw his vision of the Cross in heaven, and heard the voice saying "by this, conquer." Was he stupid enough to think that all he had to do was change the Roman standards into the shape of a Cross? Perhaps. He might have learned the secret of faith. The Cross and faith must go together. There must be a Cross so that salvation may be of faith. There must be faith so that victory can be apprehended in the Cross. For faith is the victory that answers the world.

Application

Here is the secret of the saints, the mystery of their victory; the victory that is as sure as the sovereignty of God, and which is wrought out in the blood and tears of suffering. And logically that ought to be the end of this sermon. But we are not logical, so it won't be. This, I said, is the victory of the saints and it is now necessary that I should remind you that you are saints, and try to make clear if I can, a little of what this great good news of victory means to us. Let us first hark back to what I said at the beginning.

The victory is a bond of union. In August 1939, a conference met in Amsterdam. There were representatives from all over the world—Germans, Russians, Frenchmen, Japanese, English and Indians. There was a huge crowd of young people you could see. You might have heard them singing together, and saying the Lord's prayer together, all in their own language. And the title of the conference was *Christus Victor.*

But it is often harder to say, a family together than an international conference, at which everyone is bound to be polite and well mannered. I remember speaking in a big works canteen with a man whose father is a bishop. He told the people that theirs is a huge family, and they all disagreed with one another, but one thing kept them united and loving—the love of Christ. It was God's victory over their natural disunity, it was a part of the communion of the saints. Now that is available for us; that is a part of the victory God offers us.

Second, the victory is possible in the midst of turmoil and conflict. That sounds odd. It can be particularly illustrated by Aristophanes' play, *The Acharnians.* Dikaiopolis is fed up with the war, with meagre rations and home guard duty. So, he makes a separate peace and the situation is worked out. He alone can buy what he likes. He does not have to guard the walls. While others are fighting he stays at home and feasts. Now I don't mean that Christians will contract out of life like that and run away from their responsibilities. But I do mean that in the midst of battle, when everyone else is overcome with fear and terror, the Christian is enjoying not mere peace, but victory. Whatever happens, that victory is there. Shortly after the collapse of 1940, Dr. Barth had the opportunity of writing a letter to the Christians in France. Very gently, he reprimanded them for the phrase "total defeat." "How have we Christians come to apply the word *total* to anything but God's omnipotent grace? When and how can a human defeat become total? Unless Christians involved in it were to lose their faith in the omnipotent grace of God, and with it their inward joy and their courage to bear their Christian witness?"

This victory is for you—for every saint, that is for everyone who is consecrated to God. That is the only qualification for it, that you should let yourself be God's. That is the way of the Cross, that all your fine confidence in yourself, and all your certainty that by yourself you are quite capable of winning all the victory that you need, must be nailed up and put to shame. Then to the person who is humiliated, abused, and penitent comes the victory of the Cross, and he learns with joy unspeakable that Christ crucified is Christ risen, who continually leads us in triumph.

"The Lord Reigns"—Revelation 19:6

[Preached twenty-four times from 3/31/40 at Ocker Hill to 10/26/75 at Gilesgate]

The Book of Revelation is a difficult book and it may well be that some of us at times have been tempted to give up in despair of the task of understanding its vivid pictures. If we have felt so, we need not be ashamed for we are in good company. Luther said that once he very nearly did to Revelation what he in fact did to another book (not in the Bible)—threw it in the river Elbe! The difficulty that we find in the book is understandable, but it ought not to make us, any more than Luther, forget or despise it, for if ever a work deserved the title "a tract for our times" it is this book.

A tract first for its own time. Let me remind you what those times were. This is the first Christian book to use the word *martyr* in its proper sense and that is significant. For by the time this book was put together, the noble army of martyrs was beginning to acquire noticeable proportions. The Roman Emperor on his throne had heard about the Christians, and it was no difficult matter for him to set in motion against them the vast resources of a mighty empire, the various local governments, magistrates, police, were at their beck and call; and it was not difficult to stir up the hatred of ordinary people by means of a few usefully selected and widely disseminated lies.

We can to some extent imagine how a little company of humble folk among whom were not many wise, mighty, or noble felt in the face of an onslaught such as this. No wonder that some of the Churches for whom the Revelation was written had lost their first love, were now only lukewarm. No wonder that they needed the charge to be faithful unto death. It is to this distressed and harassed little flock that our writer thunders forth the triumphant news of the victory of God. Hallelujah! The Lord God Omnipotent Reigns. Caesar has power, power to torture and kill, perhaps to exterminate.

But God has greater power and those who are in God's hands need not fear Caesar's mailed fist.

And a tract too for our times, because our times are not that different from those in the first century. For a long time, until recently, the Church had forgotten what it was like to be persecuted. Perhaps a missionary was killed now and again in the South Sea Islands, and there were Boxer riots in China. But no one could call that persecution of the Church. But now things are different. I have met Christians who have been driven from Russia, others from German, one at least from Czechoslovakia. I have met a friend of Pastor Niemöller. You see the thing is real and happening now, and happening only a few hundred miles from where we are sitting at ease. And because this book speaks in the context of persecution and suffering and death it speaks to the Church of all ages.

In a reflective mood Luther said of it "Our holiness is in heaven where Christ is, and not in the world before our eyes as one paltry ware in the market. Therefore, let offense, factions, heresy, and wickedness be and do what they may; if only the Word of the Gospel remains pure within us, and we hold it dear and precious, we need not doubt that Christ is near and with us, even if matters go hardest, as we see in this Book that through and above all plagues, beasts, evil angels, Christ is still near and with his saints, and at last overthrows them."

This book is the triumph song of those passing through the great tribulation, the tribulation Jesus promised to all his followers; above all it is the triumphant affirmation that in spite of the wicked power of human beings, of all the forces of evil and sin, that the sovereignty belongs to God to him alone. In order to prevent all misunderstanding, it will be well to say first—

What This Does Not Mean

"God's in his heaven, all's right with the world." People who have never read *Pippa Passes* by Robert Browning are apt to turn that well-known couplet into a careless, easy, sentimental assertion of an optimistic view of life that has very little contact with the real world. All is essentially right with things; evil and sin do not matter; they will look after themselves and we will be alright; everything will turn out for the best. It is certainly hardly fair to pin that view on Browning himself, for he takes little Pippa through a series of scenes of evil. The unfaithful wife and lover; men plotting the ruin of another's artistic and emotional life; vile plotting in the heart of the Church itself.

No; the saying that the Lord God reigns does not open the way to an easy view of life and the world. It does not lead to pleasant sentimentalism, what [George] Meredith called "enjoyment without obligation." Very far from that. It is not the Church, it is the people outside it that adopt a sentimental view of life. It is the people outside the Church who believe, contrary to the facts, that evolution is producing a better world. It is the people outside that are not worrying about their sins. The Church has taken off the rose-colored glasses and knows that it has sins to be forgiven.

The seer knows quite well that the reign of God is not visible now. Now, the visible king is clearly Caesar; he has his way and there is none that dare oppose. It is only in the future that humankind will be able to see the truth, and know that it is God who reigns. He knows now, and the Church knows now, because God has revealed it. That is to say, they know by faith. And it is a false faith that demands signs and philosophy for its support. God is king, be the world ever so unruly. God is king when there is least sign of his rule. It is faith, mighty faith that laughs at impossibility and seizes the gift of God; faith knows that God is on the throne when he is most invisible.

And this faith is so far from leading a person into an easy life that often it actually gets him into trouble. Luther saw that the Lord reigns, saw it through the pomp and pretensions of the Church of Rome. And because he saw it, he found himself alone against a universal Church and a European empire. Wilberforce saw that the Lord reigns, saw it through the universal custom of slavery. And because he saw it there, he too knew he had to bring the two things together and fight an unpopular battle against a popular sin. Livingstone and Pollard saw that the Lord reigns, saw it against the background of almost unrelieved heathen darkness in Africa and China. And because they saw it they took their lives in their hands to proclaim the good news. And that is why Pollard and Dymond just before they sailed for China sang a duet in the chapel at Shebbear—"Tell it out among the heathen, that the Lord is king!" The faith that the Lord is king does not lead a person to say "Well, that's alright now I can sit back and enjoy myself."

All this leads us to a positive view of what it really does mean that the Lord God omnipotent reigns. The whole of this book of Revelation is speaking of wars of one sort or another, and its message is the ultimate conquest and victory of God. It therefore speaks to us also who are involved in—

The Battle of Life

It is a message for Christian soldiers, and indeed for everyone that knows life is not a bed of roses. We must look at this in its two aspects. There is first the battle with things outside. Everyone knows we build up our churches not in isolation but through the contacts we make with others. Character is the result of the clash of personalities. We react upon one another, and relationships with others enter into the stuff of our lives. No less do we reveal and make ourselves in the way in which face the external circumstances of life; wealth and poverty, health and sickness, friendship and loneliness. Above all, we are made by our relationship to the whole business of life, with the many complicated problems and difficulties that it raises and the evil things in the world.

Now all of this is not easy. Some people find it so difficult, so hard a battle, that they just cannot face it. They shut themselves up in a world of their own phantasies, or they escape as often as they can by means of books, or pictures or the like. There are people, more perhaps than we suppose who find that the only way out is death. You would not believe the suicide rate in Cambridge (cf. the man in Burkhill's lecture).

You cannot alter this by a word of command, by an order to behave and face life squarely. An ironic historian sets side by side Frederick the Great's account of the performance of his troops at a battle with a letter of a recent recruit engaged in the battle. "Never," says Frederick "have my troops done such marvels in point of gallantry, never since it has been my honor to lead them." And the soldier tells his squalid story of men driven into battle with blows from sergeant's canes, skulking when they could behind walls, and taking the opportunity of passing through a gap and to desert in scores.

But there is another way. Capt. John Brown was asked why superior forces have failed to hold their own against him and he supposed that it was because "they lacked a cause." That is the trouble with my folk, they have no cause, nothing to fight for. You can take the same thing onto a higher plane in the words of another military leader, Cromwell: "I raised such men as had the fear of God before them, as made some conscience of what they did; and from that time forward I must say that they were never beaten."

A cause, a purpose, a leader! That is what we must have if we are to face the battle of life with steady eyes, if we are to follow the Lamb wherever he goes. But this battle is not all an outside affair, for the most of it is not in our relationships with things and people without but the battle within.

That is where the true test of the conflict lies; this is where we are most easily defeated, and where defeat spreads to other parts of the field. It is from within, as Jesus very clearly saw and said, out of the human heart, that there comes all manner of unclean and evil things. It is there that we fight with sin. There is many a person splendidly capable of mastery of life, strong enough to do great work in the world who has failed because he would not conquer himself.

There is a story told of Alexander the Great in an Elizabethan play. Alexander loves a captive girl, Campaspe. He sends her to an artist named Atelles that her portrait may be painted. Atelles and Campaspe, who does not love Alexander, fall in love. It would have been easy for the world conqueror to take Campaspe, but rather he gives her in marriage to Atelles. "Now has Alexander achieved a victory that is greater than conquering the world, for he has conquered himself." And many people have failed because they could not win the battle there. But there are also many who never care about spectacular victories who have made the greater conquest. How?

> I ask them whence their victory came,
> They, with united breath,
> Ascribe their conquest to the Lamb,
> Their triumph to his death. (Isaac Watts)

There was one who was tempted at all points as we are, who yet came out of the trial victorious. One whom not even death would move from the path of obedience and integrity, whom not even death could hold by its power. And he who overcame the clutches of death has ever since been opening the Kingdom of heaven to all believers; has been making known to them and by them that the "Lord God omnipotent reigns."

CPSIA information can be obtained
at www.ICGtesting.com
Printed in the USA
LVOW07s0509101017
551859LV00001B/2/P